Basic Real Estate and Property Law for Paralegals

First Edition

and

Basic Wills, Trusts, and Estates for Paralegals

Third Edition

Jeffrey A. Helewitz, Esq.

www.intercoast.edu
1/877-CAREERS

PUBLISHERS

111 Eighth Avenue, New York, NY 10011
www.aspenpublishers.com

About Aspen Publishers

Aspen Publishers, headquartered in New York City, is a leading information provider for attorneys, business professionals, and law students. Written by preeminent authorities, our products consist of analytical and practical information covering both U.S. and international topics. We publish in the full range of formats, including updated manuals, books, periodicals, CDs, and online products.

Our proprietary content is complemented by 2,500 legal databases, containing over 11 million documents, available through our Loislaw division. Aspen Publishers also offers a wide range of topical legal and business databases linked to Loislaw's primary material. Our mission is to provide accurate, timely, and authoritative content in easily accessible formats, supported by unmatched customer care.

To order any Aspen Publishers title, go to *www.aspenpublishers.com* or call 1-800-638-8437.

To reinstate your manual update service, call 1-800-638-8437.

For more information on Loislaw products, go to *www.loislaw.com* or call 1-800-364-2512.

For Customer Care issues, e-mail *CustomerCare@aspenpublishers.com*; call 1-800-234-1660; or fax 1-800-901-9075.

Aspen Publishers
a Wolters Kluwer business

Basic Real Estate and Property Law for Paralegals

Summary of Contents

Contents

CHAPTER 3: LAND USE   51

CHAPTER 4: CONVEYANCING   73

CHAPTER 5: REAL ESTATE CLOSING PROCEDURES   127

CHAPTER 6: CONDOMINIUMS, COOPERATIVES, AND COMMERCIAL PROPERTY   161

CHAPTER 7: LANDLORD-TENANT LAW   187

CHAPTER 8: PERSONAL PROPERTY   209

Preface

This text is designed to assist legal professionals in understanding and effectuating real estate and personal property transactions. The term "legal professional" includes legal assistants, attorneys, law clerks, legal secretaries, and all other persons whose day-to-day activities involve real estate and law. The principles, forms, and tasks discussed in the text are applicable to anyone in the legal profession who deals with these matters. In any given transaction the totality of the work may be accomplished by a lawyer or a paralegal or legal secretary working under the lawyer's supervision. However, in almost no other area of law is the non-lawyer legal professional called upon to perform such independent work.

Bsic Real Estate and Property Law for Paralegals provides an analysis of the basic legal principles involved in real and personal property law, as well as practical guidance in creating, organizing, and completing real estate transactions. Furthermore, by links to Lois Law, state-specific forms and materials are accessible to conform the material to the rules of a given jurisdiction. This text provides a complete and comprehensive guide to all aspects of property law — real estate, landlord-tenant, land use, and personal property. These topics form the mainstay of almost every general practice law office in the country, and understanding them is a fundamental skill required of all legal professionals.

Jeffrey A. Helewitz

July 2002

Preface

Jeffrey A. Helewitz

Basic Real Estate
and Property Law
for Paralegals

1

Estates in Land and Future Interests

CHAPTER OVERVIEW

The law of property has often been referred to as a "bundle of rights." This designation underscores the fact that property law encompasses more than just one simple legal concept. Rather, the law of property concerns a person's ability to possess, transfer, and access both real and personal property.

Real property is defined as land, vegetation growing on the land, structures permanently affixed to the land, and mineral resources that are located beneath the soil. **Personal property** is all property that is not classified as real property, such as clothing, furniture, electronic equipment, and so forth. An individual's ability to use, possess, and transfer real and personal property is dependent upon the legal title to that property that is vested in that individual. **Title** is the legal term indicating rights to property, and **vesting** refers to a person's ability to enforce such rights in the courts. To understand the law of property, one must first understand the different categories of title to property that a person may hold.

This chapter explores this basic legal concept with respect to property — title. When referring to the title that a person has in real property, such title is called an **estate**. However, the same title attaches to personal property as well. The rights (and obligations) incident to a specific title to property are identical regardless of whether the property is **realty** (real property) or **personalty** (personal property). For the purposes of this initial explanation, these titles are exemplified by estates in land.

Classifications of Estates

All estates, or titles, in land are divided into two broad categories: free-holds and leaseholds. A **freehold** is an estate in land that a person has for an indefinite period of time. A **leasehold** is a possessory interest in land that a person has for a period of time specified in a contract called a **lease.** The holder of a freehold estate has rights and obligations created by the law, both common and statutory. The holder of a leasehold has rights and obligations dictated by the provisions of the lease.

Freeholds

Fees

Freehold estates are divided into two sub-categories: fees and life estates. A **fee,** or **fee simple absolute,** is the largest estate in land recognized by the law. The holder of a fee interest can sell, gift, devise, and encumber that interest, and holds that interest for an indefinite period of time.

 EXAMPLE:

A woman purchases a house that rests on one-half acre of land. There are no restrictions on her title, so she holds the property as a fee simple absolute. If she wishes to sell off a portion of the land, rent her house, or use her interest in the property as collateral for a loan, she may do so, because her interest is absolute and un-restricted.

Not all fee interests are absolute. The law recognizes two types of fee simple estates that may terminate upon the happening of a particular event. Note that this interest is still indefinite, because the event may or may not occur, and the time of such possible occurrence is unknown. However, this interest does impose a certain limitation on the titleholder.

The two types of fees that may terminate at the happening of a specified event are called a fee simple determinable and a fee simple subject to a condition subsequent. These two types of terminable fees are referred to as **defeasible fees,** meaning that the interest of the titleholder may be cut off, or defeated, if the event occurs.

A **fee simple determinable** is a fee that terminates upon the happening of a specified event, at which time the title to the property is automatically transferred back to the person who created the interest, known as the **grantor,** or transferor, of the interest in the realty.

EXAMPLE:

> Grantor, who holds a fee simple absolute title to a parcel of property called Blackacre, transfers the title to his son "for so long as the property is used for residential purposes." This restriction on the use of the property creates a fee simple determinable. If the son, or anyone to whom the son transfers his interest, decides to use the property for commercial purposes, the title to Blackacre automatically reverts back to the grantor or the grantor's heirs if such use occurs after the grantor's death. This automatic reversion to the grantor of a fee simple determinable is called a **possibility of reverter,** indicating that there is a possibility that title will revert to the grantor.

A **fee simple subject to a condition subsequent** is created when the grantor transfers title to the property but reserves the right to regain the title upon the happening of an event specified in the transfer.

EXAMPLE:

> Grantor, who holds a fee simple absolute title to a parcel of property called Whiteacre, transfers title to his daughter "but if the property is ever used for commercial purposes, then Whiteacre will go back to Grantor." If the property is subsequently used for commercial purposes, the grantor may reclaim the property provided that he has specifically reserved a **right of re-entry** in the transferring document (which he has). This right, unlike the possibility of reverter, is not automatic under the law, and the grantor or his heirs may decline to exercise this right.

A fee simple determinable and a fee simple subject to a condition subsequent are very similar, and the distinguishing characteristic lies in the words used by the grantor in the transferring document. Phrases such as "for so long as," "during," "while," and so forth indicate a fee simple determinable, whereas the phrase "but if" or "upon the happening of" creates a fee simple subject to a condition subsequent. With the former, the prohibited use must be mentioned; with the latter any use except for the one specified is permitted. The consequence of this linguistic use is crucial. With a fee simple determinable the title may revert back automatically; with a fee simple subject to a condition subsequent the grantor or the grantor's heirs must actually exercise the right of re-entry or such right is lost. Also, the limitations on the use of the property extend to all persons to whom the property is transferred by and through the original transferee.

EXAMPLE:

A grantor creates a fee simple subject to a condition subsequent. Five years after the transfer the transferee uses the property in a manner that gives rise to the condition. The grantor is aware of the change in use, but does not exercise the right of re-entry. This right of re-entry, if not exercised, will be lost, and the transferee now has a fee simple absolute. If the title had been a fee simple determinable, the title would have automatically reverted to the grantor regardless of the grantor's action or inaction.

If, when creating the title, the grantor decides that he or she does not wish to regain the title but, if the specified event occurs, wishes a third person to be entitled to the property, the grantor may so indicate. The title thus created in the transfer is referred to as a **fee simple subject to an executory interest.** This simply is either a fee simple determinable or a fee simple subject to a condition subsequent in which the reversionary interest passes not to the grantor but to a third person so designated by the grantor.

 EXAMPLE:

A grantor transfers title to Greenacre to his son provided that it is used only for recreational purposes, then to his daughter. The son has a fee simple subject to a condition subsequent, and the daughter has an executory interest, in this case a right of re-entry, which she may exercise if the son uses the property for non-recreational purposes.

Historically, a type of limited fee simple existed known as a **fee tail,** meaning that the property could only pass to lineal descendants of the titleholder. Almost every jurisdiction in the country has abolished this type of title.

 EXAMPLE:

A grantor transfers his property to his son and "the male heirs of his body." This creates a fee tail in the son's male descendants, referred to as a *fee tail male.*

A fee simple estate may be held by just one person, or by two or more persons collectively. If one person holds the title, it is called a **tenancy in severalty.** The word "tenancy" comes from the French word "tenir," meaning "to hold": the person holds the title individually. If the title is held by two or more persons, the title is referred to as **concurrent ownership.** The United States recognizes five types of concurrent title to property:

1. tenancy in common
2. joint tenancy
3. tenancy by the entirety
4. community property
5. tenancy in partnership

1. Tenancy in common. A tenancy in common is an estate in property in which two or more co-tenants (titleholders) own a concurrent, but not necessarily equal, title to the property. This interest is deemed to be separate but undivided from the other tenants' interests. Each tenant in common, regardless of her percentage of ownership, is entitled to possess the entire property, but has no right to the exclusive possession of any portion of the property. Each tenant in common is free to **alienate** (transfer) her interest in the property, and there is no right of survivorship in the remaining tenants of a deceased tenant's interest. The interest of a deceased tenant in common passes to her heirs.

 EXAMPLE:

A woman inherits a summer home from her great-aunt. She decides that she does not want to use the home all the time, and to raise capital she sells a one-quarter interest to each of two friends. The three friends are now tenants in common, with the first woman owning a 50 percent interest and the two friends owning a 25 percent interest each. Despite the unequal ownership percentages, each friend has the right to possess the entire house — for example, none of them can lay claim to exclusive use of the "best" bedroom (absent an agreement to that effect).

Any co-tenant who is in actual possession of the property has the right to retain any profit derived from his or her own use of the property, and is not required to share those profits with the co-tenants who are not actually in possession. However, if the tenant in possession realizes profit from an agreement with a third person for the use of the property, this profit must be shared with co-tenants in proportion to their ownership interest.

 EXAMPLE:

Two brothers buy a parcel of real estate as tenants in common. One brother lives on the property where he grows vegetables. The second brother lives in a city 100 miles away from the property. The brother in possession does not have to share the profit he derives from the sale of the vegetables he grows on the property. However, if the brother in possession rented the property to a neighboring farmer, the brother would have to share the rent with the urban brother. The difference involves income derived from a tenant's own efforts versus income derived from leasing the possessory interest.

Each tenant in common has the legal right to **encumber** her interest, meaning that she may mortgage that interest or have that interest subject to mechanic's liens, but no one tenant may encumber the interests of the other co-tenants without their consent. ~~If the creditor of the tenant in common who encumbered her interest forecloses because the tenant failed to meet the credit obligation, the foreclosure, in most states, acts to sever the title into tenancies in severalty, proportionate to the co-tenants' interests.~~

EXAMPLE:

A tenant in common wants to raise some cash to buy some corporate shares as an investment. To raise this capital, she mortgages her one-half interest in the subject property. The price of the shares falls and the woman loses her entire investment and cannot repay the loan. The creditor to whom she mortgaged the property forecloses on the realty (see Chapter 4). After foreclosure the creditor now owns a fee simple absolute in one-half of the property, while the former co-tenant now owns a fee simple absolute in the other one-half of the property.

If the co-tenants want to terminate the tenancy in common, they have three options:

(a) they can collectively transfer their title, transferring to each a fee simple absolute in his or her proportionate share;

(b) a tenant in possession may go to court to seek an **ouster,** a court-ordered termination of a co-tenant's rights because of the co-tenant's failure to meet some specified legal obligation or abandonment of the property; or

(c) if the parties cannot agree to a suitable division, they may seek a court-ordered **partition** of the property in which the court will determine the portion each co-tenant will receive.

A tenant in common may seek contribution from the other co-tenants for all repairs, taxes, and mortgage payments made on the property that exceeds the percentage interest of the paying tenant in common, but the tenant is not entitled to be reimbursed for improvements made to the property absent an agreement by the other co-tenants or pursuant to a court order.

EXAMPLE:

Four cousins inherit a home from their grandmother as tenants in common. Two cousins want to rent the property to produce an income. Prior to such rental, one cousin pays for necessary repairs to the roof and the installation of a new boiler, and then decides to have the property artistically landscaped. This cousin may seek reimbursement for the roof repairs and the boiler but not for the landscaping, which was not a necessary repair.

Whenever two or more **grantees** acquire concurrent title to property and they are not married to each other, the law assumes that they hold title as tenants in common unless a different title is specified in the conveyance.

2. Joint tenancy. A **joint tenancy** is a form of concurrent ownership of property in which each joint tenant has an undivided interest in the whole estate, and there is a right of survivorship in the remaining joint tenants upon the death of each of them. To create a joint tenancy, the conveyance must contain what is referred to as the four unities of time, title, interest, and possession. In other words, unlike a tenancy in common that may be created by several conveyances and in which each tenant in common may own a different percentage of the whole, to create a joint tenancy all of the joint tenants must acquire the same title by the same instrument at the same time, and the title must be equal with respect to each tenant.

 EXAMPLE:

Three sisters decide to purchase some land together as an investment, and decide to hold the title as joint tenants. To create the joint tenancy, the grantor must convey this interest in the property in one document in which each sister is given a one-third interest in the realty. The document must also specify that a joint tenancy is being created.

Unlike a tenancy in common in which a co-tenant may alienate his or her interest in the property without destroying the title, with a joint tenancy, because each joint tenant owns an undivided interest, any attempt to alienate his or her interest in a joint tenancy during his or her life acts to destroy the joint tenancy. This alienation will create a tenancy in common. If more than two people hold title as joint tenants, the result would be fairly convoluted: the joint tenant who alienated her portion now holds title as a tenant in common with the former joint tenants who are collectively a tenant in common holding that interest as joint tenants.

EXAMPLE:

Abel, Baker, and Carr acquire some property as joint tenants. Abel decides to sell his interest to Dorrance. Once the sale is consummated, Abel's alienation has severed the joint tenancy. The property is now held as a tenancy in common. Dorrance holds title as a tenant in common for a one-third interest, and Baker and Carr, holding title as joint tenants, are the tenant in common for a two-thirds interest in the property. If Baker dies, the title to the joint property devolves on Carr, and the property is now a tenancy in common with Dorrance being a tenant in common for a one-third interest, and Carr being a tenant in common for a two-thirds interest. Carr received Baker's interest by right of survivorship.

As indicated by the above example, upon the death of a joint tenant his interest passes automatically to the surviving joint tenants. Any attempt by a joint tenant to transfer his interest by means of a will fails. Note that an inter vivos transfer destroys the joint tenancy and creates a tenancy in common, whereas testamentary transfers are ineffective and title passes by right of survivorship to the surviving joint tenants.

If a joint tenant encumbers his interest, this also may act to sever the joint tenancy in many jurisdictions. Furthermore, some jurisdictions have held that even entering into a contract for the sale of an interest in a joint tenancy, without the actual sale being consummated, is sufficient to destroy the joint tenancy and create a tenancy in common. Many states prohibit a joint tenant from acquiring a title by right of survivorship if the surviving joint tenant was responsible for the death of the deceased joint tenant.

Joint tenancies are not favorable to the tenants because of the restriction on the alienation of interest, and most jurisdictions require that a joint tenancy be specified as the title in the conveyance for it to be created.

3. Tenancy by the entirety. A **tenancy by the entirety** is a form of joint tenancy recognized by many states for legally married couples. A tenancy by the entirety is created with the four unities of a joint tenancy plus a fifth unity of a valid marriage.

A tenancy by the entirety cannot be encumbered or conveyed by one spouse alone; any transfer without the consent of both spouses is ineffective. As with a regular joint tenancy, there is an automatic right of survivorship in the surviving spouse, and a tenancy by the entirety may only be severed by divorce, mutual agreement, or a foreclosure by a creditor of *both* parties.

 EXAMPLE:

A married couple purchases a house as tenants by the entirety. As a couple they borrow a portion of the purchase price from a bank and give the bank a mortgage on the house to secure the loan. Several years later, the wife, an inveterate gambler, borrows money to pay her gambling debts and gives her creditor a mortgage on the house. When both of the loans are in default, only the bank can foreclose because both spouses signed the mortgage; the wife's creditor is unable to foreclose because he is the creditor of the wife alone.

A tenancy by the entirety affords protection to the married couple because neither spouse alone has the legal ability to destroy the title, and the right of survivorship will remain intact. This provides more benefits to a couple than a regular joint tenancy.

4. Community property. Nine jurisdictions in the United States currently recognize community property as a title for married couples. Community property is a title to property given to property acquired by a married couple during the marriage if no other title is specified on the conveyance, or if that title is specifically selected. With community property, each spouse is deemed to be the outright owner of one-half of the property, meaning that each is able to alienate his or her portion, and there is no automatic right of survivorship.

 EXAMPLE:

A married couple in New Mexico, a community property state, purchases a parcel of undeveloped real estate as an investment. The wife is killed in a car accident, and in her will she leaves all of her real property to her sister. Because the couple did not specify a different title when purchasing the land, the property is considered to be community property, and the wife was free to will her interest to whomever she wished. Consequently, the property is now held by the husband and the sister as tenants in common.

5. Tenancy in partnership. For business partners, the law has described a fifth type of concurrent ownership known as a tenancy in partnership. A **tenancy in partnership** is only available to persons operating a business as a general or a limited partnership. All of the business property, unless otherwise designated, is deemed to be held as a tenancy in partnership. The attributes of such title are:

(a) no one partner may possess the partnership property for other than partnership purposes without the other partners' consent;
(b) no one partner may sell the property, otherwise than in the regular course of business, without the other partners' consent;
(c) the personal creditors of the individual partners may not attach this property to satisfy the personal debts of the individual partners; and

(d) the heirs of a deceased partner are only entitled to receive the value of the deceased partner's interest in the property — the title to the property itself passes to the surviving partners by operation of law.

The purpose behind the creation of a tenancy in partnership is to assure business partners that the property that is acquired by and for the business will remain the property of the collective partners to be used exclusively for business purposes.

 EXAMPLE:

> Three friends decide to go into business together to buy and sell gemstones. Each partner contributes a certain amount of capital, and they purchase a quantity of colored gemstones for the business. Later, one of the partners defaults on a loan that he had taken out to go on a vacation. This partner's creditor cannot attach the gemstones to satisfy the debt because they are held in tenancy in partnership. Conversely, if the three partners collectively borrowed the money to buy gemstones, this creditor could attach the gemstones because it is a debt of the partnership, not the individual partner.

Life Estates

The second subset of freehold is known as a **life estate,** whereby a person holds title for a "lifetime," which is deemed to be an indefinite period. At the termination of the "life," title to the property will automatically pass to someone else whose identity is specified in the conveyance that created the life estate.

 EXAMPLE:

> In her will a woman leaves a house, which she owned as a tenancy in severalty, to her "beloved husband for life, then to our children." The husband has inherited a life estate, meaning that he has a possessory interest in the property only during his lifetime, and on his death the children will inherit the property as tenants in common (the woman did not specify any type of title for the children so the law will assume a tenancy in common).

The person whose life determines the duration of the estate is referred to as the **measuring life.** In the most common situation, the grantee is the measuring life, as exemplified above. However, under certain circumstances the holder of the life estate may only hold this possessory interest during another person's life. This type of estate is referred to as a **life estate pur autre vie**.

EXAMPLE:

In the previous example, assume that the widower does not wish to live in the house but wants to travel. To raise capital he conveys his interest in the property to a third person. This person now has a life estate pur autre vie, holding title only so long as the widower, the measuring life, lives. At the widower's death, the title passes to the children according to the terms of their mother's will.

The **life tenant,** the person who holds title to the life estate, is entitled to the ordinary use and profits from the property, but is precluded from doing anything that would injure or reduce the interests of the person who will ultimately acquire the fee estate. The person who eventually receives the fee interest in the property after the termination of the life estate is referred to as the **remainderman** (the children from the previous example). To determine whether the use of the land is considered ordinary or detrimental to the remainderman, see Chapter 2.

Leaseholds

The second broad category of estates is the leasehold. As the term would imply, a leasehold is an interest in property that a person holds pursuant to a contract known as a **lease.** A person who has a transferable interest in property may grant the use of that property to some one. If this transfer is accomplished by means of a lease, the transferor is called the **lessor, or landlord,** and the person who acquires the right pursuant to the lease contract is called the **lessee or tenant.** A leasehold differs from a freehold interest in that it is a possessory interest only, and it terminates at a set period of time as determined by the lease.

A leasehold is formed by contract, in which the lessor gives the lessee possession of the property for a specified period of time, and the lessee agrees to pay the lessor a fee for such use known as **rent.** Leasehold rights and obligations are determined by the contract between the parties as well as statutory and common law. These legal rights and obligations come under the heading of **landlord-tenant law,** which is fully discussed in Chapter 7.

EXAMPLE:

The widower from the previous example decides that, rather than conveying his entire interest to a third person, he will just rent the house for one year and use the rent to travel. He contracts with the third party to rent the property, and then leaves on a trip. The third person now has a leasehold rather than a life estate pur autre vie. *Query:* What would happen if the widower died in a plane crash two days after the lease was executed? See Chapter 4.

Future Interests

One of the primary concerns of property law is to ensure that at some point one person (or a collective group) has a sufficient interest in the property to be able to exercise all rights of a fee holder. This legal ability to exercise rights of ownership and possession is called *vesting.* The area of property law known as future interests is concerned with seeing that all property titles are vested within a reasonable period of time. In the example above, the widower has a presently vested life estate and the children have vested remainder interests in fee, which take effect in the future, at the death of their father.

Earlier in the chapter the concept of the possibility of reverter, the right of re-entry, and reversions were all introduced. Each of these estates is a future estate because even though the holder of such right has a property interest, the ability to exercise that right is delayed until some point in the future.

Classifications

The law recognizes four classifications of future estates:

1. **Indefeasibly vested remainder:** This type of estate is created in a person who is both in existence and ascertainable at the time the conveyance creating such interest comes into existence. The interest is indefeasibly vested because it occurs automatically at the natural termination of a previous estate.

EXAMPLE:

In her will a woman conveys her house to her niece Betty for life, then to Betty's daughter Joan. Betty has a life estate and her daughter Joan has an indefeasibly vested remainder. When Betty dies, title automatically passes to Joan. Joan's right is currently vested because she can stop Betty from doing anything that would injure or diminish the value of the property.

2. **Vested remainder subject to open:** This estate is created when a vested remainder is given not to a named person but to a class of persons and that class may be added to. "Subject to open" means that the title is shared by persons who may be added to the class.

 EXAMPLE:

In the preceding example, assume that the woman's will leaves the property to "my niece Betty for life, then to Betty's children." At the date of the woman's death, Betty has one child, Joan. However, because Betty may have more children before she dies, Joan's interest is subject to being proportionately diminished by the addition of more siblings to the class. Joan's interest is a vested remainder subject to open.

3. **Vested remainder subject to complete divestment:** This is a **vested remainder that is subject to a condition subsequent** as discussed above. The interest may be totally lost (divested) if the condition occurs.

 EXAMPLE:

A man conveys his house to his wife for life, then to his son provided that the son always uses the property for residential purposes, otherwise to his daughter. The son has a vested remainder in fee subject to a condition subsequent. If he uses the property for non-residential purposes, he will be divested and the title will pass to his sister.

4. **Contingent remainder:** This is a remainder interest that may or may not vest — it is conditioned upon either a condition precedent or is created in a person who is unborn or unascertainable at the time of the conveyance.

A remainder subject to a condition precedent is exemplified by a conveyance that gives a remainder interest provided that some condition is met before the remainder becomes a present estate.

 EXAMPLE:

A man conveys his house to his wife for life, then to his son provided that the son becomes a priest. The son's interest is contingent upon his taking orders, which means that it may never vest in him if the condition is not met.

A contingent remainder created in unborn or unascertained persons occurs when the person who will hold the eventual title is not in existence at the date of the conveyance creating the interest.

 EXAMPLE:

A woman conveys her house to her sister for life, then to the children of her brother. If the brother has no children at the time of the conveyance, the interests of the unborn children are deemed to be contingent (upon their birth). Note that if the brother had at least one child at the time of the conveyance, the child's interest would be a vested remainder subject to open.

Any time a future interest either cuts off an earlier estate or only comes about after a gap following the natural termination of an earlier estate, it is referred to a an **executory interest.** These interests are not considered vested, and therefore are treated under the law in the same fashion as a contingent remainder.

 EXAMPLE:

Grantor to *A* for life, then two years after *A*'s death to *C*'s children. *C*'s children's interest is executory because it follows a gap (two years) after the termination of the preceding estate.

The Rule Against Perpetuities

In order to avoid the situation in which vested titles to land are held up indefinitely because of contingent remainders, the law mandates that, for a transfer of property to be valid, all interests created by the transfer must vest (be legally enforceable) within a predetermined period of time from the date of the instrument creating those interests. This legal doctrine is called the **Rule Against Perpetuities,** and its application has worried and confused legal professionals for centuries. Simply stated, the Rule mandates that all interests must vest, if at all, within 21 years after the death of the lives in being at the effective date of the initial conveyance, plus the period of gestation (pregnancy). In order to understand how the Rule affects estates, each component of the Rule must be analyzed.

"All interests" refers to every interest, vested, contingent, or executory, that is created by the document of conveyance.

"Must vest" means the vesting of each of these interests is required to be legally enforceable.

"If at all" means that if any one of these interests, regardless of how remote, fails to vest within the stated period, none of the interests vests because the transfer is considered invalid.

"Within 21 years after the death of the lives in being at the effective date of the conveyance" refers only to those persons who are alive at the date the instrument becomes effective and who, either directly or indirectly by being the progenitor of an interest taker, acquire some interest in the conveyance. These persons also include anyone who is *in utero* at that date. Persons who do not fall into this discrete grouping are not considered to be lives in being. This provision of the Rule sets the maximum time period for the vesting of all interests created by the conveyance.

 EXAMPLE:

In his will a man leaves his property to his "wife for life, then their children for life, then to their grandchildren." In this example the effective date of the conveyance is the day of the man's death when the will takes effect. The wife has an immediately vested life estate. The children are all lives in being because all of a person's children must be either alive or in utero at the date of the person's death, and all of them have vested life estates. The man's grandchildren, who are uncertain at this date, have contingent remainders, but they will all be ascertained at the date of his children's death and their interests vest immediately upon the death of those children who are all lives in being. Consequently, this transfer does not violate the Rule Against Perpetuities.

 EXAMPLE:

A man makes an inter vivos transfer, as an anniversary gift, to his "wife for life, then to our children for life, then to our grandchildren." In this instance the transfer is invalid according to the Rule. The transfer takes effect immediately. The man and his wife can have a new child two years after this conveyance. Assume that the man, his wife, and their children who were alive at the date of the conveyance are all subsequently killed in a car accident, only leaving the afterborn child alive. According to the transfer, this child takes a life estate, and after his death the property would go to his children. The baby is not a life in being, and if he lives more than 21 years before dying and leaving a child, this grandchild's interest will vest more than 21 years after the death of the lives in being — the man, his wife, and the children alive at the date of the conveyance.

As demonstrated above, the date of the conveyance is the crucial aspect of applying the Rule. In its classical application, the provisions of the transfer are determined by looking at all possibilities, regardless of how improbable, to ascertain whether the provisions of the Rule will be violated. If, under any conceivable scenario, an interest would vest beyond the period of the Rule, the entire transfer fails. To determine whether this might occur, follow these steps:

1. determine the effective date of the transfer;
2. determine who are the lives in being at that date;
3. create an afterborn child;
4. assume all lives in being then die; and
5. using the afterborn, follow through with the provisions of the transfer. If it is possible that an interest will vest more than 21 years after all lives in being die, the entire conveyance fails and the property reverts to the grantor or the grantor's heirs.

Several states have enacted **salvage doctrines** to save conveyances from being found invalid for possible violation of the Rule Against Perpetuities. The most common of these doctrines are:

1. Age contingency: If the transfer would be invalid because a person's interest is delayed until after the person's twenty-first birthday, the transfer is read as though the person would take an interest at age 21.
2. Administrative contingency: If the transfer would violate the Rule because some contingent event is mentioned in the transfer, the doctrine assumes that the contingency will take place within the period of the Rule.
3. Gifts to person by title rather than by name: The traditional example of this was a gift that wills to "my son for life, then to his widow for life, then to her children." It is conceivable that the woman the son is married to at the testator's death will die, and the son will remarry a woman who was not alive at his parent's death. This man's second wife will be the "widow," and she is not a life in being. The last gift will be to her child who takes after her death, and so the Rule may be violated. This salvage doctrine states that the term "widow" is deemed to refer to the person who meets that description at the time the transfer takes effect, not anyone who may subsequently meet that designation.
4. Wait and see: Many jurisdictions have enacted statutes that will only apply the provisions of the Rule if a violation actually occurs. This means that the court will not look prospectively to improbable situations, but will let the transfer take effect until an actual violation of the Rule occurs. If the "improbable" does take place, the transfer is only deemed ineffective from that point forward.
5. Year limitation: Many states have bypassed the Rule entirely by enacting statutes that permit transfers to continue for a specified

number of years (usually 90) at which point the last interest must vest.

When drafting or analyzing a conveyance that purports to create successive estates, the legal professional must perform the following steps:

1. examine the provisions to determine whether the transfer may violate the Rule; and
2. determine whether the state in control of the conveyance has provided for any salvage doctrine that will save the transfer from violating the Rule.

Practical Tips

- To determine the title, obtain an **abstract of title** from the county recorder's office that provides a detailed indication of how the property has been transferred over the years.
- Keep a receipt for the abstract, which is an expense.
- If there is a break in the chain of the title, advise the attorney immediately.
- Review the transfer documents to make sure the Rule is not violated.
- Make a summary of all key documents for easy review.
- Create an information sheet for missing information that must be obtained.
- Review the property descriptions to make sure there are no discrepancies in the different transfers.

Chapter Review

The purpose of this chapter is to introduce the various types of titles to property that a person may possess. Although the discussion generally is focused on titles to realty, it must be remembered that these same titles, rights, obligations, and restrictions apply to personalty as well.

Interests in real property are known as estates, and the law divides estates into two broad categories: freeholds and leaseholds. Freehold estates are those interests in property that the tenant holds for an indefinite and uncertain period of time. Freeholds are subdivided into fee estates and life estates. These titles may be held by one person or by a group of persons collectively.

The second classification of estates, the leasehold, is an interest in property that is created by contract. The rights and obligations of the parties are determined by the provisions of the lease entered into by them. A complete discussion of the law of leaseholds appears in Chapter 7.

Not all estates in property are presently exercisable. Some interests are created to take effect in the future, known as future interests. These future interests can have an important effect on a person's estate, and, to this end, several legal theories have come into existence over the years to clear titles to property.

The Rule Against Perpetuities was enacted to mandate that all transfers of property will create vested (i.e., legally enforceable) rights within a period of time specified in the Rule. Traditionally, if any future interest would vest beyond the period of the Rule, the entire conveyance was deemed invalid. To avoid invalidating conveyances, many jurisdictions have enacted salvage doctrines to bypass the dictates of the Rule. Further, any attempt to restrict the transferability of legal interests in property is deemed invalid in many states if such restriction extends beyond a statutorily determined period of time.

The law of property is one of the bulwarks of the U.S. legal system, and legal professionals must be conversant with the rights, duties, and liabilities imposed on titles to property.

Ethical Concern

All legal professionals who are not attorneys must be careful not to give legal advice. In the case of real property law, because so much of the work is performed by legal assistants, it is very tempting for the paralegal to provide advice to clients. This is an ethical violation for the legal assistant and for the attorney who supervises the legal assistant.

Key Terms

Abstract of title
Alienate
Co-tenant
Community property
Concurrent ownership
Contingent remainder
Defeasible fee
Encumber
Estate
Executory interest
Fee
Fee simple absolute
Fee simple determinable
Fee simple subject to a condition
  subsequent
Fee simple subject to an executory
  interest

Fee tail
Four unities
Freehold
Grantee
Grantor
Indefeasibly vested remainder
Joint tenancy
Landlord
Landlord-tenant law
Lease
Leasehold
Lessee
Lessor
Life estate
Life estate pur autre vie
Life tenant
Measuring life

Ouster   Tenancy by the entirety
Partition   Tenancy in common
Personal property   Tenancy in partnership
Personalty   Tenancy in severalty
Possibility of reverter   Tenant
Real property   Title
Realty   Vested remainder subject to
Remainderman   complete divestment
Rent   Vested remainder subject to a
Right of re-entry   condition subsequent
Right of survivorship   Vested remainder subject to open
Rule Against Perpetuities   Vesting
Salvage doctrines

Exercises

1. Research how your state applies the Rule Against Perpetuities and whether it has any salvage doctrines.
2. Discuss the advantages of holding title to property as a tenant in common, a tenant by the entirety, and community property.
3. Give three examples by which a life estate pur autre vie may be created.
4. Discuss the difference between a contingent and an executory interest.
5. Discuss several problems that may occur if a conveyance is made to a class of persons rather than to named individuals.

Situational Analysis

A couple has lived together for eight years but has not married. They decide to purchase a home together and want to make sure that each one's rights are protected. The woman is providing the bulk of the purchase price. How should the couple be advised to protect their interests? What factors must be considered?

Edited Cases

The following cases highlight the difference between joint tenancies and other forms of title that may have the outward appearance of a joint tenancy.

Drucker v. Cornish
152 Cal. App. 3d 509, 1984 Cal. App. LEXIS 1683

Jane Denham Cornish, executrix of the estate of Janet C. Drucker, deceased, appeals the orders determining Ann C. Hall to be the owner as surviving joint tenant of (1) a bank account at La Jolla Bank & Trust Company (La Jolla account) and (2) the proceeds of a $25,000 treasury bill. Although the source of the La Jolla account and the treasury bill was a joint tenancy account between Drucker and Hall, those items were in Drucker's name alone at the time of her death. Because the joint tenancy was not a true joint tenancy we reverse with instructions to enter orders in favor of the executrix.

In August 1981, Hall petitioned under Probate Code section 851.5 for a declaration that she was the sole owner as surviving joint tenant of the La Jolla account opened by Janet Drucker, deceased. Finding Hall owned the account, the court granted her motion for judgment on the pleadings and ordered Cornish to give the money in the account to Hall. This court reversed the judgment in an unpublished opinion (4 Civ. No. 26554) because Hall had not established a joint tenancy account by a writing as required by Civil Code section 683 and Financial Code section 852. The opinion said:

> Nevertheless, this case should be remanded for trial because Hall contends the funds deposited by Drucker into the account were withdrawn from a separate account held in joint tenancy by Drucker and Hall. The significance of this contention was not pursued by the superior court due to the erroneous award of judgment on the pleadings based on the writings. If at trial Hall can prove the source of the funds was indeed a joint tenancy account owned by Drucker and herself, the new account opened by Drucker ordinarily would also be held in joint tenancy despite the lack of a sufficient writing.
>
> > Contrary to the common law rule, if money is taken from a joint tenancy account in a California bank during the joint lives of the depositors, property acquired with the money so withdrawn, or another account into which the money is traced, has the character of property held in joint tenancy, unless there has been a change in the character by some agreement between the parties.
>
> (9 CALJUR (3d ed. 1974) Banks, etc., at 115, p. 326.)
> A joint tenancy account does not lose its status as such when one of the joint tenants withdraws the funds and reinvests them (*Estate of Harris*, 9 Cal. 2d 649; *Taylor v. Crocker-Citizens Natl. Bank*, 258 Cal. App. 2d 682; *Cordasco v. Scalero*, supra, 203 Cal. App. 2d 95; *Wallace v. Riley*, 23 Cal. App. 2d 654; *Estate of McCoin*, 9 Cal. App. 2d 480). Therefore, although a finding of a joint tenancy cannot be supported by any of the writings in evidence here, given the proper evidentiary showing, a joint tenancy may be proved by tracing the source of the funds in the account. The award of judgment on the pleadings to either party would be improper.

Before the superior court heard the matter, Hall filed another petition against the estate for proceeds of a $25,000 treasury bill in Drucker's name at the time of her death asserting it, like the La Jolla account, was traceable to a joint tenancy bank account at San Diego Trust and Savings Bank (San Diego account). The two petitions were consolidated for hearing. The court found that when Drucker established the La Jolla account by withdrawing funds from the San Diego account she did not intend to terminate the joint tenancy between herself and Hall. Accordingly, the court ruled Hall was entitled to both the La Jolla account and the treasury bill.

Our earlier decision precluded the court on retrial from finding the La Jolla account to be in joint tenancy form. We specifically held:

> The superior court also erred when it found the documents presented (the signature card and the checking-savings fund transfer authorizations) were sufficient to create a joint tenancy. Under Civil Code section 683 and Financial Code section 852, a joint tenancy bank account may only be created by a writing which contains specific language referring to a joint tenancy and/or a right of survivorship; "the intention to create a joint tenancy must appear expressly in the instrument allegedly giving rise to it. Without such a declaration, no joint tenancy results." [Citation.] Even where two parties have created a common bank account to which both have equal access and where they have been informed by a bank officer a joint tenancy has been created, no joint tenancy will result absent a writing which specifically states the parties' intent to create a joint tenancy.

(*In re Estate of Drucker* (Nov. 23, 1982) 4 Civ. 26554 [unpub. op.], at pp. 4-5.)

> The absence of a writing sufficient to create a joint tenancy precludes the admission of parol evidence to prove a joint tenancy was intended by Drucker. [Citations.]

(Id., at p. 6.)

Thus, the only avenue available to Hall and the critical issue before the court on retrial was whether the San Diego account was a true joint tenancy between the decedent and Hall. The general statement contained in our opinion to the effect that property acquired with joint tenancy money is joint tenancy property unless the parties have agreed otherwise did not mean that Hall could satisfy her burden by merely tracing the source of the treasury bill and the La Jolla account to an account which she and Drucker held in joint tenancy form. Borrowing from *Estate of Zeisel* (1983) 143 Cal. App. 3d 516 [192 Cal. Rptr. 25]

> It begs the question to argue [that Hall] is the surviving joint tenant of the account standing in the name of [Drucker] at the time of [her] death and that she is therefore conclusively presumed to have been a joint tenant of the accounts on which her name was placed in the first instance. She was not a joint tenant of the successor account unless she was a true joint tenant of the original account, and in determining whether [any] presumption is applicable we may not assume the answer to the ultimate question at issue.

(Id., at p. 524.)

The nature of each party's interest in a joint tenancy bank account turns on the intent of the parties establishing the account. (*Paterson v. Comastri* (1952) 39 Cal. 2d 66, 71-74 [244 P.2d 902]; *Wallace v. Riley* (1937) 23 Cal. App. 2d 654, 665-666 [74 P.2d 807].) Where each party contributes funds into the joint tenancy account each has a present vested interest in those funds even though the contributions may be unequal. Even though one party may make no contributions whatsoever, the parties may none-theless agree each has an interest in those funds allowing either party to use the funds under the terms of their agreement.

Frequently, however, individuals establish a joint tenancy account as part of an estate plan intending to make a gift to the surviving noncontrib-uting joint tenant effective upon the contributing joint tenant's death. The California Supreme Court judicially recognized this purpose in *Paterson v. Comastri, supra,* 39 Cal. 2d 66. (See also *Estate of Zeisel, supra,* 143 Cal. App. 3d 516.) This type of arrangement is the legal equivalent of a revoca-ble living trust in which the contributing joint tenant is the trustor and both joint tenants are trustees. As trustee the noncontributing joint tenant must comply with the trust terms. Where the contributing joint tenant in-tends to preclude the noncontributing joint tenant from a present lifetime interest the funds must be used solely for the trustor's benefit during the trustor's lifetime. It is only upon the trustor's death that the noncontribu-ting joint tenant becomes entitled to the balance in the joint tenancy ac-count.

Viewed in this light, the trustor may invade part or all of the trust corpus or even revoke the trust to use the funds for purposes other than making a gift to the person named earlier as trust beneficiary. Under such circumstances, if the trustor were to die without redepositing the funds withdrawn from the trust, the beneficiary is not entitled to the property acquired by the trustor from trust funds. When the noncontributing joint tenant, as trustee, violates the trust and takes the funds for his own pur-poses the trustor can trace those funds into any property acquired by the errant trustee. Thus, the rule stated in our earlier opinion applies only in the latter situation. The facts in each of the cases reciting the general rule support our conclusion. (See *Estate of Harris* (1937) 9 Cal. 2d 649 [72 P.2d 873]; *Taylor v. Crocker-Citizens Natl. Bank* (1968) 258 Cal. App. 2d 682 [65 Cal. Rptr. 771]; *Cordasco v. Scalero* (1962) 203 Cal. App. 2d 95 [21 Cal. Rptr. 339]; *Wallace v. Riley, supra,* 23 Cal. App. 2d 654; *Estate of McCoin* (1935) 9 Cal. App. 2d 480 [50 P.2d 114].)

Here, the joint tenancy relationship between Hall and Drucker was well defined. Hall, the noncontributing tenant, had the duty to use the funds deposited by Drucker during Drucker's lifetime to defray Drucker's household expenses, medical bills and taxes. Hall's use of those funds for any other purpose had to await Drucker's death for only then did Hall, as the surviving joint tenant, have the right to those funds. When Drucker decided to transfer part of what in effect was trust corpus from the San Diego account into the La Jolla account and later purchase a treasury cer-tificate in her name alone, Hall lost her right to those funds. (See *Paterson v. Comastri, supra,* 39 Cal. 2d at p. 71.) Hall was named as a 25 percent beneficiary in Drucker's will. Lacking admissible evidence of Drucker's testamentary intent other than the intent she expressed in her will and lacking any evidence establishing the San Diego account as a true joint tenancy account, Hall is not entitled to the property standing in Drucker's name alone at the time of Drucker's death.

Orders reversed with instructions to enter orders in favor of the executrix.

Case Questions

1. What factors did the court use to arrive at its result as to the nature of the title to the account?

2. What could the parties have done so that the court would have reached the opposite decision?

Estate of Hamburg
151 Misc. 2d 1034, 574 N.Y.S.2d 914 (1991)

In this SCPA 2103 discovery proceeding, the administratrix, decedent's daughter, seeks to recover the sum of $280,000.00 plus interest from the respondents, decedent's son, Howard, and his wife, Sheila. The parties agree that the funds which had been deposited into the accounts containing the names of decedent and Howard had initially belonged solely to the decedent and that Howard, prior to the decedent's death on March 3, 1989, at the age of 90, had withdrawn $280,000.00 from the accounts and deposited the proceeds into accounts in the names of himself and Sheila. Decedent's surviving distributees are his three children.

Petitioner contends that respondents are liable for the total amount of the withdrawals because the accounts were convenience accounts rather than true "joint accounts" [see Banking Law sec. 675]. In the alternative, petitioner argues that the accounts were the product of undue influence, fraud or lack of capacity. Should petitioner fail to prevail on any of these alternative theories, she seeks to recover one-half of the amount of the withdrawals on the ground that Howard forfeited any survivorship interest that he might have had in the accounts by withdrawing the entire balance there from prior to decedent's death without having obtained decedent's consent or authorization.

Respondents contend that all of the accounts should be viewed as valid joint accounts and that it should be concluded that decedent expressly or impliedly approved of all of the withdrawals. Additionally, respondents contend that decedent was competent at all relevant times. Lastly, respondents assert that they are entitled to a setoff in excess of $95,000.00 for claims other than funeral expenses. They argue that these claims are valid and that excluding Howard's testimony under CPLR 4519 would result in the provisions of CPLR 4519, as applied to the facts of this case, constituting an unconstitutional taking of property without due process. As required by CPLR 1012(b), the Attorney General was notified of the constitutional issue raised. However, he opted not to intervene but requested that a copy of the court's decision be served upon him.

The parties stipulated that respondents are to be reimbursed for decedent's funeral expenses in the sum of $5,883.00 and that all of the checks drawn on a Citibank checking account in the names of decedent and Howard were used for decedent's benefit. The reason that the sum at issue is equal to the sum initially deposited in the accounts is that the interest was periodically withdrawn and used for decedent's living expenses. However, petitioner rejects the respondents' claims for a setoff for the following reasons: respondents have failed to meet the burden of proof required to establish the validity of the claims; the subject matter of these claims should be treated as gifts rather than obligations; repondents, in part, are seeking to recover interest lost on the funds which they wrongfully withdrew from decedent's own funds; most, if not all, of the proof adduced with regard to these claims was from Howard's own lips and is, therefore, barred under CPLR 4519; and a substantial portion of the claim is barred by the statute of limitations.

Employees of three of the depositories for the accounts at issue testified about the respective practices of their employers. The overall thrust of their testimony was that the account in each institution was viewed as a joint account by the bank. Their testimony indicated that it was not unusual for the stamp marked "payable to either/or survivor" to be placed only on the passbook and not on the signature card even though the bank viewed the account as a joint account.

Howard testified in support of his claim of a setoff against the estate. Inasmuch as this was not a jury trial, with the consent of the parties the court reserved decision upon petitioner's objections that most of Howard's testimony had to be considered communications or transactions with the decedent and, consequently, inadmissible under CPLR 4519. Respondents contend that they are entitled to be reimbursed in the sum of $43,823.00 for interest withdrawn from accounts in their names and deposited into checking accounts used for the benefit of decedent. Howard testified about these transactions and about the records he kept of the transactions. Howard also contended that, after he had withdrawn the $280,000.00 in dispute, it was deposited into money market accounts and certificates of deposit, that he regularly withdrew the interest totaling $22,789.00, and deposited this interest into checking accounts used for the decedent's benefit, and that the sum of $23,400.00 in principal from these accounts was similarly withdrawn and deposited into checking accounts for decedent's benefit. Lastly, Howard estimated that the cost for the gas and tolls to drive to his father's apartment for a period of seven years and three months totalled $6,239.00 and that he should be reimbursed for this expenditure.

Of course, should it be concluded that respondents are entitled to the funds withdrawn from the accounts, there is no need to pass upon their claim for a setoff. The enactment of the predecessor of sec. 675 of the Banking Law relieved the surviving co-tenant of an account containing the survivorship language required by the statute of the burden of establishing that the deceased co-tenant intended to create a survivorship account [see *Matter of Creekmore*, 1 N.Y.2d 284]. However, the ownership interest of the surviving co-tenant may, nevertheless, be successfully attacked if it is established that the deceased depositor lacked the competency to form the intent required to make a valid gift or if it can be established that the account was the product of undue influence or fraud [*Matter of Kleinberg v. Heller*, 38 N.Y.2d 836, 840 (concurring op.); *Matter of Creekmore*, supra; *Haynos v. Krupczyk*, 14 A.D.2d 507].

Although it should be clear whether or not accounts were created in such a manner as to constitute "prima facie evidence" of the intent of the depositors "to vest title" in the survivor [Banking Law sec. 675(b)], the courts are frequently required to determine this issue. As evidenced by the testimony of employees of three different banks, the banks' practice of stamping survivorship language on the passbook or on other documents instead of on the signature cards must take the blame for much of this litigation. Hopefully, now that the legislature has created a statutory "convenience" account [Banking Law sec. 678, L. 1990, Ch. 436], the banking industry will create signature cards which clearly contain the required statutory language indicating whether the account is a "survivorship" account or a "convenience" account.

Although this court has previously expressed the opinion that some of the lower court's interpretations of *Matter of Fenelon* [262 N.Y. 308], the seminal case discussing the requirements to create the statutory presumption of a survivorship account, are more rigid than the *Fenelon* holding requires [see *Estate of Hoffman*, N.Y.L.J., June 29, 1989, p. 26, col. 3], this court is constrained to follow the recent appellate holdings that the statutory presumption of title vesting in the survivor does not arise unless the depositor has signed a signature card, or perhaps some other document, containing the necessary survivorship language [*Matter of Coon*, 148 A.D.2d 906, 907, citing *Matter of Timoshevich*, 133 A.D.2d 1011, 1012; *Matter of Burns*, 126 A.D.2d 809, 811]. Although the absence of the statutory presumption does not preclude the surviving co-tenant from establishing a right of survivorship, it does place the burden of proof upon the survivor to establish that the deceased depositor intended to create a survivorship account [*Matter of Coon*, supra, 908, citing *Matter of Thomas*, 43 A.D.2d 446, 449].

Here, if the court had to determine whether the accounts at issue were "survivorship" accounts, it would conclude that the accounts in the Emigrant Savings Bank totaling $60,000.00 were joint accounts with right of survivorship and that all of the accounts in the other depositories were not. The signature card for the initial Emigrant account signed by the decedent was sufficient to constitute "prima facie evidence" of an intent on the part of the depositors to vest title in the survivor because it contained an "X" in the box next to the words "Joint (either / or survivor)" and no proof was adduced to rebut this evidence. With regard to the accounts in all of the other depositories, no signature card was presented which contained both the decedent's signature and the required statutory language that it was payable to either "or the survivor of them" [Banking Law sec. 675(a)] and, consequently, there is no statutory presumption as to survivorship. Moreover, no admissible credible proof was adduced to sustain respondent's burden of otherwise proving that decedent intended to create survivorship accounts.

Nevertheless, under the facts herein, the result is the same regardless of whether the accounts created a "survivorship" interest or a tenancy in commmon. If the accounts were "survivorship" accounts, Howard destroyed his rights of survivorship by dint of having withdrawn, without the decedent's consent or ratification, more than his moiety interests while decedent was still alive and he would be liable to the estate for the excessive withdrawal of one-half of the amount withdrawn inasmuch as he withdrew all of the funds on deposit. [*Matter of Kleinberg v. Heller*, supra, 843]. If the accounts did not create a joint tenancy with right of survivorship, they created a tenancy in common entitling Howard to one-half of the sum on deposit [EPTL 6-2.2(a); *Matter of Timoshevich*, supra, 1012, citing *Matter of Chorney*, 66 Misc. 2d 963, 967].

Inasmuch as Howard is claiming a right to the funds at issue against the administratrix, CPLR 4519 precludes him from testifying "in his own behalf . . . concerning a personal transaction or communication" between himself and the decedent. The words "personal transaction" and "communication" have been afforded a broad construction. Thus, a person who is disqualified under CPLR 4519 cannot testify about anything that was gleaned by any of this witness's senses in the presence of the decedent nor can such testimony be used to establish directly or indirectly that a particular transaction occurred or did not occur between the decedent and the witness or that the decedent should or should not have had certain information or a particular impression [Richardson on Evidence (10th ed.) sec. 402].

Respondents are correct in asserting that, where funds were deposited in an account which was payable to either the depositor or her son, the court held that the depositor, in support of her claim that the son had wrongfully withdrawn all of the funds prior to his death, should have been permitted to testify that her "intent" in adding his name to the account was solely for her "convenience" [*Brezinski v. Brezinski*, 84 A.D.2d 464]. Regardless of whether permitting the depositor of the funds to testify as to her own intent can be considered as the commencement of a trend to whittle away at the exclusions required by CPLR 4519, it cannot be molded into the foundation for holding that CPLR 4519 permits an adverse party to testify about events which would be germane to decedent's understanding as to whether certain payments made to or for the benefit of the decedent were either a gift or repayment of an obligation.

Here, Howard could not testify that he withdrew the accounts at issue and then delivered the funds to decedent [*Matter of Wood*, 52 N.Y.2d 139]. It would be a distinction without a difference to permit Howard to testify that he withdrew the funds at issue, then deposited the same amount to an account in his own name, and then either transferred them into accounts which contained decedent's name or used that amount for decedent's benefit. It follows that if Howard's testimony as to these transactions is barred by CPLR 4519, his notebook, which purportedly reflects such transactions, as well as his testimony further explaining the transactions are also barred by CPLR 4519. Similarly, Howard's testimony as to the number of times that he visited the decedent in support of the claim for gas and tolls is barred by CPLR 4519 [*Matter of O'Neil*, 20 A.D.2d 741].

Without accepting Howard's elaborations and explanations as to the various banking transactions for the decedent's benefit as admissible, the passbooks in the names of the respondents as well as the Citibank checking account in the names of decedent and Howard are admissible for whatever probative value that they might have without any further elaboration other than the stipulation of the parties that the joint Citibank checking account was used for the decedent's benefit.

Based upon the above findings of fact and conclusion of law, petitioner is entitled to recover from respondents the sum of $134,117.00 (the $140,000.00 improperly withdrawn from the accounts minus $5,883.00 reimbursement for funeral expenses) plus interest at the statutory rate from the date of decedent's death. The Chief Clerk shall mail a copy of this decision to the Attorney General.

Case Questions

1. How does this decision tally with the *Drucker* decision?
2. Briefly discuss the nature of the evidence presented and questioned in this case.

2 Rights Incident to Titles in Realty

CHAPTER OVERVIEW

The preceding chapter introduced the various titles that may be acquired to create an interest in property. As discussed in that chapter, these titles apply to interests in all property, real or personal. This chapter and the five that follow focus on rights that are incident to a person holding a title in real property only.

Chapter 1 began with the adage that the law of property really concerns a "bundle of rights." This chapter underscores that axiom by discussing several different rights that are incident to owning or possessing realty in which the only common denominator is the realty itself. That is, for the most part, these rights and obligations are not conceptually related outside of their relationship to the land. The seven rights that are examined in this chapter are:

(a) adverse possession, the manner in which the owner of realty may lose his or her title to all or part of the land to an interloper;
(b) surface rights, the right of a landowner to have the land supported by the neighboring property;
(c) water rights, the right of a titleholder in realty to use and exploit the natural resources located beneath the land;
(d) nuisance, the right of the titleholder to the quiet enjoyment of the use of the property;
(e) fixtures, the manner in which personal property may become permanently affixed to and considered part of the land;
(f) waste, the right of the titleholder to prevent the reduction in value of the property; and

(g) emblements, the right to use and enjoy the vegetation that grows on the land.

Adverse Possession

Adverse possession is a method whereby a person may acquire title to all or part of another person's real estate by operation of law. Titles acquired by adverse possession arise when a person, not the titleholder, takes physical possession of the property for a statutorily determined period of time without the true owner attempting to oust the trespasser. To acquire title by adverse possession, certain requirements must be met:

(a) The statutory period: Each jurisdiction, by statute, specifies the time period for determining whether a person has acquired title by means of adverse possession. Typically, the period ranges between 10 and 20 years, depending upon the particular state.

 EXAMPLE:

Blackacre is located in a state in which a person may acquire title by adverse possession after possessing the property for ten years. The owner of Blackacre, an undeveloped parcel, lives over 800 miles away and has never visited the site; the property was purchased as an investment for future development. An interloper comes onto the land in 1991 and puts up a shack on the property. The interloper uses the property as a residence. In 2001, after ten years have elapsed, the interloper may have the court declare him the owner of Blackacre by adverse possession.

(b) The possession of the property must be open and notorious: This requirement mandates that the interloper's possession be visibly apparent so that the true owner would be deemed to have notice of the fact that someone was in possession of the property.

 EXAMPLE:

In the preceding example, the fact that the interloper constructed a shack on the lot and actually resided in the shack for the statutory period would be deemed sufficiently "open and notorious" to meet this requirement. If the owner had visited Blackacre the shack and the evidence of habitation would have been obvious.

(c) Actual and exclusive possession: This requirement indicates an actual use and possession of the property in question. If the interloper only occupies a small part of the property, he or she may only acquire title by adverse possession to the part actually used. However, if the interloper occupies a reasonable portion of the property, and has some colorable title to the rest of the land, it will be considered as actual possession of the entire lot.

EXAMPLE:

Whiteacre is a ten-acre tract of undeveloped land. An interloper comes onto the property and builds a small house with a flower and vegetable garden on one-half acre of the property. The interloper then constructs a small and simple stone fence around all of Whiteacre. This use of the property would probably be considered possession of all of Whiteacre.

The fact that two or more people may be taking possession does not destroy the requirement of "exclusive" use, provided that one of the persons is not the true owner.

EXAMPLE:

A brother and sister find an abandoned house on an acre of property. They take possession of the house for the statutory period. The siblings may acquire title by adverse possession as tenants in common. Conversely, if the house had been inherited by the sister from their father and the brother resented that fact and continued to reside in the house along with the sister, he would not acquire title by adverse possession because he is residing with the true owner.

(d) Continuous possession: To acquire title by adverse possession, the interloper must possess the property for the entire statutory time limit in one continuous period — unconnected periods of possession cannot be totaled together to meet the statutory period. However, the use of the property by the interloper does not have to be continuous if such use would be inconsistent with the nature of the property in question. Also, an interloper may tack his possessory period to another's period, provided that there is privity between the interlopers.

EXAMPLE:

An interloper obtains possession of a run-down beachfront house that she uses for vacations during the warm weather periods and for holidays during the winter months. This use of the property is consistent with the nature of the property, and therefore this use would be deemed continuous.

EXAMPLE:

An interloper has lived on a parcel of land for seven years when he dies. He wills his interest to the property to his daughter who continues to live on the land for the remainder of the statutory period (ten years). Because there was privity between the parties, the seven years can be tacked on to the three years for the full possessory period of ten years.

(e) Hostile possession: The person who is claiming title by adverse possession must evidence that he or she possessed the property without the permission of the true owner. If the true owner agrees to the possession, explicitly or implicitly, the possession is not considered to be hostile and the statutory period will not run.

EXAMPLE:

In the earlier example in which a house was inherited by a sister but was inhabited by the brother as well as the sister, as long as the sister permits the brother to reside with her, the brother's possession is not considered to be hostile. Whenever the owner remains in possession of the property, all other persons are legally considered to be in possession with the owner's permission.

If the property in question is held by two or more people as co-tenants (see Chapter 1), the possession by one tenant is never considered to be adverse to the other co-tenant because all co-tenants have equal rights of possession. For a co-tenant to be in possession adverse to the interests of the other co-tenants, the tenant-in-possession must attempt to oust the co-tenant by a court order or by an explicit assertion that he or she is claiming exclusive title.

EXAMPLE:

Two brothers inherit a farm as tenants in common. One brother decides to live on the farm and work the land while the other brother returns to the city. Merely leaving the farm and going to the city does not constitute an abandonment of the property by the urban brother, thereby making the farming brother's possession adverse; the urban brother must make an affirmative act of abandonment in order to start the other brother's period of adverse possession.

Once all of the statutory requirements have been met, the claimant interloper may go to court for an order to **quiet title** in which the court will vest title in the claimant by adverse possession (see Chapter 5). The adverse possessor has now become the true owner of the property.

Surface Rights

Surface rights refer to a property owner's right to have the land supported in its natural state by all adjoining land (**lateral support**). This means that if one landowner uses his property in a manner that causes a neighbor's land to subside, the landowner will be held strictly liable for the resulting injuries to the land. Being held **strictly liable** means that the person who causes the injury is held legally responsible for the injury regardless of how careful he was in performing the action that caused the injury.

 EXAMPLE:

A young couple have just purchased their first house and are remodeling the property. They want to create a small ornamental pond, and hire a landscaper to excavate the pond on a corner of their property. Unbeknownst to the parties, there is a fault beneath the surface, and when the landscaper digs down a few feet a portion of the land collapses, including a part of their neighbor's garden. The couple is strictly liable for the injuries resulting from the collapse of the land to the neighbor's garden.

If the property that is injured has buildings constructed on it, and the damage to the surface causes injury to the structures, the landowner who caused the damage will be held liable if the collapse would have occurred to the property in its natural state. Otherwise, the person who caused the damage to the lateral support will only be liable if he or she acted negligently.

 EXAMPLE:

A woman is remodeling her townhouse. The townhouse shares a wall with the house next door. While the digging is taking place the work causes the neighbor's wall to collapse two feet. If the neighbor can prove that the land would have collapsed even if no house were on it, the woman will be held strictly liable for the damage to the house. If the damage to the wall was only occasioned because of the weight of the house built on the land the woman will only be held liable if the digging was done in a negligent manner.

In addition to lateral support, a property owner is entitled to **subjacent support,** meaning that anyone who is occupying the area beneath the property must support the surface and all buildings on the property that existed when the use commenced. The underground user will be held strictly liable for any resultant injuries to the land and the buildings on it. If a building is erected after the underground use began, the underground user will only be liable for damage to that structure if the user was negligent and that negligence caused the injury.

 EXAMPLE:

A landowner permits an oil company to drill for oil on his property. The property in question has a house located on it. After the drilling has begun, the landowner uses some of the money he received from the oil company to build a garage. Two months later, due to a weakness in the underground rock that could not have been discovered prior to the drilling, the land gives way and damages the house and the garage. The oil company will be held strictly liable for any resulting injury to the house, but will only be liable for injury to the garage if it can be shown that the company was negligent in its work and that negligence caused damage to the garage. The house was on the property when the use began, but the garage was added after the work had started.

Water Rights

The owner of land has certain rights of use, and limitations of use, of the water located on the land. These rights depend upon whether the water is a watercourse, ground water, or surface water.

(a) Watercourse: A **watercourse** is a stream, a river, or a lake, and four separate legal concepts have developed with respect to the rights incident to these types of waters:

    i.   The riparian doctrine. The **riparian doctrine** holds that a landowner has the unfettered right to use all watercourses that abut or are surrounded by his or her land. The person who holds riparian rights may use the water only for the land that gives rise to this right, but this use may be limited by the particular jurisdiction.

    ii. Natural flow theory. Pursuant to the **natural flow theory,** the landowner may only use the water in a manner that does not damage the quality, quantity, or velocity of the water for adjoining landowners.

EXAMPLE:

A farmer owns a parcel of land through which a small river flows. In order to irrigate the land, the farmer constructs dykes in the river to direct the water. This causes a tremendous diminution in the amount of water that flows onto his neighbor's property. The neighbor can enjoin the farmer from such use because it destroys the natural flow of the river.

> iii. **Reasonable use.** This doctrine, which is the most prevalent, states that riparian owners may make a reasonable use of the water, meaning that all use is permissible provided that it does not substantially interfere with the rights of other riparian owners. To determine whether the use is "reasonable," the courts consider six factors:
>   • the amount of the alteration in the flow of the water
>   • the purpose for which the water is being used
>   • whether the use causes any pollution to the water
>   • the amount and extent of the use
>   • the flow of the water
>   • any other factors that the court deems significant
> Under this theory, permissible use is determined on a case-by-case basis.

 EXAMPLE:

A landowner constructs a waterwheel to harness the flow of a river on her property to generate electricity. This use causes a reduction in the flow of the river, and some downstream neighbors complain that this use has caused some pollution and a reduction in the amount of water that flows onto their property. The court will consider all factors to determine whether the landowner's waterwheel is a reasonable use of her riparian rights.

> In determining whether the use of the watercourse by the riparian owner is permissible, the courts will always look to see whether such use furthers a natural or artificial purpose. Natural use is always favored over an artificial use.
> iv. **Prior appropriation doctrine.** Under this theory landowners acquire use of the watercourse by historical actual use. Provided such use does not cause a natural decline in the flow of the water, the courts allocate priority by the time of the appropriation of the watercourse. Under this theory, an appropriated right may be lost by the abandonment of the use by the landowner.

EXAMPLE:

In 1985 a landowner diverted a stream that runs on his property to create an ornamental pond. This diversion caused a minor reduction in the velocity of the water. Later, the adjoining property is purchased by a couple who want to use the stream for irrigation but cannot because of the decrease in velocity. The court may consider that the first landowner has prior rights to the stream, under the prior appropriation doctrine, or may decide that such use causes a significant reduction in the velocity of the water for the neighbors.

(b) Ground water: **Ground water,** also called **percolating water,** refers to underground water. Four different theories have developed with respect to the rights to this water, depending upon the particular jurisdiction:

   i. **Absolute ownership doctrine.** Twenty eastern states adhere to this doctrine, which permits the landowner to all unrestricted use of such water.

   ii. **Reasonable use doctrine.** Twenty-five states favor this concept, which permits the owner of the land all use of such water except for export.

   iii. **Correlative rights doctrine.** This doctrine is favored in California; it permits all the owners of overlying land reasonable use of the ground water.

   iv. **Appropriation rights doctrine.** This doctrine, followed by several states in the west, allows use based on the historical use of such water, in the same manner as the prior appropriation doctrine for watercourses.

(c) Surface water: **Surface water** is defined as water that accumulates on the land, such as rainfall, that does not flow by means of a river or stream. About half of the states consider surface water to be a **common enemy,** meaning that the landowner may do anything he or she wishes to cause drainage and removal of surface water. The other states permit landowners to use only reasonable methods of draining the surface water.

   The legal problems associated with surface water only concern drainage rights.

EXAMPLE:

During the fall rains, a small river tends to overflow, causing surface water on the property through which it flows. One landowner has created a system of canals to run off the water, which causes a higher level of surface water on his neighbor's land. Another neighbor has constructed a channel to drain the surface water into a storage tank. The landowner who has constructed the canals may be liable to his neighbors for the increase in the surface water on the neighboring property, depending upon the jurisdiction in which the land is located. The landowner who stores the water would be totally free to make such storage use of surface water.

Nuisance

Nuisance is a theory that is based in tort law that affects a person's property rights. The law distinguishes two types of nuisance: public and private.

    Public nuisance. A **public nuisance** is any act that unreasonably interferes with the health, safety, or property rights of the community at large. This injury can only be asserted by the government on behalf of the community; a private property owner may only assert a claim based on a public nuisance if the property owner can demonstrate some particular individual injury to his or her property. An example of a public nuisance would be using a building for hazardous waste detention that affects the property rights of the surrounding property owners.

    Private nuisance. A **private nuisance** is a substantial and unreasonable interference with another person's use or enjoyment of property that he or she possesses. "Substantial interference" refers to any act that is offensive to the average person. The law does not consider the action to cause a substantial interference if the interference arises because of a person's hypersensitivity or the particular use to which the subject property is put.

EXAMPLE:

A nightclub has just opened on a residential street. The couple who own the house directly opposite the club are constantly awakened by the noise from the nightclub and the increased traffic from the club's patrons. The couple may be able to enjoin the club from operating if they demonstrate that the noise generated by the club creates a substantial interference with the enjoyment of their property.

If the basis of the claim of nuisance is the "unreasonable interference" with the use or enjoyment of the property, the claimant must be able to demonstrate that this interference with use or enjoyment of the property outweighs the utility of the defendant's conduct. In making its decision, the court will always bear in mind that a person is entitled to the reasonable use of his or her property, considering:

- the neighborhood in which the property is located;
- the effect on the land value to the property in question; and
- the ability of the defendant to use a different method of operation.

 EXAMPLE:

A revivalist church has just opened in a residential neighborhood. The person who lives next door to the church asserts that the Sunday morning services are so loud that they interfere with the quiet enjoyment of his property. In determining whether the church's activities are a nuisance, the court will look at the actual amount of noise generated and the particular characteristics of the neighborhood.

Note that the right against interference from nuisance attaches not only to the owners of the property, but also to anyone who has the lawful possession of the property, such as a tenant.

Fixtures

A **fixture** is defined as a chattel that has been so affixed to real property that it is deemed to have become a part of the realty. A **chattel** is simply an item of personal property.

The determination as to whether a chattel has retained its identity as personal property or has become incorporated into the realty depends on two factors:

1. whether the intent of the party affixing the chattel was to make it a permanent part of the real estate; and
2. whether the chattel has been affixed in such a manner that its removal would be inconsistent with its use or would damage the structure to which it has been attached.

 EXAMPLE:

A landowner decides to construct a house on a vacant lot. The bricks, tiles, cement, and so forth, all of which are chattel, are incorporated into the structure during the construction of the building and they are totally incorporated as real property. Other chattels, such as water pipes, are so integral to the structure that their removal would cause severe damage to the structure; they are thereby deemed fixtures, permanently attached to the land.

EXAMPLE:

A homeowner is decorating her new house. She has wall-to-wall carpeting installed in the dining room, whereas in the living room she decides to use area rugs. The wall-to-wall carpeting has become a fixture because it was installed for a particular use with the house. Conversely, the area rugs are not fixtures because area rugs are intended to be moved around.

In situations in which title to the realty is divided among two or more persons, such as a life estate followed by a remainder interest or a tenant's possessory title in the landlord's property (see Chapter 7), the law assumes, absent an agreement to the contrary, that the person with the possessory interest lacks the intent to have a chattel permanently affixed to the realty because he or she has a terminable interest.

EXAMPLE:

A couple rent an apartment for a two-year period and decide to put linoleum on the kitchen floor. The linoleum is considered to be personal property, not a fixture, unless the lease specifies a different result.

Many problems are encountered when homeowners attempt to sell their property and the prospective buyer assumes certain items, such as chandeliers, switch plates, and so forth, are fixtures, whereas the sellers consider the items as personal property that they intend to take with them. To avoid conflicts, whenever property is sold the seller should indicate at the outset which items will not be deemed fixtures.

Waste

Waste is the damage caused to real property by a person who does not have a fee simple title to the property that affects the value of the property for the successor fee holder. The doctrines associated with waste apply to life tenants and lessees because their interests terminate in favor of the holder of a fee title.

The law classifies four different types of waste:

1. **Voluntary waste:** This type of waste occurs when the tenant intentionally or negligently damages the property, or extracts its natural resources in a manner inconsistent with the rights of a life tenant or a lessee.

EXAMPLE:

A life tenant decides that he does not want the two-car garage that is on the property. He calls a construction company and has the garage demolished. The tenant's voluntary action has diminished the value of the property and therefore constitutes voluntary waste.

 EXAMPLE:

A woman inherits a life estate in a diamond mine. As a life tenant of such property she is entitled to engage in ordinary mining activities. However, the woman decides to hire miners to extract the diamonds 24 hours a day, 7 days a week, to extract all the diamonds in the mine. This use is beyond the ordinary and reasonable use of the mine and may be considered waste to the interests of the remainderman.

2. **Permissive waste:** This type of waste results when the tenant fails to protect the property from damage from the elements. The life tenant is expected to make ordinary repairs on the property to maintain it in the same condition it was in when he or she acquired possession of the estate.

 EXAMPLE:

A couple inherit a life estate in a brick house. They only use the house periodically, and when water starts seeping in they simply mop up the floor. Brickwork needs to be pointed every few years, but the couple are unwilling to go to the expense of maintaining the brickwork. When the damage from the water becomes so severe that the bricks start falling out, the couple will be held liable for permissive waste.

3. **Ameliorative waste:** This category of waste is distinguishable from the other forms of waste because the action of the tenant increases rather than decreases the value of the property. Historically, a remainderman was entitled to receive the property in the same state it was in when the earlier estate took possession, thereby including all changes to the property within the category of waste. The modern trend of the court is to deny the remainderman any action for ameliorative waste, unless the remainderman can demonstrate that the "improvement" in fact lessens the value of the property to him.

EXAMPLE:

A life tenant of a house decides that he wants to add a two-car garage to the property. The garage increases the value of the property. Historically, this construction would be considered waste to the remainderman. Today, such construction would not be considered waste, unless the remainderman could show that the building was an eyesore that will have to come down or that it was constructed in a manner that violates the zoning laws of the community.

4. **Equitable waste:** This type of waste concerns land that is used for agricultural purposes and arises when the life tenant fails to exercise good husbandry thereby causing decreased production value of the land. It is fairly close to voluntary waste, but attaches to this particular type of property.

EXAMPLE:

A man inherits a life estate in a farm. During his tenancy he only grows corn on the land and fails to rotate crops. This causes depletion in the mineral content of the soil, lessening the value of the land. The remainderman could sue on a claim of equitable waste.

If a tenant has committed waste on the property, the remainderman has a cause of action. The remainderman may either seek **damages,** a monetary amount to compensate the remainderman for the degree of injury sustained by the waste, or an **injunction,** a court order requiring that the tenant stop the action that constitutes waste to the property.

Emblements

Emblements are the resources incident to the land, such as crops, minerals, timber, and so forth. All persons with a possessory interest in real property are entitled to take and use the profits, or emblements, on the land, provided that such use does not go beyond an ordinary and reasonable use that would adversely affect the interests of the remainderman or the owner.

Emblements fall into two broad categories:

1. **fructus naturales** — these are items naturally growing or living on the land that can be used by the possessor during the period of lawful possession.
2. **fructus industriales** — these are items that are specifically planted by the possessor; the fruits growing on the land as the result of

the possessor's own efforts. The possessor is entitled to one final taking of such fruit after the termination of the tenancy, provided that the fruit was growing on the land at the time of the termination of the tenancy.

 EXAMPLE:

A woman acquires a life estate in a small house situated on a few acres of land. The land has several cherry trees growing on it, as well as wild flowers. The woman decides to create an herb garden for vegetables and herbs. During the tenancy the woman may use all of the cherries, flowers, vegetables, ands herbs that grow on the land. On her death, her heirs may enter the land to remove the vegetables and herbs that were planted and growing at the time of her death, but have no right to the cherries or the wildflowers.

Practical Tips

- Determine the appropriate law in the jurisdiction with respect to surface and water rights before making any changes to the land.
- If representing a landowner, make sure that the owner visits the land periodically to prevent squatters from taking adverse possession.
- If representing a squatter, make sure that he or she has stayed on the land in an open and notorious manner.
- If representing an adverse possessor, make sure that the title is affirmed by a court and recorded with the county recorder's office.

Chapter Review

Any person who acquires an interest in realty also acquires certain other specific rights that automatically attach to the title in land. This is true regardless of whether the title was acquired by sale, inheritance, lease, or adverse possession. Conversely, the titleholder may lose his or her title if a third person obtains possession of the property for a statutory period in a manner that is open, notorious, continuous, and adverse to the rights of the true owner.

The rights that are incident to titles in realty fall into two broad categories: those that permit the titleholder to exert dominion over the land itself, and those that provide the titleholder with freedom from interference with his or her enjoyment or use of the property.

The rights that permit the titleholder to exert dominion over the land are water rights (the right to use watercourses that run on the property and surface water), the right to extract minerals, and the right to fixtures, which are chattels that become permanently affixed to the land.

The rights that afford the titleholder protection from interference with the use and enjoyment of the property include the right to be free from nuisance and the right to seek judicial relief from waste to the property caused by a life tenant or lessee.

A title in realty affords the holder not only the ability to use the land, but also a bundle of other rights that permit her to protect that interest and exert control over actions that affect the land itself.

Ethical Concern

Law and interpersonal relationships often conflict. This is especially true with respect to water and surface rights. The owner of real property must be aware of the impact that asserting these rights for his or her land may have on the neighboring land. Even though the right may be legal, it may cause many personal problems between neighbors.

Key Terms

Absolute ownership doctrine
Adverse possession
Ameliorative waste
Appropriation rights doctrine
Chattel
Common enemy
Correlative rights doctrine
Emblements
Equitable waste
Fixture
Fructus industriales
Fructus naturales
Ground water
Lateral support
Natural flow theory
Nuisance

Percolating water
Permissive waste
Prior appropriation doctrine
Private nuisance
Public nuisance
Quiet title
Reasonable use
Reasonable use doctrine
Riparian doctrine
Strict liability
Subjacent support
Surface rights
Surface water
Voluntary waste
Waste
Watercourse

Exercises

1. Research the statutory period for adverse possession in your state.
2. Research which of the water rights doctrines applies in your state.

3. List several factors that you would use to determine whether a particular chattel is a fixture or removable personal property.
4. Differentiate and give your own examples of the different types of waste.
5. Briefly discuss the factors that a court might use to determine whether a given action constitutes nuisance to a property owner.

Situational Analysis

A brother and sister inherit a large farm from their grandfather. The sister is an attorney who works in a large city; the brother is unemployed. The brother takes up residence on the farm to till the soil. Because of the size of the farm, the brother only farms one-half of the property. Ten years later, a couple claim title to the other half of the property by adverse possession, stating that they have lived in a cabin on the land for ten years. What evidence would be needed to support the couple's claim? What impact does this claim have on the sister's rights? What other information do you need?

Edited Cases

The first case, *The Prudential Ins. Co. of Am. v. Spencer's Kenosha Bowl, Inc.*, discusses the concept of waste, and the second decision, *Myers v. Beam*, analyzes the doctrine of adverse possession.

The Prudential Insurance Company of America
v. Spencer's Kenosha Bowl Inc.
137 Wis. 2d 313, 404 N.W.2d 109 (1987)

Spencer's Kenosha Bowl, Inc. (Spencer's) appeals from a judgment awarding $369,188.21 in damages to the Prudential Insurance Company of America (Prudential). The award is for waste committed by Spencer's upon real estate against which Prudential holds a mortgage. Spencer's raises four issues on appeal: (1) whether Spencer's, as a successor owner which did not assume the mortgage indebtedness, may be held liable for waste, including passive or permissive waste; (2) whether Prudential's waste claim was properly included in a foreclosure action; (3) whether the trial court properly calculated the amount of the waste judgment against Spencer's; and (4) whether the waste finding is sufficiently supported by the evidence. Because we resolve all of the issues against Spencer's, we affirm.

The property involved in this litigation is a commercial building constructed in 1970 and situated on real estate located in the city of Kenosha.

Spencer's purchased the property in 1975 from Delco Development Co. (Delco) which had previously mortgaged the property to Prudential. It is undisputed that Spencer's did not assume Delco's mortgage indebtedness when it purchased the property. Prudential subsequently foreclosed on the property after the mortgage note was in default.

In April, 1983, the Honorable Frederick Kessler, the judge then assigned to the case, granted Prudential's request for foreclosure of the property. The amount owed on the mortgage note at the time of the sheriff's sale was fixed at $994,497.80. The property sold for $635,000 in May, 1984. Following the sale, the Honorable Richard G. Harvey, Jr., the judge subsequently assigned to the case, held a hearing on Prudential's claim that Spencer's had committed waste upon the property. In his decision on the waste issue, Judge Harvey found that Spencer's had committed waste in the following amounts:

Property Taxes	$198,743.34
Roof	37,890.00
Ceiling Tile and Grid	103,064.52
Electric Facilities	14,647.16
Drywall-wood	36,251.85
Restroom	766.66
Exterior Canopy	13,090.83
Cleanup Costs	16,381.00
Floor Tile Damage	24,000.00
	$444,835.36

However, because the amount of the waste exceeded the amount of the debt less the foreclosure sale proceeds, Judge Harvey lowered Prudential's waste award so that it equaled the amount of the debt deficiency.

Spencer's initially argues that a grantee who does not assume the mortgage of a grantor-mortgagor cannot be held liable for any waste committed on the mortgaged property. Whether a mortgagor has a cause of action for waste is a question of law. See *Williams v. Security Savings & Loan Ass'n*, 120 Wis. 2d 480, 482, 355 N.W.2d 370, 372 (Ct. App. 1984). As a result, we review this question independently of any conclusions made by the trial court. Id.

Waste is a species of tort. See *Jaffe-Spindler Co. v. Genesco, Inc.*, 747 F.2d 253, 256 (4th Cir. 1984). It is defined as "the unreasonable conduct by the owner of a possessory estate that results in physical damage to the real estate and substantial diminution in the value of the estates in which others have an interest." *Pleasure Time, Inc. v. Kuss*, 78 Wis. 2d 373, 381, 254 N.W.2d 463, 467 (1977). Although a mortgagee only has a lien on the mortgaged property, see sec. 708.01, Stats.; *State v. Phillips*, 99 Wis. 2d 46, 50, 298 N.W.2d 239, 241 (Ct. App. 1980), he or she is entitled to maintain a legal action for waste against a mortgagor. See *Jones v. Costigan*, 12 Wis. 757, 760-65 (1860).

We conclude that the waste doctrine permits a mortgagee to maintain an action for waste against a nonassuming grantee of a mortgagor. In *Scott v. Webster*, 50 Wis. 53, 6 N.W. 363 (1880), the supreme court held that senior mortgagees in possession of property were accountable to a junior mortgagee for waste committed on the property. Id. at 64, 6 N.W. at 365. There, the senior mortgagees removed a large amount of timber from the property which substantially diminished its value. Id. at 60-61, 6 N.W. at 363. Prior to the timber removal, the senior mortgagees purchased an equity of redemption which entitled them to possession of the property. Id. at 62, 6 N.W. at 364. Consequently, the senior mortgagees were both owners and mortgagees of the property. Id. at 63, 6 N.W. at 364-65. The court reasoned that with respect to the junior mortgagee, the senior mortgagees were mortgagees in possession and as such must be held liable for the waste they committed while in possession of the property. Id. at 63-64, 6 N.W. at 365.

Here, as in *Scott*, Spencer's legally had possession of the property and, under the trial court's findings, committed acts which resulted in a substantial diminution in the property's value. It is undisputed that Prudential, as a mortgagee, had an interest in the property. See *Phillips*, 99 Wis. 2d at 50, 298 N.W.2d at 241. As a result, all of the essential ingredients for a waste cause of action as set out in *Pleasure Time* are met. See *Pleasure Time*, 78 Wis. 2d at 381, 254 N.W.2d at 467. Moreover, we consider the court's reasoning in *Scott* as an indication of the liberality to be allowed a mortgagee when enforcing or protecting the lien interest. See also *Atkinson v. Hewett*, 63 Wis. 396, 23 N.W. 889 (1885) (mortgagee allowed to recover for wasteful conduct of trespasser). We do not deem the nonassuming grantee's status so unique that it warrants insulation from a waste action and prevents the mortgagee from preserving and protecting a security interest.

Our conclusion is also supported by the supreme court's language in *Edler v. Hasche*, 67 Wis. 653, 659-61, 31 N.W. 57, 59-61 (1887). There, Edler and Brandt were mortgagee and mortgagor, respectively. As in this case, Hasche purchased the mortgaged property from Brandt "subject to the mortgage." Id. at 659, 31 N.W. at 59. While the court left for a later proceeding the question of Hasche's liability for the mortgage debt and strongly suggested that the evidence might not support a finding that Hasche had assumed the mortgage, the court nonetheless recognized that Hasche's removal of a building was waste for which he was liable to Edler. The court stated that "Hasche's liability for waste . . . upon every principle of justice is clear and must be affirmed." Id. at 661, 31 N.W. at 60-61.

The import of *Edler* on this case is clear. Regardless of successor liability on the mortgage debt, the court in *Edler* affirms the principle that a nonassuming grantee can be liable to a mortgagee for waste committed to the secured property. Consequently, Spencer's nonassuming grantee status does not affect its liability for waste.

As an extension of this issue, Spencer's attempts to draw a distinction between its liability for active and passive waste. Passive or permissive waste results from negligence or omission to do that which would prevent injury. See *Finley v. Chain*, 374 N.E.2d 67, 79 (Ind. Ct. App. 1978) (overruled on other grounds by *Morris v. Weigle*, 383 N.E.2d 341, 345 n.3 (Ind. 1978)).

Active or voluntary waste requires an affirmative act which results in the destruction or alteration of property. See *Jowdy v. Guerin*, 457 P.2d 745, 748 (Ariz. Ct. App. 1969). At common law, an individual could be held liable for waste only if the acts were tortious and intentional. See Leipziger, The Mortgagee's Remedies for Waste, 64 Cal. L. Rev. 1086, 1093-94 (1976). No waste cause of action lay for negligent waste. Id. at 1094, 1130-32.

Whether a particular act is waste depends upon the circumstances. *Pleasure Time*, 78 Wis. 2d at 381, 254 N.W.2d at 467. Modern Wisconsin law does not distinguish between passive and active waste. However, early Wisconsin law recognized that waste could "be either voluntary or permissive." *Melms v. Pabst Brewing Co.*, 104 Wis. 7, 9, 79 N.W. 738, 739 (1899). Moreover, Wisconsin law has dealt with fact situations where the actions characterized as waste can be described as either active or passive. See, e.g., *Scott*, 50 Wis. at 53, 6 N.W. at 363 (waste resulting from removal of timber); *Jones*, 12 Wis. at 757 (removal of doors and windows from house); *Pleasure Time*, 78 Wis. 2d at 381, 254 N.W.2d at 467-68 (waste alleged involved demolished and deteriorated buildings); *First Nat'l Bank v. Clark & Lund Boat Co.*, 68 Wis. 2d 738, 741, 229 N.W.2d 221, 223 (1975) (failure to pay taxes).

We conclude that the modern waste definition is broad enough in Wisconsin to include both active and passive waste. The common law "limitations are not well rationalized in the cases and seem to have come about largely by accident." *Leipziger*, supra, at 1094. Conduct which results either in active or passive waste "may injure or threaten property rendering the debt unsafe." *Finley*, 374 N.E.2d at 79. Consequently, the mortgagee's security may be impaired by either passive or active waste and the policy for allowing the mortgagee recovery is the same regardless of the type of waste involved.

Next, Spencer's argues that the entry of judgment was not warranted because the amount of the waste found to have been committed was less than the amount obtained from the sale of the property. Spencer's, however, cites no legal authority for this proposition and, as a result, we are not required to consider it. See *State v. Schaffer*, 96 Wis. 2d 531, 545-46, 292 N.W.2d 370, 378 (Ct. App. 1980). Moreover, Spencer's argument seems to be a distortion of the common law rule that, in lien jurisdictions, a mortgagee cannot recover until his security has been substantially impaired which occurs only when waste has reduced the value of the encumbered property to less than the unpaid balance of the debt. See *Leipziger*, supra, at 1097. It is undisputed in this case that the waste found by the trial court reduced the value of the encumbered property in the fashion required by this rule.

Spencer's also challenges the trial court's calculation of the damages based on the debt deficiency. Spencer's argues that this is in fact an award of a deficiency judgment on a mortgage which it never assumed. However, in lien jurisdictions, a trial court must determine the extent of reduction in the value of the security interest in the property, not just the amount of injury to the real estate. See *Finley*, 374 N.E.2d at 78. Where, as here, the amount of waste committed on the property is greater than the amount of the debt deficiency, the extent of reduction in the value of the mortgagee's security interest will always be equal to the debt deficiency. Consequently, we do not view the trial court's award as a deficiency judgment but, rather, as an independent award litigated within the context of a foreclosure proceeding.

Finally, Spencer's argues that the trial court's finding that Spencer's had committed waste by failing to maintain the property is not supported by the evidence. Whether a particular act constitutes waste is left to the trier of fact. *Pleasure Time*, 78 Wis. 2d at 382, 254 N.W.2d at 468. Factual findings will not be overturned unless clearly erroneous. Sec. 805.17(2), Stats.

We conclude that the trial court's finding that Spencer's failed to maintain the property is supported by the evidence. The record reveals that at the time of Spencer's occupancy in 1975, the building's roof was only five years into its twenty-year expected life span; that the roof was in full compliance with the state building code when Spencer's took occupancy in 1975; that an expert witness testified that the leaks in the roof had existed for some time and had resulted in extensive damage to the interior fixtures; that the roof was first cited for being in violation of the state building code in 1983; and that when this action was commenced the roof had completely deteriorated and needed total replacement. Consequently, the trial court concluded that most if not all of the roof's deterioration and subsequent damage to the building occurred while Spencer's had possession of the property. This finding is not clearly erroneous.

Judgment affirmed.

Case Questions

1. How does the court support the statement that "waste is a form of tort"?

2. What factors does the court rely on to determine that waste has occurred?

Myers v. Beam
551 Pa. 670, 713 A.2d 61 (1998)

Appellants Jay and Helen Myers sought to acquire title by adverse possession to a strip of land adjoining their property, and the court of common pleas granted their petition. The court found that all elements necessary to establish title by adverse possession were present. The Superior Court, however, reversed due to appellants' attempt to acquire title by seeking a quitclaim deed from appellees' predecessors in title before the expiration of the statute of limitations for adverse possession. The Superior Court held that the request for a quitclaim deed was an acknowledgement of the superiority of the record owners' title inconsistent with the requirement that adverse possession must be hostile. Thus the element of hostility is the only element of adverse possession at issue.

Appellant argues that we should follow the reasoning of Judge Tamalia, who dissented from the conclusion of the majority of the Superior Court panel. He cited *Burns v. Mitchell*, 252 Pa. Super. 257, 381 A.2d 487 (1977), to the effect that even if a trespasser seeks a quitclaim deed from the record owner, such a trespasser is not acknowledging superior title in the record owner, but is merely seeking to improve the marketability of his own title.

Burns, however, is factually distinguishable. The disputed land in *Burns* adjoined the lots of the two parties, neither of whom held record title. Burns obtained title by adverse possession. She later acquired a quitclaim deed to the disputed land. Burns held that the quitclaim deed only gave Burns record title to property she had already acquired by adverse possession. Under these circumstances, Burns merely improved the marketability of her title after establishing ownership by adverse possession.

In this case, by contrast, appellants sought a quitclaim deed from the record owner; moreover, they did so approximately eight years prior to the running of the statute of limitations for adverse possession. It is therefore apparent that the *Burns* precept — namely, that it is perfectly consistent to claim title by adverse possession and also seek a quitclaim deed — is inapplicable under the facts of this case.

It is also argued that it is not essential to establish hostility in a claim of adverse possession if all other elements of adverse possession are present. This argument is based on *Tioga Coal Co. v. Supermarkets General Corp.*, 519 Pa. 66, 75, 546 A.2d 1, 5 (1988). *Tioga* stated that "if the true owner has not ejected the interloper within the time allotted for an action in ejectment, and all other elements of adverse possession have been established, hostility will be implied, regardless of the subjective state of mind of the trespasser." Id. Appellants argue that if the *Tioga* rule is applied to this case, where every element of adverse possession, with the sole exception of hostility, is undisputedly present, then title by adverse possession has been properly proved, as hostility is implied when the other elements are present.

This is a misinterpretation of the holding and rationale of *Tioga*. The opinion stated that the above holding "is consistent with a requirement that adverse possession be characterized by hostility as well as the other elements of the cause of action. . . ." Id., 519 Pa. at 75, 546 A.2d at 5. *Tioga* manifestly cannot be interpreted as disposing of the requirement of hostility. The record in *Tioga* was silent as to evidence of hostility.

To interpret and apply the holding of *Tioga* in this case, it is essential to recognize that the facts of the cases differ materially. The record of *Tioga* was silent as to hostility; there was no evidence tending to prove or disprove hostility. In those circumstances, the court inferred the existence of hostility. In this case, however, there is evidence tending to disprove the existence of hostility. To rely on *Tioga* to establish the existence of hostility in this case would not only be an extreme extension of *Tioga*, but would essentially eliminate hostility as one of the required elements of adverse possession. Such an interpretation is impermissible given the above-quoted statement in *Tioga* that its holding "is consistent with a requirement that adverse possession be characterized by hostility as well as the other elements of the cause of action. . . ." Id., 519 Pa. at 75, 546 A.2d at 5. Here, seeking a quitclaim deed destroyed the element of continuous hostility in the adverse possession of appellants, and *Tioga* is not capable of being interpreted as supplying that element by implication.

We therefore hold that the Superior Court was correct in reversing the court of common pleas, thereby denying title by adverse possession on account of appellants' attempt to acquire a quitclaim deed from appellees.

Order of the Superior Court affirmed.

Case Questions

1. What is the effect of the quitclaim deed on the assertions in this case?

2. What does the court say about the requirement of hostility?

3 Land Use

CHAPTER OVERVIEW

Land use refers to the right of enjoyment and access to land that may be permitted to persons who are not the legal owners or possessors of the land. In this regard, this right to the use of the land affects both the person with current legal title to the property as well as a person who will eventually acquire that title.

Five major topics are discussed under the heading of land use. The first concerns restrictions that may be placed on the titleholder with respect to the nature of the use to which the property may be put. These restrictions are known as covenants and they affect all persons who acquire title to the property from the person who originally received the property subject to the covenant.

An easement is the right of passage over or use of another person's realty, which may be acquired in several ways. Once the easement is established, the easement holder has rights to such use that may be enforced against the titleholder.

A license refers to the power a person may have to perform a particular act, or series of acts, on another person's property, such as having the right to receive the fruit from a neighbor's cherry tree.

Any person who has lawful possession of realty, by common and statutory law, owes certain duties of care to anyone who is physically present on the property, even if that person is considered to be a trespasser — a person who has no lawful authority to enter onto the land.

Finally, all owners of property may be subject to certain governmental restrictions. The government — federal, state, and local — has the legal authority to limit the nature of the use of geographic sections within their jurisdiction under the concept of zoning regulation.

This chapter continues the exploration of the "bundle of rights" associated with the law of property by examining these limitations imposed on a person's use of his or her own land.

Covenants

A **covenant** is a written promise to do or not to do something on or with the land. Covenants are often referred to as **real covenants** to imply their effect on realty. Most are typically are found in the deed that conveys the property (see Chapter 4), and are considered to "run with the land," meaning that these provisions limit not only the person who originally acquired the deed that included the covenant, but to all subsequent titleholders as well.

 EXAMPLE:

A widow decides to generate some capital by selling off a large tract of undeveloped land that she inherited. She wishes to keep the area purely residential, and so in the deeds she executes as she parcels off the property she includes a covenant that the grantee will not construct a multi-family dwelling on the property. This restrictive provision creates a covenant that runs with the land, thereby ensuring that the property will remain residential.

As a general proposition, a person is not legally bound to any provision that he or she did not specifically indorse. However, under real property law, a person will be bound to a covenant that runs with the land regardless of his or her actual assumption of the provision if the following five requirements are met with respect to the creation of the covenant:

1. Intent: In order for the covenant to run with the land it must be evidenced that the grantor who created the covenant specifically meant that it bind the use of the property. This intent will usually depend upon the exact wording of the covenant, but may be inferred as well.

 EXAMPLE:

The widow from the previous example has divided her tract of land into 20 parcels. In 19 of her deeds she specifically includes the covenant with respect to single-family dwellings. This indicates her intent. On the last parcel she inadvertently neglects to insert the covenant. Her intent *may* be determined from the words of all the other deeds that created the subdivision.

2. Notice: This requirement means that, for a subsequent purchaser to be bound by a covenant, he or she must have notice of the existence of the covenant. This notice could either be actual, because it appears in the conveyance the purchaser acquires, or implied, because the covenant appears in the record books where title to real property is officially recorded (see Chapter 4).

EXAMPLE:

A young couple purchases a parcel of land from the widow in the preceding examples. Twenty-five years later they decide to sell their house. The conveyance to the man who purchases their house does not include the covenant, but the deed with the covenant was filed with the recorder's office when the widow first sold the property. The man is bound by the covenant because the recording of the covenant provides notice to him as a subsequent purchaser of the property.

3. Horizontal privity: **Horizontal privity** means that the original parties to the covenant must share some interest in the property (usually the covenant), such as being the buyer and the seller, the landlord and the tenant, or the mortgagor and the mortgagee. This common interest creates privity.
4. Vertical privity: **Vertical privity** means that the person who acquired the property from the person who first acquired the property with the covenant has acquired the entire interest of that original party.

EXAMPLE:

In the previous example, the widow and the young couple have horizontal privity because of the contract for the sale of the land. The man who buys the property from the couple has vertical privity because the couple owned a fee that they sold to the man — he acquired their entire interest.

5. Touch and concern the land: To create a covenant, the subject of the covenant must **touch and concern the land,** meaning that its provisions must restrict a person from doing something on the parcel of land (such as not constructing multi-family dwellings) or require that the person do something on the particular parcel (maintaining the land in its natural state).

If all of the preceding five requirements are established, a real covenant that runs with the land has been created. If this type of covenant exists, the successor in interest to the original party may enforce that covenant in a court of law. The original parties would be the persons who first created the covenant, such as the widow and the young couple from the preceding example. The successor in interest is anyone who acquired title from the person who first obtained the title subject to the covenant, such as the man who bought the house from the young couple in the preceding example. (See Chapter 1 for a discussion of a fee simple subject to a condition subsequent.) To enforce the covenant, the successor in interest must prove the following:

(a) the original parties intended that the covenant could be enforced by a successor in interest;
(b) there is privity with respect to the party seeking enforcement and the original party; and
(c) the covenant touches and concerns the land.

If all of these requirements are satisfied, the party seeking enforcement of the covenant may seek damages — monetary relief — for the injury caused by its breach.

EXAMPLE:

The man who purchased the property from the young couple in the previous example decides to modify the house to make it a two-family dwelling. This construction would violate the covenant. The man's neighbor, who also purchased his property from the widow, may go to court to seek damages if such construction takes place because the man is subject to the covenant as is the neighbor whose deed from the widow contained the same provision.

The provisions of a real covenant may terminate if the person who could enforce the covenant executes a **release,** a document that relinquishes legal rights; the property is condemned by the government (see below); or the property is reacquired by the promissee or the promissee's successor in interest (the above-discussed widow). The reacquisition of the property by the original grantor is called a **merger** of the interests.

Closely associated with the concept of real covenants are equitable servitudes. An **equitable servitude** is a form of a covenant that is distinguished from real covenants by the remedy that is being sought by the party seeking to enforce its provisions. If the injury results from a covenant, the injured party may seek monetary damages; if the injury results from an equitable servitude, the injured party may only seek an injunction or specific performance — equitable rather than legal remedies.

As with covenants, an equitable servitude may be created by a writing, but unlike a covenant an equitable servitude may also arise by implication. Typically, equitable servitudes arise by implication when a common scheme for a subdivision can be discerned, as with the example of the widow's property discussed above. To be bound by an equitable servitude, any person who acquires a tract of land in a subdivision must have notice of the servitude. Such notice may be actual, by means of the deed of purchase; by record, if it appears in the county record books; or by inquiry, by visual inspection of the property.

To be bound, in addition to notice, the equitable servitude must "run with the land" in the same fashion as a covenant. The primary differences between a covenant and an equitable servitude are:

(a) a covenant *must* be created by a writing whereas an equitable servitude may arise by implication;

(b) no privity, horizontal or vertical, is necessary for an equitable servitude;

(c) notice for an equitable servitude may arise by inquiry; and

(d) the remedy for the breach of a covenant is money, whereas the remedy for the breach of an equitable servitude is an injunction.

Equitable servitudes terminate in the same manner as covenants.

Covenants and equitable servitudes may be viewed as limitations on the use of the land that create fees simple determinable or fees simple subject to a condition subsequent, depending on the wording (see Chapter 1).

Easements

An **easement** is the right of access or use of another person's realty and, unless otherwise terminated, is deemed to exist in perpetuity. Easements are divided into two broad categories: easements appurtenant and easements in gross.

Easements appurtenant are rights of access and use of adjoining property. The tract of land that has the right over the adjacent property is called the **dominant tenement,** and the property that is subject to the use of the easement holder is called the **servient tenement.** Easements appurtenant attach to the land and pass along with the transfer of the title to the land.

 EXAMPLE:

> Fred and Ricky own adjacent lots. Fred wants to extend his driveway, but the construction will encompass six inches of Ricky's property. By agreement, Ricky permits Fred to use the six-inch strip but retains ownership of the area. Years later, Ricky sells his property to Lucy. Lucy acquires title to the property subject to the use by Fred of the six-inch strip for his driveway.

An **easement in gross** is an easement that is held by an individual for his or her own enjoyment over non-adjacent property. An example of an easement in gross would be the right a homeowner gives to children in the neighborhood to use his property to reach their school even though they do not live on the adjoining property. If the easement in gross is for non-commercial purposes it is not transferable by the easement holder (the children), but if it is for a commercial purpose it may be transferred.

EXAMPLE:

A property owner has been approached by a cellular telephone company that wants to erect a pole on the property. For a fee the property owner agrees. Because the easement is commercial in nature, the telephone company may transfer its easement rights.

Easements may be created in one of four ways:

1. **Express grant:** The express grant is a writing that may appear in the deed conveying the property or by a separate document. The person who grants the easement must be the owner of the servient tenement upon which the right of the easement will attach. The grantor of the easement may only grant the easement for the period of his title, either fee, life estate, or by lease. The grantee is the owner of the dominant tenement that benefits from the easement. An example of an easement created by express grant would be the previous example involving Fred and Ricky in which Ricky agreed to let Fred use part of his land to build a driveway.
2. **By implication:** An **implied easement** arises by the actual use of the adjacent property without consent. This is created by operation of law and so no writing is necessary. The implied easement may arise by the continuous use of the property because such use is necessary for the enjoyment of the dominant tenement. An example would be a vacation home that has access to a lake either by public road that takes two miles or by a private road over a neighboring property that would take only half a mile. If the vacation homeowner uses this private road for a significant period of time, an implied easement will be created.
3. **By necessity:** An **easement by necessity** occurs when a tract of land has no access to a public road except by going over a neighboring property. In this "landlocked" situation, the dominant tenement has the easement right to gain access to the road, but the servient tenement can determine the exact route for this access.

EXAMPLE:

A tract of land is subdivided in a manner by which a property owner's access to the public road can only be gained by going over his neighbor's property. The neighbor must let the property owner have such access, but may limit that access to a particular strip of land. If access to the public road eventually extends directly to the dominant tenement property, the easement will terminate.

4. **By prescription:** An **easement by prescription** is an easement that is created in the same manner as acquiring full title to property by adverse possession (see Chapter 2). To acquire the right, the easement holder must use the adjoining property in manner that is:
   (a) open and notorious;
   (b) adverse to the interest of the servient property;
   (c) continuous and uninterrupted; and
   (d) for the statutory period mandated by the state statute.

An easement by prescription differs from adverse possession in that the person acquiring the easement is only acquiring the right of use and access rather than title to the property itself.

Easements may terminate in one of eight ways:

1. by the condition that was stated in the grant of the easement

EXAMPLE:

"You may use my property to gain access to the lake until the new public shortcut is constructed."

2. when the same person acquires title to both the dominant and servient tenements, thereby merging the titles
3. if the easement holder executes a release of his rights, which may be gratuitous or for consideration
4. if the easement holder abandons the easement, either for a statutory period or by a physical act such as constructing a fence surrounding the dominant tenement, thereby closing his access to the servient tenement
5. if the dominant tenement orally states his intention of abandoning the easement and the servient tenement relies on this oral expression to her detriment, the dominant tenement will be estopped from reclaiming the easement

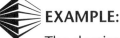

EXAMPLE:

The dominant tenement says that he no longer wishes to use the easement. Based on this statement, the servient tenement constructs a wall around the property. The dominant tenement will be barred from claiming easement rights because the servient tenement constructed the wall based on those statements.

6. the servient tenement can terminate the easement by prescription — using the property in a manner that is inconsistent with the easement holder's rights for the statutory period
7. if the easement was created by necessity, the easement automatically terminates when the necessity no longer exists
8. the easement will terminate if the property is condemned by the government or is unintentionally destroyed

While an easement is in effect, the servient tenement is precluded from engaging in any activity that would interfere with the easement right of the dominant tenement.

 EXAMPLE:

The owner of a servient tenement no longer wants his neighbor to trample over his property, so he constructs a wall around his land. The neighbor who has the easement right may sue the servient tenement to have the wall taken down so as not to interfere with his easement rights.

Easements create significant rights for the dominant tenement and impose significant liabilities on the servient tenement. Whenever a person acquires title to property she should determine whether any easement attaches to that property.

Licenses

A **license** is the right to do an act or a series of acts on another person's land. Unlike an easement that creates a perpetual right of use, a license arises at the pleasure of the property owner and may be rescinded by the property owner at any time. A license merely grants the **licensee,** the license holder, the permission to enter onto the other person's property, whereas an easement creates a property right in the easement holder.

 EXAMPLE:

Blackacre borders a large lake. The owner of Blackacre let his neighbors use a path across Blackacre to get to the lake. The owner also lets his friend from the city use Blackacre to fish in the lake. The neighbors may have an easement over Blackacre, whereas the city friend merely has a license. The owner of Blackacre can stop his friend from using Blackacre but the neighbors may have acquired certain property rights to the use of Blackacre for access to the lake.

Duty of Care

Any person who is a lawful possessor of real property owes certain duties of care to third persons who come onto that property. The nature and extent of that duty depends on the category into which the third person may fall. Generally persons who enter onto the land fall into one of three categories:

1. **Trespassers** are those persons who enter onto realty without permission. Because these persons have no lawful right to be on the land, the person in possession only owes such people slight care. This means that the possessor must alert such persons only of artificial structures on the property, or natural circumstances that are not readily discernible, that may injure trespassers. An example might be the posting of a sign indicating that there are bear traps located on the property to alert the trespasser to a dangerous situation.
2. **Licensees** are persons who are permitted to enter the property with the possessor's permission for a purpose that generally benefits the licensees. This category would include all social guests of the property owner/possessor. Licensees are entitled to the ordinary standard of care, meaning that they must be warned about dangerous conditions, such as a loose step or a broken chair, that may or may not be readily apparent.
3. **Invitees** are persons who are asked onto the property to benefit the property owner/possessor's pecuniary interest, such as customers in a retail store. The property owner/possessor owes invitees the highest standard of care, which requires that the invitee be warned of all potential defects that might cause injury.

Despite these differences, the modern trend of the law is to require the ordinary standard of care to all persons who enter onto property, regardless of the nature and reason for that entrance.

There is one important exception to the foregoing, and that exception involves any situation that would cause children to be attracted to the property. In this instance, the property owner/possessor is held to the highest standard of care so as to protect children, and may be held strictly liable under a legal doctrine called **attractive nuisance.** This doctrine relates to situations that would lure children to the property, such as a swimming pool, construction site, natural gorge, and so forth. If the property owner/possessor knows or should know that children will be drawn to the property, she is expected to take all reasonable precautions to protect the children from harm.

EXAMPLE:

A property owner has just built a swimming pool on his property and the children in the neighborhood continually come onto the property to swim in the pool. It is dangerous for small children to swim unsupervised, and therefore the homeowner is required to construct a fence around the pool to keep the children away from the pool for their own good.

Zoning

The government is empowered to restrict land use for the purpose of protecting the general health and welfare of the public. To effect this mandate, local governments enact **zoning regulations** that restrict land use. Provided that there is some rational basis between the zoning regulation and the general welfare of the community, such government restrictions on land use are deemed to be constitutional, meaning that it is not considered to be a deprivation of property. However, to ensure the constitutionality of the zoning regulation, a proposed regulation is subject to a public hearing so that members of the community may present arguments for and against the proposed regulation. See Exhibit 3.1.

Exhibit 3.1: California Statutes

Zoning Statutes

§ 658542.1. Single-family residence zone; permit for dwelling unit for senior citizen occupancy; application of section

Notwithstanding Section 65906, any city, including a charter city, county, or city and county may issue a zoning variance, special use permit, or conditional use permit for a dwelling unit to be constructed, or which is attached to or detached from, a primary residence on a parcel zoned for a single-family residence, if the dwelling unit is intended for the sole occupancy of one adult or two adult persons who are 62 years of age or over, and the area of floor space of the attached dwelling unit does not exceed 30 percent of the existing living area or the area of the floor space of the detached dwelling unit does not exceed 1,200 square feet.

Basically, zoning consists of designating geographic areas for specific purposes, such as residential, commercial, public (parks, town halls), and mixed use. Furthermore, within these areas the zoning regulation may prescribe the nature of the buildings that may be constructed within the zone, such as single-family dwellings, multi-family dwellings, and so forth. Enforcement of the zoning regulations rests with a governmental body known as a **zoning board.**

Various problems may arise with respect to zoning regulations. First, if a particular use of the property has existed for a long period of time prior to the zoning regulation that would not permit such a use, the property owner may continue such use provided that it can be demonstrated that such use actually pre-dated the regulation.

 EXAMPLE:

At the turn of the twentieth century a farmer built a small shed next to the road to sell his farm produce. Over the years the entire area became residential, and most of the farms were sold off. The farmer's great-grandchild continues to use the shed, slightly enlarged, as a store. The area has just been re-zoned for residential use only, and the neighbors want the store to stop operating. The great-grandchild may be able to continue running the store by documenting a preexisting use.

If a preexisting use has been established, that use may continue, but any change in the specific use would thereafter have to conform to the current zoning regulations.

Second, zoning regulations may also require certain architectural standards to maintain a uniform style in a community. Therefore, when a homeowner intends to make structural changes to his or her house, it may require prior approval of the zoning board.

 EXAMPLE:

A woman has just purchased a colonial house in a city's historical district. She wants to modernize the house for twenty-first century use. Before she may make any changes to the outside of the building, she must obtain approval of the zoning board.

Third, if a person wants to use his property in a manner inconsistent with current zoning regulations, he may be able to obtain a **variance** from the zoning board, giving him permission to use the property in this manner. Before permitting a variance, most boards require a public hearing so that members of the community may express concerns about the effect of the variance on the community.

Exhibit 3.2: California Statutes

Building Code

§ 65850.2.   **Use of regulated substances or sources of hazardous emissions; development projects or building permit applications for projects not requiring development permits; information lists and application forms; completion of application or approval; risk management plans; fees**

(a) Each city and each county shall include in its information list compiled pursuant to Section 65940 for development projects, or application form for projects which do not require a development permit other than a building permit, both of the following:

(1) The requirement that the owner or authorized agent shall indicate whether the owner or authorized agent will need to comply with the applicable requirements of Section 25505 and Article 2 (commencing with Section 25531) of Chapter 6.95 of Division 20 of the Health and Safety Code and the requirements for a permit for construction or modification from the air pollution control district or air quality management district exercising jurisdiction in the area governed by the city or county.

(2) The requirement that the owner or authorized agent shall certify whether or not the proposed project will have more than a threshold quantity of a regulated substance in a process or will contain a source or modified source of hazardous air emissions.

(b) A city or county shall not find the application complete pursuant to Section 65943 or approve a development project, or a building permit for a project which does not require a development permit other than a building permit, in which a regulated substance will be present in a process in quantities greater than the applicable threshold quantity, unless the owner or authorized agent for the project first obtains from the administering agency with jurisdiction over the facility, a notice of requirement to comply with, or determination of exemption from, the requirement to prepare and submit an RMP. Within five days of submitting the project application to the city or county, the applicant shall submit the information required pursuant to paragraph (2) of subdivision (a) to the administering agency. This notice of requirement to comply with, or determination of exemption from, the requirement for an RMP shall be provided by the administering agency to the applicant, and the applicant shall provide the notice to the city or county, within 25 days of the administering agency receiving adequate information from the applicant to make a determination as to the requirement for an RMP. The requirement to submit an RMP to the administering agency, shall be met prior to the issuance of a certificate of occupancy or its substantial equivalent. The owner or authorized agent shall submit to the city or county certification from the air pollution

Exhibit 3.2: *(Continued)*

control officer that the owner or authorized agent is in compliance with the disclosures required by Section 42303 of the Health and Safety Code.

(c) A city or county shall not issue a final certificate of occupancy or its substantial equivalent unless there is verification from the administering agency, if required by law, that the owner or authorized agent has met, or is meeting, the applicable requirements of Section 25505 and Article 2 (commencing with Section 25531) of Chapter 6.95 of Division 20 of the Health and Safety Code, and the requirements for a permit, if required by law, from the air pollution control district or air quality management district exercising jurisdiction in the area governed by the city or county or has provided proof from the appropriate district that the permit requirements do not apply to the owner or authorized agent.

(d) The city or county, after considering the recommendations of the administering agency or air pollution control district or air quality management district, shall decide whether, and under what conditions, to allow construction of the site.

(e) Nothing in this section limits any existing authority of a district to require compliance with its rules and regulations.

(f) Counties and cities may adopt a schedule of fees for applications for compliance with this section sufficient to recover their reasonable costs of carrying out this section. Those fees shall be used only for the implementation of this section.

(g) As used in this section, the following terms have the following meaning:

(1) "Administering agency," "process," "regulated substance," "RMP," and "threshold quantity" have the same meaning as set forth in Section 25532 of the Health and Safety Code.

(2) "Hazardous air emissions" means emissions into the ambient air of air contaminants which have been identified as a toxic air contaminant by the State Air Resources Board or by the air pollution control officer for the jurisdiction in which the project is located. As determined by the air pollution control officer, hazardous air emissions also means emissions into the ambient air of any substance identified in subdivisions (a) to (f), inclusive, of Section 44321 of the Health and Safety Code.

(h) Any misrepresentation of information required by this section shall be grounds for denial, suspension, or revocation of project approval or permit issuance. The owner or authorized agent required to comply with this section shall notify all future occupants of their potential duty to comply with the requirements of Section 25505 and Article 2 (commencing with Section 25531) of Chapter 6.95 of Division 20 of the Health and Safety Code.

Zoning regulations are typically enforced by the government by seeking an injunction against any person who violates a zoning regulation without having obtained permission by means of a variance from the zoning board.

Closely associated with zoning regulations are **building codes** that mandate minimum requirements for construction, electricity, plumbing, and so forth, of all structures. See Exhibit 3.2. Such laws regulate the material and methods used in construction of a building, and buildings may not be occupied without obtaining a **permit** and inspection by the locality's governmental agency that oversees these laws. If a structure does not meet the standards of the building codes and is declared to be dangerous for occupancy, the government may be able to **condemn** the building, meaning that it may be destroyed for the welfare and safety of the public.

Probably the most dramatic governmental interference with land use is its ability to take over private property for public purposes, such as the construction of a road, under the doctrine of **eminent domain.** To meet constitutional guarantees, no private property may be taken by the government without adequate compensation. Questions may arise as to the adequacy of the proffered compensation, but the property owner has no choice but to sell the property to the government.

EXAMPLE:

A man purchased some undeveloped land ten years ago as an investment. At the time he paid $10,000 for the property. Over the years the surrounding area has become populated, and the man believes his investment is now worth $100,000. The local government informs him that they will need to acquire his property to create roads, utilities, and so forth, due to the new population in the area. The government only pays him $45,000 for the property. The man must transfer title to the government, but may challenge the adequacy of the consideration in court.

Practical Tips

- Check the title at the recorder's office to determine whether any easement exists on the land. If representing the easement holder, make sure all easements are recorded; if representing the servient tenement, see if the easement can be removed.
- Make sure all valid easements and liens are recorded.
- Make no change to existing structures until all zoning requirements and restrictions have been determined.
- Prepare any documents that may be necessary to validate the need for a zoning variance.

- Maintain evidence of all licenses that may be granted to avoid any future problems.
- Become familiar with members of the local zoning board.

Chapter Review

The right to own and possess land is not absolute. Certain limitations and restrictions may be imposed on the use of realty that severely limit the titleholder's unfettered enjoyment of the property.

The most prevalent types of restrictions on land use are covenants and equitable servitudes, restrictions on the use of property that arise when the property is transferred. These limitations create rights in persons not the property owner to see that these restrictions are enforced, either by means of seeking monetary damages for violations of the real covenants or injunctions against violations of equitable servitudes.

Easements create rights of use of and access over one person's property by another, and this use and access can have important effects on what the property owner may or may not do to his or her own land. Unless specifically terminated, easements are deemed to exist forever, and the owner of the property that is subject to the easement cannot do anything that would interfere with the easement holders' rights.

Closely related to easements are licenses — permissions by the property owner/possessor to third persons to enter the land for a particular act or for a series of acts. However, unlike easements, licenses are not rights, and unless established by contract, are totally revocable by the property owner/possessor at will.

All persons in lawful possession of realty are required to maintain the property in a manner that renders it safe for third persons who enter onto the land. Historically, the law distinguished the standard of care owed by the property owner/possessor by the nature of the third person — trespasser, licensee, or invitee — but the modern trend of authority imposes the ordinary standard of care on the property owner/possessor regardless of the status of the third person. There is one exception to this modern trend that exists for attractive nuisances, hazardous situations that could cause children to wish to enter the property. In this instance the property owner/possessor is held to a standard of strict liability.

Finally, a person's ability use his or her property may be restricted by several governmental regulations, such as zoning regulations, building codes, and the power of eminent domain.

Ethical Concern

Just because a trespasser is injured on the land does not mean that the landowner is in any way responsible. It is unethical to institute a legal claim against a landowner for injuries that a trespasser caused through his or her own fault. Such frivolous actions may result in sanctions imposed by the court.

Key Terms

Attractive nuisance	Implied easement
Building code	Invitee
Condemn	Land use
Covenant	License
Dominant tenement	Licensee
Easement	Real covenant
Easement appurtenant	Release
Easement by necessity	Servient tenement
Easement by prescription	Touch and concern the land
Easement in gross	Trespasser
Eminent domain	Variance
Equitable servitude	Vertical privity
Express grant	Zoning regulations
Horizontal privity	Zoning board

Exercises

1. Determine the statutory period for acquiring an easement by prescription in your jurisdiction, as well as the other requirements to create such an easement.
2. Briefly discuss the methods whereby an easement may be terminated.
3. Research the zoning regulations for your neighborhood. Determine the procedures for obtaining a variance from your zoning board.
4. How would you determine "reasonable compensation" for the taking of private property by the government in a case of eminent domain?
5. Research some cases of attractive nuisance decided in your state.

Situational Analysis

By agreement, Alan was given the right to use a portion of Betty's property as a driveway for a period of one year until he could construct a driveway of his own. The year ended four months ago and Alan continues to use Betty's property and has not constructed his own driveway.

What are the respective rights of the parties? What information might you need to arrive at your conclusion?

Edited Cases

The following two judicial decisions underscore certain principles introduced in this chapter. Problems with easements are discussed in *Price v. McNeil*, and licenses are analyzed in *Chicago & North Western Transp. Co. v. City of Winthrop*.

Price v. McNeil
2001 Ala. Civ. App. LEXIS 221

Gary Price and Martha Price (the "servient estate") own real estate subject to an easement that is now owned by Deborah McNeil (the "dominant estate"). They are adjacent landowners. The servient estate sued the dominant estate, alleging that the dominant estate had wrongfully obstructed their use of the easement by erecting a locked gate. The trial court eventually ruled in favor of the dominant estate, concluding that the dominant estate had an "exclusive" easement that barred any use by the servient estate. The servient estate appealed to the supreme court, which transferred the case to this court, pursuant to Ala. Code 1975, Sec. 12-2-7(6). We reversed the trial court's judgment, holding that, as a matter of law, the easement was not "exclusive." See *Price v. McNeil*, 771 So. 2d 1054 (Ala. Civ. App. 2000) (*Price I*). We instructed the trial court on remand "to determine the extent to which the [servient estate is] allowed to use the easement." 771 So. 2d at 1057. On remand, the trial court ordered that the dominant estate can maintain the locked gate, but that the servient estate is to have a key and that they can use the key to open the gate and then lock it back after each use. The servient estate appealed to the supreme court, which again transferred the case to this court pursuant to Ala. Code 1975, Sec. 12-2-7(6).

In *Price I*, we instructed the trial court on remand to follow the principles set forth by our supreme court in *Blalock v. Conzelman*, 751 So. 2d 2 (Ala. 1999), and *Duke v. Pine Crest Homes, Inc.*, 358 So. 2d 148 (Ala. 1978), to determine to what extent the servient estate may use the easement. The *Duke* court stated that a servient estate may use an easement as follows:

> It is well settled in Alabama that the owner of the servient estate may himself use the land upon which an easement has been dedicated so long as [his use] does not conflict with the purpose and character of the easement. . . .
> . . . We wish to make it clear that the servient owner must not in any way interfere with or impinge upon the rights secured by the dominant estate under the express grant of the easement . . . . Nor must use by the servient owner create any such additional burden upon the easement as would interfere with those rights granted by the express terms of the easement.

358 So. 2d at 150, 151 (citation omitted).

The *Blalock* court stated:

> Moreover, pursuant to the general rule, the [dominant estate and servient estate] have concurrent rights to the use of the easement, and neither party can prevent the other from using the easement in a manner consistent with the purposes for which the easement was created. Thus, the existence of the easement creates mutual rights and obligations.
>
> "The landowner may not, without the consent of the easement holder, unreasonably interfere with the latter's rights or change the character of the easement so as to make the use thereof significantly more difficult or burdensome." Conversely, the easement holder "can not change its character, or materially increase the burden upon the servient estate."

751 So. 2d at 6 (citations omitted).

The servient estate argues that the placement of the locked gate across the easement, regardless of the fact that they now have a key to unlock the gate each time they want to cross the easement, is an "undue burden" on the servient estate. The evidence in the record indicates that the dominant estate placed the gate at the point where the easement accesses a public road. The dominant estate testified that she erected the gate in order to protect "her property" from trespassers. The easement crosses the servient estate for several hundred feet before entering the dominant estate. The servient estate argues that the locked gate should be placed at the point where the easement enters the dominant estate.

The dominant estate's easement is "[a] perpetual easement for ingress and egress." In *Blalock*, the dominant estate had an easement "for ingress and egress to and from said property." The dominant estate used the easement for a driveway. The servient estate altered the driveway and planned to remove trees and shrubbery along the easement. The dominant estate sued the servient estate, seeking to enjoin it from removing the trees and shrubbery. The trial court enjoined the servient estate from removing the trees and shrubbery. The supreme court reversed, stating:

> At its core, the [dominant estate's] action is about vegetation, that is, the [dominant estate] asserts a right to certain trees and vegetation growing in the area of the easement. However, the easement created by the deeds conveying lots 1 and 2 is only "for ingress and egress to and from [lot 1] as shown in [the re-survey]." Nothing in those deeds addresses vegetation. Thus, the [dominant estate] seeks to change the essential character of the easement from that of a right of way, to — in effect — one of shade and air. See *Metcalf v. Houk*, 644 N.E.2d 597, 600 (Ind. Ct. App. 1994) ("Generally an easement for ingress and egress confers only the right to pass over the land and not to control the real estate or install improvements"); see also *Upson v. Stafford*, 205 Ga. App. 615, 616, 422 S.E.2d 882, 884 (1992) (the holder of an access easement had no right to a "buffer of trees" between his easement and adjoining property); *Solow v. Liebman*, 175 A.D.2d 120, 121, 572 N.Y.S.2d 19, 20 (1991) (holder of an access easement "had no right, as a matter of law," to prevent the owner of the servient estate from removing trees from the easement).
>
> Moreover, the presence or absence of vegetation is not material to the [dominant estate's] ability to use the easement. It is, however, highly material to [the servient estate's] ability to use the easement.

751 So. 2d at 6.

The easement in this case is likewise limited to an easement for "ingress and egress." We hold that, just as the control over the vegetation was held not to be material to the use of the easement in *Blalock,* the placement of the gate across the easement for the protection of the dominant estate, regardless of whether the servient estate is provided a key to the gate, is not material, or reasonably necessary, to the use of this easement. See *Clark v. Kuhn,* 171 Ore. App. 29, 15 P.3d 37 (2000) (holding that the dominant estate's placement of a gate across the easement is not reasonably necessary for the purpose of using an easement for ingress and egress); and *Drew v. Sorensen,* 133 Idaho 534, 538, 989 P.2d 276, 280 (1999) (holding that the placement of a gate across the easement, which barricaded a significant area of the servient estate, is an "unreasonable burden" on the servient estate and is not "reasonable and necessary" to maintenance of the easement). See also *Ballington v. Paxton,* 327 S.C. 372, 488 S.E.2d 882 (S.C. Ct. App. 1997) (holding that the servient estate could maintain on the easement a locked fence that did not unreasonably interfere with the dominant estate's use of the easement).

Therefore, we reverse the trial court's judgment providing that the dominant estate may maintain a gate on the easement as long as the servient estate is provided a key to the gate. As stated above, the dominant estate, as a matter of law, cannot maintain a locked gate on the easement, because the gate imposes an unreasonable burden on the servient owners. On remand, the trial court is instructed to enter a judgment consistent with this opinion.

Case Questions

1. How are the rights of the dominant tenement infringed in this case?

2. How does the court conclude that both the dominant and servient tenement have concurrent rights?

Chicago and North Western Transportation Company v. City of Winthrop
257 N.W.2d 302 (Minn. 1977)

Plaintiff, Chicago and North Western Transportation Company, brought this action for reimbursement, pursuant to the terms of a license agreement, for amounts expended in connection with a Federal Employers' Liability Act (FELA) claim by one of its employees. The trial court granted motion of defendant, City of Winthrop, for summary judgment, and plaintiff has appealed to this court. Because the license and defendant's contractual obligations thereunder were not extinguished by a conveyance of the land, we reverse.

On October 22, 1957, plaintiff's predecessor in interest, the Minneapolis and St. Louis Railway Company, signed an agreement with the defendant, City of Winthrop, whereby defendant was given a license to

construct and maintain a sewer upon the railroad's right-of-way. The
agreement provided that defendant would indemnify the railroad for liability for any injury resulting from the maintenance of the sewer. In 1960,
all the assets of the Minneapolis and St. Louis Railway, including the right-
of-way at issue, were conveyed to the Chicago and North Western Railway
Company. In 1966, defendant desired to alter or change its sewer facilities
and a new license agreement was executed between the Chicago and
North Western Railway Company and defendant. The 1966 agreement expressly superseded the earlier agreement and contained the following indemnity clause:

> Fifth. It is understood by the Licensee that said facility is subject to and may in-
> crease the dangers and hazards of the operation of the railroad of the Railway
> Company, and that this license is subject to all risks thereof. Therefore, and as a
> material consideration to the Railway Company for entering into this license and
> without which the Railway Company will not enter into same, the Licensee agrees
> to assume and pay for all loss or damage to property whatsoever, and injury to
> or death of any person, or persons whomsoever, including all costs and expenses
> incident thereto, however arising from or in connection with the existence, con-
> struction, maintenance, repair, renewal, reconstruction, operation, use or removal
> of said facility, or any defect therein or failure thereof, . . . and the Licensee forever
> indemnifies the Railway Company against and agrees to save it harmless from
> any and all claims, demands, law suits or liability for any such loss, damage,
> injury and death, costs and expenses, even though the operation of the Railway
> Company's railroad may have caused or contributed thereto.

The agreement also provided that the license could be revoked by the railroad upon 30 days' notice and that the license was not assignable or transferable without the written consent of the railway company being first
obtained.

In 1972, the Chicago and North Western Railway Company conveyed
certain assets, including the right-of-way involved here, to the Chicago
and North Western Transportation Company, the plaintiff herein.

On September 19, 1973, John Grogan, an employee of plaintiff, was
injured by the lid of one of the manholes constructed by defendant on the
railroad's right-of-way. The plaintiff paid Grogan $3,900 in settlement of
his FELA claim, in addition to medical and other expenses amounting to
$1,033.34. The plaintiff then brought the instant action against defendant,
City of Winthrop, for indemnification pursuant to the 1966 license agreement. The defendant denied liability and made a motion for summary
judgment on the grounds that the 1966 license agreement was revoked by
the conveyance in 1972 of the right-of-way involved, and that plaintiff did
not give defendant notice of the injury within the period specified in Minn.
St. 466.05. The trial court granted said motion solely upon the grounds
that the 1972 conveyance had revoked the 1966 agreement as a matter of
law.

The Restatement, Property, Sec. 512, defines a license as —

> an interest in land in the possession of another which
>   (a) entitles the owner of the interest to a use of the land, and

(b) arises from the consent of the one whose interest in the land used is affected thereby, and

(c) is not incident to an estate in the land, and

(d) is not an easement.

Because a license is generally revocable, it is not an encumbrance upon land. It is actually a justification for acts done under the license, a sort of immunity from trespass.

1. The Restatement, Property, Sec. 519, comment b, has recognized a distinction between the license itself and a contract which creates it. In the instant case the 1966 agreement is actually a contract providing that in consideration for the railroad's granting a license to the city to construct and maintain a sewer on the railroad's right-of-way, the city would assume various duties, among which was the duty to indemnify the railroad for any liability resulting from injury caused by the sewer. It is expressly stated in the 1966 agreement that the defendant's obligations were in consideration for the granting of the license. If this agreement in 1966 were solely a license, there would have been no need for the city to consent thereto as it did in this case.

2. The purpose of the rule that a license is generally revoked by a conveyance of the land is to protect the marketability of titles. Since the protection is only for the benefit of the new landowner, only he can invoke it. *Johnson v. Hegland,* 175 Minn. 592, 222 N.W. 272 (1928). In the instant case plaintiff, after the conveyance to it in 1972 and after knowledge of the existence of the license, continued to allow defendant to use its license to maintain the sewer on the railroad property. Under the circumstances the conveyance of 1972 did not operate automatically as a revocation of the license or the defendant's contractual obligation thereunder to indemnify the plaintiff.

Reversed.

Case Questions

1. Why does the court say that a license is not an encumbrance?
2. Why does the license document not need to be recorded?

4 Conveyancing

CHAPTER OVERVIEW

Conveyancing refers to the legal process whereby title to real estate is transferred from one person to another. Transfer of realty typically takes one of three forms: gifts, in which the titleholder, the **donor,** gives the property to another, the **donee,** without an exchange of consideration (for free); testamentary transfers, in which title is transferred pursuant to the titleholder's will or by operation of law on the titleholder's death; and by contract, the general bargain and sale exchange of property.

A detailed discussion of the law surrounding testamentary transfers is beyond the scope of this text, and a discussion of the law of gifts appears in the last chapter of this book. This chapter concentrates on the process involved in the sale of real property. The process of effectuating a sale of realty generally follows a simple four-step format:

1. The parties to the sale enter into a contract for the sale of the property that contains certain **warranties,** or guarantees, with respect to the nature of the interest being transferred.
2. After the contract is executed, the buyer checks the seller's title to the property and demands that any defects in the title (see below) be cured prior to the closing date. Also, during this period the buyer will enter into a mortgage agreement with a bank or financial institution if financing will be necessary to complete the purchase.
3. On the **closing** date, title passes from the seller to the buyer by the delivery to the buyer of a validly executed deed. The delivery of the valid deed extinguishes any contract rights that may have

existed between the parties, and all legal rights of the buyer and seller are now based on the provisions of the deed.

4. The buyer records the deed in the county recorder's office in the county in which the property is located in order to protect his or her title against any subsequent transfer of the title by the former owner (seller).

This chapter explores each of these steps in the sale of realty in detail.

Contracts for the Sale of Realty

Land Sales Contracts

Pursuant to the Statute of Frauds, in order to be enforceable in a court of law, all contracts for the sale of an interest in realty must be in writing. This provision of the Statute of Frauds may also apply to the lease of property as well (see Chapter 7). To meet this statutory requirement, the document must

1. be an actual writing;
2. be signed by the party who is to be charged, i.e., the party against whom the document is attempting to be enforced; and
3. contain all of the essential terms of the agreement, including the parties to the contract, a legally sufficient description of the property being transferred, and the purchase price.

 EXAMPLE:

A father wishes to sell his home to his son and daughter-in-law. To meet the provisions of the Statute of Frauds, the father drafts a contract in which he identifies himself as the seller and the son and daughter-in-law as the buyers; specifies the purchase price; and identifies the property by the description that appears in his deed to the land. This document contains sufficient information to make it enforceable under the Statute of Frauds.

A court may enforce a contract for the sale of real estate that is not in writing or sufficiently detailed if the parties to the agreement have completely or partially performed their obligations, such as paying the purchase price, living on the property for a significant period of time, or making substantial improvements on the land.

 EXAMPLE:

A father decides to sell his farm to his son. The father and son do not sign any contract, but the son takes possession of the land, farms the property for over five years, pays all property taxes on the land, makes payments to the father as part of the oral purchase agreement, and makes substantial improvements to the house and farm buildings. After five years the father decides to sell the farm to a third party. In this instance, based on the son's performance, the court would probably enforce the oral agreement between the father and son.

In addition to the provisions of the Statute of Frauds, a contract for the sale of realty must meet all of the requirements of every valid contract:

1. There must be a valid **offer,** which is defined as a proposal by one party, the **offeror,** to another to enter into a valid contract. The offer must contain all of the essential terms of what will be the contract — parties, price, description of the land, and so forth.
2. The person to whom the offer was made, the **offeree,** must agree to all of the terms of the proposal as specified by the offeror. An offeree may not vary any of the essential terms of the offer.
3. The agreement must be supported by legally sufficient **consideration.** Consideration is generally defined as a benefit conferred or a detriment incurred at the request of the other party. For contracts for the sale of realty, the consideration is the land and the purchase price. To have a valid contract, both parties must give and receive something of value (the land and the money).
4. The parties must actually intend to enter into the agreement. A presumed contract will fail if it can be demonstrated that one or another of the parties was forced into entering into the agreement, was mistaken as to the provisions of the agreement, or any other factor can be demonstrated that indicates a lack of intent to contract.
5. The parties must have **contractual capacity,** which is the legal ability to enter into a contract. Generally, this means that they must have attained the age deemed by the state statute to be a legally sufficient age to contract (18 years of age is considered to be legally sufficient in every state, but many jurisdictions provide for younger persons to enter into certain types of contracts — the provisions of each state statute must be individually analyzed). Also the person must have the mental ability to understand the nature of the agreement.
6. Finally, the contract provisions may not violate any law.

The moment at which the contract comes into effect is crucial in determining the parties' rights.

First, once the contract exists, if either side breaches the contract — fails to fulfill his or her contractual obligations — the other side is entitled to certain remedies in court. The non-breaching party may be entitled to **damages,** a monetary award based on the degree of financial injury the non-breaching party has suffered based on the breach, or the non-breaching party may be entitled to **specific performance,** a non-monetary remedy available pursuant to the court's equitable powers. Specific performance is generally only permitted for unique property, and all land, under the law, is considered to be unique. Therefore, the non-breaching party may be able to have the court order the breaching party to purchase or convey the realty in question.

Second, once the contract is validly formed, the risk of loss of the property may be transferred. In the United States there are two theories concerning the risk of loss or destruction of real property. The first is known as the **doctrine of equitable conversion.** Under this concept, once the contract is signed the buyer is considered to be the owner of the realty, and the seller is considered only to have the right to receive the purchase price. Consequently, if the property is damaged or destroyed after the contract is signed (but before title passes — see below) the resultant loss may be borne by the buyer. The second theory, more recently adopted, is called the **Vendor and Purchaser Risk Act.** Pursuant to this theory, the risk of loss remains with the seller until the buyer takes actual possession of the property and makes some improvement to the realty. Each state's statute must be examined to determine which theory is prevalent in a particular jurisdiction.

 EXAMPLE:

Buyer and seller enter into a valid contract for the sale of Blackacre. The seller remains in possession of the property until the closing date, which is set for six weeks after the contract is signed. Two weeks after the signing, a hurricane totally destroys Blackacre. If the jurisdiction follows the doctrine of equitable conversion, the risk was on the buyer and the seller has the right to receive the complete purchase price for the property. Conversely, if the jurisdiction has adopted the Vendor and Purchaser Risk Act, the risk remained with the seller and the buyer may either avoid the contract or demand a reduction of the purchase price to reflect the destruction of Blackacre.

The typical contract for the sale of real estate usually contains the following specific provisions in addition to the foregoing general contract requirements (see Exhibit 4.3 at the end of this chapter):

(a) *The parties:* The parties to the contract must be named, including their addresses and indicating the legal titles by which they are making the purchase and sale, such as the officer of a corporation, a partner, and so forth.

(b) *Consideration:* The contract must recite the consideration for the agreement — the purchase price, including any method of payment that will be made, such as an **installment sale** in which the purchase price is to be paid over a specified number of years. The recitation of the consideration should also include any and all financing provisions that have been made with respect to the sale of the property (see below). The consideration should also detail the description of the property. See Exhibit 4.1. Real property is described according to several methods:

(i) **Plat description:** This method of land description is based on a **survey,** which is a written evaluation and description of real property. The plat indicates the dimensions and boundaries of the property, and is often used in a description of planned subdivisions. The plat will include the following information:

- the state, county, and district in which the property is located,
- the subdivision name and lot, block, and unit name; and
- a reference to the **plat book** that appears in the county recorder's office.

(ii) **Metes and bounds description:** This method indicates the area following a course from a specified starting point, usually a natural or artificial focal point such as a monument,

---

Exhibit 4.1: Real Property Description

ALL that certain lot or piece of ground situated in the City of Pittsburgh, County of Allegheny, and Commonwealth of Pennsylvania, bounded and described as follows, to wit:

BEGINNING at a point on the Westerly line of South Graham (formerly Graham) Street distant 371.961 feet Northerly from the intersection of the Westerly line of South Graham Street and the Northerly line of Baum Boulevard as formerly located; thence along said line of South Graham Street in a Northeasterly direction, 40.00 feet to a point; thence extending back in a Northwesterly direction a distance of 150.00 feet to the Easterly line of Vintage Way; thence Southerly by said line of Vintage Way and parallel with South Graham Street, a distance of 40 feet to a point; thence in a Southeasterly direction and preserving the same width throughout of 40.00 feet, a distance of 150 feet to South Graham Street, at the place of beginning.

HAVING erected thereon a residential dwelling being municipally known and numbered as 432 South Graham Street.

BEING FURTHER DESIGNATED as Block & Lot 51-G-255 in the Deed Registry Office of Allegheny County, Pennsylvania.

BEING the same property which Susan E. Carr, unmarried by her deed dated October 15, 1993 and recorded in the Recorder's Office of Allegheny County, Pennsylvania, in Deed Book Volume 9205, Page 104, granted and conveyed unto Edward J. Petrick, Jr., unmarried, the grantor herein.

---

and then follows a course so many feet or yards to another point in a given direction. Eventually the course returns to the starting point to create an enclosed area, which is the property in question.

(iii) **Rectangular survey description:** The method of dividing land into rectangular lots was established in 1785 and is used by approximately 30 states. The system is based on lots formed by the intersection of hypothetical lines: the **principal meridians,** which are north-south lines, and **base lines,** which run horizontally east-west. In this fashion the states that use this method have divided up the land into specified rectangular quadrants.

(c) *Title:* The agreement should specify the exact nature of the title the seller possesses. In order for the property to be salable, the seller is expected to provide the buyer with a **marketable title.** A marketable title is one that gives the buyer title to the property free from all **encumbrances.** Encumbrances are any defects in the chain of title that could potentially cause a lawsuit over the right to the property. The most commonly encountered encumbrances are:

(i) **Liens,** which are creditors' claims on the property to satisfy debts. Liens may take the form of government liens for non-payment of taxes, **mechanics' liens** for work performed on the property, or a general lien imposed by the court in order to satisfy claims of general creditors of the titleholder.

 EXAMPLE:

A homeowner hires a contractor to construct an addition to her house. The homeowner pays the contractor a portion of the total price when the work begins, but fails to pay the contractor the balance due when the work is completed. The homeowner has no valid complaint with respect to the quality of the work performed by the contractor. Automatically, under the common law, the contractor has a mechanic's lien on the property for the balance of the payment owed to him.

 EXAMPLE:

A property owner fails to pay his real estate taxes on some undeveloped property he is holding as an investment. The government imposes a tax lien on the property.

 EXAMPLE:

A property owner is found liable, by a competent court, of having severely injured a woman by failing to observe the ordinary standard of care while driving his car. The woman is awarded a large judgment by the court, but the property owner refuses to pay. The injured woman may be able to have a lien imposed on the property to satisfy the judicially imposed debt of the property owner.

Liens are generally recorded on the title to the property at the county recorder's office and represent a claim on the property.

(ii) Mortgages, which are a special category of security interest held by a person who extends financing for the purchase of realty. Mortgages are discussed in detail later in this chapter.

(iii) **Clouds on title,** which are any breaks in the chain of title that could give rise to a lawsuit with respect to ownership of the property. Titles and transfers of title should be recorded in the county recorder's office, but occasionally such recording is neglected, or a grantor may attempt to pass title to several persons, all of whom claim ownership. The specifics of recording title are discussed later in this chapter.

Any potential claim or challenge to title renders the title unmarketable. However, the seller is only required to provide a marketable title at the closing (see below), so any encumbrance that is in fact cured by the closing does not render the title unmarketable. Furthermore, a purchaser may be willing, under the contract, to purchase an **insurable title,** one in which the title is not totally clear but which is capable of having insurance issued to cover any potential claim. If a purchaser is willing to accept anything less than a fully marketable title, the contract for sale must specify which encumbrances the buyer is willing to accept.

(d) *Closing.* The *closing,* or **settlement,** is the date on which all parties to the sale and purchase of the land agree to perform all of their contractual obligations. The sales contract should specify the date, place, and time of the closing. If no closing date is indicated in the contract, most courts will impose a closing date "within a reasonable time" from the date of the execution of the contract.

At the closing the seller is typically required to present the following:

(i) a deed to the property that is in a form that can be recorded at the country recorder's office, specifying the title that is to be acquired by the buyer;

(ii) a **closing statement** that sets forth any adjustments to the costs of the purchase;

(iii) a certified rent roll if the property in question is leased, including a letter sent to the tenants indicating the change in ownership;

(iv) all permits, certificates of occupancy, and licenses issued to the property by government agencies, securing the use and habitability of the property;

(v) an affidavit that the seller knows of no proceeding or threatened proceeding against the property;

(vi) plans of any improvements designed for the property;

(vii) all keys to the property; and

(viii) all other documents that the seller would reasonably suppose would be necessary for the purchaser as the new titleholder of the property.

The buyer is required to present the following at the closing:

(i) an **assumption agreement** whereby the buyer assumes all liabilities on the property and agrees to perform all current obligations of the seller with respect to the property;

(ii) a copy of the *closing statement*; and

(iii) the purchase price or the portion of the purchase price that the parties have agreed is to be paid at the closing.

(e) *Transfer of possession.* The sales contract should specify the date on which possession of the property passes from the seller to the buyer. Usually this occurs at the closing, but may be advanced or postponed depending on the wishes of the parties.

 EXAMPLE:

The contract for the sale of a house indicates the closing date to be October 1. The buyer would like to take possession on September 15 to settle in, and the seller agrees to vacate the property by midnight on September 14. The agreement with respect to the transfer of possession should appear in the contract.

(f) *Risk of loss.* As discussed above, depending on the jurisdiction, the shifting of the risk of loss or damage to the property may pass from the seller to the buyer at the date of the contract or when possession actually transfers. However, the parties may specify who bears the risk for various types of damage to the property, as well as who will be responsible for maintaining insurance on the property.

(g) *Earnest money.* **Earnest money,** sometimes referred to as the **deposit** or the **down payment,** is the portion of the full purchase price the buyer gives at the time of the signing of the sales contract. Earnest money may be given credit as a partial payment or as a penalty should the buyer default, or back out, of the contract. The sales contract should specify exactly what the earnest money represents, and the funds should be placed in a trust, or **escrow,** account until the sale is consummated. Note that this trust account does not belong to either party until the obligations of the contract have been fulfilled. Furthermore, the contract should indicate who will be entitled to any interest earned on the funds in the account until the funds are finally transferred.

(h) *Rights of the broker.* If the parties utilize the services of a real estate broker, the contract should identify the rights of the broker with respect to a commission, including when the commission is to be paid and by whom. A **commission** is the fee the broker earns for his or her services.

Contracts with real estate brokers with respect to their commissions, known as **listing agreements,** fall into several categories:

(i)   **Open listing:** With this type of agreement the property owner engages several brokers to help sell the property, and any commission goes to the one who completes the sale.

(ii) **Exclusive listing:** In this type of agreement the property owner only hires one broker, but retains the right to sell the property himself. If the owner sells the property, the broker receives no commission.

(iii) **Exclusive right to sell:** With this agreement the broker is the only one who may sell the property, and she receives a commission if anyone, including the owner, consummates the sale.

See Exhibit 4.2.

(i)   *Assignments.* An **assignment** is the transfer of contractual rights. Generally, most contracts are freely assignable, or transferable, provided that the assignment does not unduly burden the other party to the contract, or the contract was not one that was based on the personal confidence of the transferring party. Such types of confidences in a real estate contract would arise when financing is an issue and one party is lending the other the funds to acquire the property. This type of agreement is based on the personal creditworthiness of the borrower, so the contract is usually nonassignable unless the lending party agrees. Furthermore, the parties to a contract may specify that the contract is or is not assignable, and if it is assignable, what conditions, if any, must be met prior to the transfer.

EXAMPLE:

"Purchaser shall have the right to assign this agreement provided that the Seller be given 30 days' prior written notice and agrees to the assignment in writing within 10 days of the transfer. Seller may withhold agreement of the assignment if the Seller, in his sole discretion, believes the assignee to lack sufficient financial resources to conclude the sale."

(j)   *Warranties.* A warranty is a statement by a party to a contract in which the party guarantees certain aspects of the agreement. If the party making the warranty fails to fulfill its obligations, the injured party may sue for a breach of the warranty. If the warranty goes to the heart of the contract, a breach of the warranty may be considered a breach of the entire contract.

Exhibit 4.2: Real Estate Listing Agreement

T 486—Real Estate Listing Agreement: Non-exclusive. 11-78   JULIUS BLUMBERG, INC.,
                                                                                            PUBLISHER, NYC 10013

REAL ESTATE LISTING AGREEMENT

BROKER:	OWNER:	PREMISES:
Address		
	Address	
Telephone No.		
Broker is Licensed in the State of }	Telephone No.	Date:
Commission:		

Owner hereby lists the above Premises with Broker for sale in accordance with the information, terms and conditions set forth above and following:

Licensed broker 1. *Broker is a licensed real estate broker under the laws of the state set forth above.*

When Commissions earned 2. *Broker shall not earn the Commission unless:*

    a) a contract of sale has been signed by the Owner and a purchaser upon terms acceptable to the Owner in the Owner's sole judgment

    b) the contract was brought about through the Broker's efforts

    c) the deed conveying title is delivered in accordance with the contract and the full purchase price is paid.

Failure to close title 3. *If a contract of sale has been signed by Owner and a purchaser and title does not close,*

    a) because owner does not have good title conveyable in accordance with the contract, broker is not entitled to the Commission.

    b) Broker is not entitled to the Commission unless Owner intentionally defaulted.

    c) because purchaser defaults, Owner is not required to enforce purchaser's obligations and Broker is not entitled to the Commission.

Price change 4. *The purchase price at which the Premises are listed with Broker may be changed by Owner without liability to Broker. Owner is not liable to Broker for any expenses, fees or disbursements paid or incurred by Broker in connection with Broker's efforts to sell the Premises.*

Commission Payable 5. *If earned, the Commission payable to Broker, shall be paid upon the delivery of the deed.*

Termination, withdrawal 6. *Owner may terminate this agreement or withdraw the Premises from sale at any time by either oral or written notice to Broker without liability.*

Non-exclusive 7. *Owner may list Premises with other Brokers*

Margin headings 8. *The margin headings are for convenience only.*

This agreement contains all the terms and conditions of the listing and shall not be changed except by a written agreement signed by both Owner and Broker.

This agreement has been signed by Broker and Owner on the date set forth above.

Broker: ....   Owner:

By ....

    ....

Forms may be purchased from BlumbergExcelsior, Inc. or any of its dealers. Reproduction prohibited.

The typical warranties given by a seller are:
- the seller has title to the property equal to the title being conveyed
- the seller will fulfill all contractual obligations
- the seller has the right to enter into the contract
- there are no claims on the property
- the seller will cause no change in the zoning of the property
- the seller knows of no governmental action against the property
- utilities are available to the property
- the property is accessible by public roads
- the property contains a minimum number of acres or square feet

The typical warranties given by the purchaser are:
- the purchaser has the right to enter into the contract
- the purchaser can finance the purchase
- the purchaser will perform all contractual obligations
- there are no actions pending against the purchaser that will affect the purchaser's ability to perform the contract obligations
- the purchaser will do nothing that diminishes the seller's title prior to the closing

(k) *Time is of the essence clause.* Many contracts specify that **time is of the essence,** meaning that all obligations must be fulfilled on the dates and times specified in the agreement or the contract will be deemed breached, thereby relieving the other party from all further obligations. If such a clause does not appear in the contract, the courts usually infer "reasonable time" for the parties to perform.

(l) *Conditions.* A contractual **condition** is a fact or event, the occurrence or nonoccurrence of which creates or extinguishes an absolute duty to perform. What this means is that the parties are expected to fulfill their contractual obligations *unless* the fact or event specified occurs. Many real estate contracts include a **condition precedent** with respect to financing the sale. A condition precedent is a fact or event that must occur before the party must perform a contractual obligation. In this instance, the condition may specify that the purchaser's obligation to buy is conditioned upon his obtaining financing for the purchase within a specified number of days. If the buyer makes a reasonable effort to secure financing and fails to obtain the necessary funds, the buyer will no longer be obligated to purchase the property.

(m) *Notice.* The contract should specify the manner in which the parties to the agreement wish to receive notice of the various events that are noted in the contract. Typically such notice mandates written notice be posted by certified mail to an address indicated in the contract. All parties to the contract must give all required written notice in the manner specified in the agreement.

(n) *Other provisions.* Real estate contracts, like all contracts, contain certain **boilerplate,** or standard, formalized provisions with respect to the definitions of the terms used in the agreement, for example, which state's law is to apply to its interpretation, arbitration provisions, and so forth. These clauses appear in all contracts and are not specifically related to real property transactions.

(o) *Execution.* The term **execution** refers to the signing of the agreement. The parties should sign according to their position, for example, as an individual, an officer of a corporation, a partner for the partnership, and so forth. The contract does not need to be notarized or witnessed, and the contract itself is generally not recorded with the county recorder's office. After the closing, the deed (see below) is the document that will be used to record the transfer of the title from the seller to the buyer.

After the contract for the sale of the property is executed, the buyer will usually conduct a **title search** to make sure that the seller's title is clear and capable of being transferred subject to the contract. If a cloud on the title appears that the seller does not cure by the closing, the purchaser may avoid the sale or may acquire **title insurance** to protect against a claim by a party asserting title to all or part of the property. The methods for recording titles will be discussed below.

See Exhibits 4.3 and 4.4 at the end of this chapter for examples of a Contract of Sale and a Rider to a Residential Contract of Sale.

Deeds

A **deed** is a document that is used to transfer title to real property. To be valid, the deed must:

1. be in writing;
2. be signed by the grantor;
3. reasonably identify the parties; and
4. describe the land in question in a legally sufficient manner (see above).

If the deed neglects to name the **grantee,** the person who is acquiring the title, the court will assume that the person in possession of the deed is the grantee. However, if the land is not sufficiently described, the deed is considered to be incomplete. The property will be considered sufficiently described, even if not in accordance with its legal description as it appears in the county recorder's office, if it gives sufficient information so that a reasonable person could identify the property. The court will permit oral evidence to complete the description of the land if the description given provides a reasonable lead to the land in question, but cannot accept oral evidence if the overall description is totally inadequate.

EXAMPLE:

A man owns three tracts of land in the same county. In the deed he indicates that he is transferring title to the property he refers to as Honeywell Cottage. The court will permit oral testimony to indicate which of the three parcels the grantor calls "Honeywell Cottage" because the description in the deed is sufficient to provide a lead as to which property is meant.

In order to transfer the title, the deed must be delivered to the grantee. This delivery must indicate a present intention on the part of the grantor to pass the title, even if the right of possession to the property is delayed. This delivery requirement can be satisfied in several ways:

(a) a manual delivery to the grantee or the grantee's agent. Note that a delivery to the grantor's agent with instructions to pass the deed to the grantee does not constitute delivery to the grantee. The delivery must be a direct transfer to the grantee's control.

EXAMPLE:

A woman intends to give some property she owns to her niece. She executes a deed and gives the deed to her lawyer, telling the lawyer to send the deed to the niece. Because the lawyer is the woman's agent, no delivery has yet taken place. When the lawyer gives the deed to the niece, or the niece's lawyer, the delivery is then complete.

(b) a recording of the deed in the county recorder's office; or
(c) a notarized statement by the grantor indicating the intention to transfer the title.

Once a deed has been delivered, the grantor cannot revoke the deed unless the transfer was subject to a condition.

EXAMPLE:

A man gives the deed to his house to his son, telling the son that the property will be his (the son's) on the man's death. The man's death is a condition to the transfer and so the man may revoke the deed prior to his death.

Finally, to complete the transfer, the grantee must accept the deed; most courts assume acceptance unless the grantee indicates a rejection of the property.

There are three types of deeds used to convey title to property: the general warranty deed, the special warranty deed, and the quitclaim deed. The differences between these types of deed concern the warranties, known as **covenants,** that they contain.

See Exhibit 4.5 at the end of this chapter for an example of a deed.

General Warranty Deed

The general warranty deed usually includes the following covenants, referred to as the **common law covenants:**

1. **Covenant of seizin:** This covenant states that the grantor has the title to the property he or she is purporting to convey and also has possession of the property at the time of the conveyance.
2. **Covenant of right to convey:** This covenant specifies that the grantor has the legal authority to convey the title. In most instances having the title to the property will satisfy this covenant.
3. **Covenant against encumbrances:** In this covenant the grantor warrants against any liens, mortgages, or clouds on title on the property (see above).

These three preceding covenants are breached, if at all, at the time of the closing.

4. **Covenant of quiet enjoyment:** This covenant states that the grantor warrants that the grantee will not have his or her possession of the property disturbed by anyone with a lawful claim to the property. Note that this does not protect the grantee from specious lawsuits filed by persons who have no lawful claim to the property.
5. **Covenant of warranty:** In this covenant the grantor agrees to defend the grantee against claims to the property made by third persons, and to reimburse the grantee for any loss that the grantee may suffer from claims by persons with a superior title. Note that the covenant for quiet enjoyment concerns possession, whereas this covenant concerns title.
6. **Covenant of further assurances:** In this covenant the grantor agrees to do all things necessary to perfect title in the grantee should any claim against title occur in the future. The distinction between the covenant of warranty and the covenant of further assurances is one of degree; with the former the grantor will protect the grantee from loss, with the latter the grantor will go further and do all things necessary to establish lawful title in the grantee. This last covenant does not form a part of what is called the **usual covenants** and is often deleted, but is always included if the deed calls for the "common law covenants."

Special Warranty Deed

This deed is created by state statute and protects the grantee against two specific acts of the grantor:

1. that the grantor has not conveyed the property to anyone other than the grantee; and
2. that the property is free from any encumbrances created by the grantor.

This type of deed protects the grantee only from these two specific acts, and only if they were caused by the grantor herself. The scope of this type of deed is more limited than the general warranty deed.

Quitclaim Deed

This deed simply conveys to the grantee whatever title the grantor has; no representations are made with respect to the nature of that title or interest. It contains absolutely no covenants whatsoever, and the grantee acquires whatever title that grantor has, which could be none at all.

EXAMPLE:

A man convinces two foreign tourists in New York City to purchase the Brooklyn Bridge from him. He executes a quitclaim deed in their favor, and they pay him a sum of money. When they discover that he had no title to the bridge at all, the couple has no claim against the man for breach of warranty, because he has conveyed exactly the interest he possessed. (Note that the couple may institute other proceedings against the man not based on property law.)

The rights of the grantee and the grantor are determined by the nature of the covenants in the deed conveying the property. However, if a person conveys a title he or she does not possess, but then subsequently acquires that title, the law, under a doctrine known as **estoppel by deed,** will inure that title to the benefit of the grantee of the deed (not for a quitclaim deed, however). See Exhibit 4.6 at the end of this chapter for an example of a quitclaim deed.

EXAMPLE:

A woman purports, by general warranty deed, to sell some property to a third person. The buyer is unaware that the property in question is owned by the woman's father, and the woman only resides on the land. Several months later the woman's father dies and she inherits the property. Pursuant to the doctrine of estoppel by deed, the title now vests in the purchaser.

Mortgages

A **mortgage** is a security interest given by a debtor to his or her creditor to guarantee the repayment of a loan. Simply put, if the person who is purchasing the property requires financing, he or she will obtain a loan from an individual or institution who then becomes the buyer's creditor. To secure that loan, which is evidenced by a written document referred to as a **bond** or a **note,** the lender will require the borrower to provide another document, the mortgage, that gives the lender the right to attach specified property (the realty) to satisfy the debt should the borrower default on the loan. The borrower/debtor is referred to as the **mortgagor,** the one who gives the security interest, and the lender/creditor is referred to as the **mortgagee.**

 EXAMPLE:

A young couple wants to purchase their first home but cannot pay the complete purchase price. To acquire the property, the couple arrange for a loan from their bank. To ensure that the bank will not lose the money loaned, the bank insists that the couple give it a mortgage on the house. Should the couple default on the loan, the bank as the mortgagee will have the right to attach the house to satisfy the outstanding debt.

Because the mortgage represents an interest in land, pursuant to the Statute of Frauds the mortgage must be in writing in order to be enforceable. However, certain transactions that do not meet this requirement may still be enforced under a concept known as an **equitable mortgage.** This doctrine arises whenever a person acquires a deed to property under circumstances in which the apparent intention is to transfer a deed as a security interest rather than as a title. If this situation can be proved, a court may find, under its equitable jurisdiction, that the person in possession of the deed does not have title to the property but merely a security interest in the land.

 EXAMPLE:

A man needs money to pay for his daughter's college education. He is the sole owner of a house he inherited from his father. The man approaches a friend for a loan, and the friend agrees, provided that the man transfers the deed to his house to him until the loan is repaid. The father gives the man the deed, and the friend loans the money. When the loan is repaid, the "friend" claims that the money was intended as a sale of the house, not a loan. Under these circumstances, the court may find that the friend has only an equitable mortgage.

Note that some jurisdictions require some other documentary evidence in addition to the deed to meet the requirements of an equitable mortgage.

A mortgage may be used as a security interest not only for the purchase of realty, but also for improvements on the property and to secure a preexisting obligation.

Any transferable interest in real property may be mortgaged; however, the mortgagor is incapable of mortgaging any interest greater than the one he or she possesses. Consequently if a husband who holds title to property as a tenant by the entirety mortgages his interest, the mortgagee may only attach the property if the wife joins in the mortgage or the wife predeceases the husband, thereby creating a tenancy in severalty in the surviving spouse (see Chapter 1).

A legal axiom holds that the mortgage follows the note. In other words, if the underlying debt obligation is found invalid, so is the mortgage that attaches to it. The validity of the mortgage is controlled by the validity of the underlying note.

 EXAMPLE:

A woman is defrauded into signing a loan agreement and gives a mortgage to secure the debt. If the court deems that the loan agreement is void because of the fraud, the mortgage automatically becomes void as well.

The mortgagor is required to inform and obtain approval from the mortgagee before any changes are made to the subject property because such changes affect the mortgagee's interest. Most mortgages require the mortgagor to obtain **mortgage insurance** to provide funds should the mortgagor be found in default. Also, many mortgage agreements provide for **acceleration payments** if the mortgagor does anything to impinge on the mortgagee's rights, such as changing the nature of the property or defaulting, thereby making the remainder of the unpaid debt immediately due.

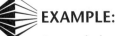 **EXAMPLE:**

A couple has acquired a house by borrowing money from the bank to which they have executed a mortgage. The mortgage includes an acceleration provision in case the couple default on the note or make substantial changes to the nature of the property without first obtaining the bank's consent. Ten years later the couple decide to demolish the freestanding garage on the property. If they do so without the bank's consent they may be obligated to repay the outstanding debt at once, because the property is now arguably less valuable (see the discussion on waste in Chapter 2).

If the mortgagor transfers the property, the transferee acquires the property either subject to the mortgage or by assuming the mortgage. A transfer **subject to the mortgage** means that the transferor remains principally liable on the debt, and the property can be attached if the transferor defaults. This could mean that the transferee will lose the property if the transferor fails to discharge the debt to the mortgagee.

A transfer in which the transferee **assumes the mortgage** means that the transferee now becomes liable for the underlying debt, and the transferor will only be liable secondarily (if the transferee defaults). To effectuate an assumption of the mortgage:

1. there must be a writing stating that the transferee intends to assume the mortgage; and
2. there must be a document that indicates the assumption of the mortgage.

A transferee who acquires property as an inheritance acquires the property subject to the mortgage, meaning that the estate of the deceased mortgagor is obligated for the debt, not the heir.

EXAMPLE:

A couple has lived in a small house for three years and are now planning a family and want to purchase a larger home. They sell the house to an elderly woman who wants a small home. The woman agrees to assume the mortgage so that she can buy the property for a lower purchase price, the difference being made up by the mortgage. One year later the woman dies and the house is willed to her granddaughter. The woman's estate must discharge the mortgage. If the estate assets are insufficient, the mortgagee may be able to attach the house to satisfy the obligation, and the granddaughter will inherit nothing. Furthermore, the original young couple may be liable for any money still outstanding after the house is sold by the mortgagee.

If the mortgagor defaults, the mortgagee is permitted the following remedies:

1. Action in default — the mortgagee can sue the mortgagor in a court of law for the amount of the loan that is outstanding.
2. **Judicial foreclosure** — the mortgagee can request the court to order a **foreclosure** sale of the property in which the property is attached and sold at public auction. If the proceeds of the resulting sale exceed the amount of the debt, the excess is given to the mortgagor; if the proceeds of the sale are insufficient to satisfy the debt, the mortgagee may then proceed against the mortgagor in an action for debt for the difference.
3. **Foreclosure by advertisement** — several jurisdictions, such as New York, permit the mortgagee, provided that such right appears in the mortgage, to foreclose on the property without court order if the mortgagee places a notice of the foreclosure sale for a statutory period of time.

Note that the mortgagee may not proceed in an action in debt and a foreclosure simultaneously. The mortgagee must select which cause of action to pursue first, and if the results of that action are insufficient to satisfy the note, the mortgagee may then seek the alternative remedy.

A mortgagor may be able to stop or redeem a foreclosure under a concept known as **redemption**. Redemption refers to the mortgagor's payment of the debt so as to be able to reclaim title to the property. There are two types of redemption procedures:

1. **Redemption in equity** — at any time prior to the foreclosure sale the mortgagor may redeem the property by satisfying the debt. Virtually every jurisdiction permits this type of redemption.
2. **Statutory redemption** — several jurisdictions also permit a mortgagor to redeem the property within a statutory period of time after the foreclosure sale by satisfying the underlying debt. Note that this form of redemption creates uncertainty for the purchaser of the property in the foreclosure sale, and so is generally not favored.

Mortgages are an important facet of real estate conveyancing because few people are able to purchase property without some form of financing. The mortgage becomes an important aspect of the closing as well (see Chapter 5).

Mortgages, like deeds, are recorded with the county recorder's office to protect the mortgagee, and mortgages form an encumbrance on the property. In many instances, property owners will refinance their property, thereby creating several mortgages on the same realty. The impact of multiple mortgages on the mortgagee is determined by the nature of the priorities afforded under the particular state law (see below).

See Exhibit 4.7 at the end of this chapter for an example of a Uniform Residential Loan Application.

Priorities and Recording Statutes

The concept of "priority" refers to the right afforded to persons each of whom has acquired an interest in realty. When multiple persons all assert claims to the same property the law and the courts must devise a system whereby the divergent rights can be satisfied and in which order. To this end, every jurisdiction has enacted **recording acts** that establish a chain of priority with respect to claims against property. The recording acts provide public notice to all persons asserting an interest in realty as to who may have a right to the property.

There are three types of recording acts in effect, and the specifics of each state's statutes must be individually analyzed. The three methods to establish priority are:

1. **Notice:** Under this type of recording statute, a subsequent bona fide purchaser for value of the property will prevail over an earlier grantee who fails to record his or her interest. Because the subsequent purchaser had no actual or constructive notice of any other interest in the property at the time of the creation of the interest, he or she will prevail.

EXAMPLE:

A man sells some property to Buyer One on August 15, but Buyer One does not record the transaction at the county recorder's office. On August 20 the man sells the same property to Buyer Two, who immediately records the transaction. In a lawsuit to determine title, Buyer Two, will prevail in a notice state because he had no notice of the sale to Buyer One at the time of his purchase. Note, however, if Buyer Two did not purchase the property but was given the property as a gift from the man, the title would vest in Buyer One because Buyer Two did not give value to acquire the title.

2. **Race:** In this type of jurisdiction, the first to record prevails regardless of the date of the transaction creating the interest.

EXAMPLE:

Assume that in the prior example Buyer Two knew of the sale to Buyer One but convinced the man to sell the property anyway. Buyer Two records the conveyance before Buyer One. In a pure race jurisdiction Buyer Two would prevail because his actual knowledge of the earlier conveyance is irrelevant since he recorded first. In a notice jurisdiction Buyer One would prevail.

3. **Race-notice:** Under this type of statute, the subsequent purchaser for value must record first *and* have no notice of an earlier conveyance.

EXAMPLE:

Using the parties from the previous examples, assume that Buyer Two has no notice of the sale to Buyer One. After the sale to Buyer Two, Buyer One records. The next day Buyer Two records. Buyer One prevails because Buyer Two did not record first.

In those jurisdictions that require notice to obtain a priority, the transferee must perform a title search to determine whether an earlier claim has been recorded. A title search is merely the process of examining the record books for the subject property at the county recorder's office.

Record offices use one of two methods to record titles. The first method is referred to as a **tract index** or **block and lot index,** in which the searcher looks at the record pages that are indexed by the physical description of the land (see above). The other method utilized by record offices is the **grantor-grantee index** in which the search is conducted by the names of the parties, looking first for the immediate transferor as a grantee, then his or her grantor as grantee, and so on back in the chain of title.

Once a claim is recorded, it protects the claimant from subsequent purchasers or claimants because recording provides notice. Consequently, to protect the rights of the parties, all interests in realty should be recorded in the county recorder's office, which is the official office for recording interests in realty.

Practical Tips

- The legal professional must be accurate and specific in creating a deed.
- Be careful in the description of the property — reference to prior deeds is useful.
- If the seller is the representative of an estate, the representative's name and address must appear on the documents, including his or her authority to act for the estate.
- Check whether the recorder's office requires a cover sheet.
- In many counties, personal checks are not permitted for filing fees — only certified or attorney checks will be allowed.

- Review the lien law of the particular jurisdiction to make sure all requirements for recording liens are met.
- Carefully review all mortgage documents.

Chapter Review

Conveyancing is the process whereby title to realty is transferred from one person to another. The most common method of conveyancing is by means of a sale. To effectuate a sale of realty, two documents are necessary: the contract for the sale of the property and the deed that transfers the title to the property.

All agreements that concern an interest in realty are required to be in writing to be enforceable pursuant to the Statute of Frauds. Furthermore, all contracts for the sale of real estate must meet all of the general contract law requirements to create any valid contract: offer, acceptance, consideration, capacity of the parties, legality of the subject matter, and contractual intent. In addition to these general requirements, certain provisions are specific to real estate transactions, such as the allocation of risk, the date of the closing, financing provisions, and so forth.

At the closing the seller presents to the buyer a deed that transfers the title. The nature of the deed determines the nature of the covenants, or warranties, that the grantor is making to the grantee with respect to the nature of the protection of the title being transferred. There are three types of deeds in common use: the general warranty deed that contains the common law covenants; the special warranty deed that only protects against specific acts committed by the grantor; and the quitclaim deed in which no warranties at all are given.

In order to consummate the sale, most purchasers require a loan. To secure the loan, the lender typically has the borrower give a mortgage — a security interest in the property — to the lender that gives the lender certain rights with respect to the property. The mortgage creates an encumbrance on the title, and affects the rights of all subsequent grantees.

To protect rights with respect to realty, all interests — the deed, all mortgages, and all appropriate liens — should be recorded at the county recorder's office in the county in which the property is located. This recordation puts all subsequent claimants on notice of prior rights to the land.

Ethical Concern

To complete a conveyance of real property much specific information is required. To speed up the process there may be a real temptation to provide information that may not be accurate but seems reasonable to save time and expense. Such conduct is considered to be an ethical violation as a falsification of a legal document. Take the time to check all facts that appear on a contract of sale or a deed.

Key Terms

Acceleration payment
Assignment
Assume the mortgage
Assumption agreement
Base line
Block and lot index
Boilerplate
Bond
Condition
Condition precedent
Closing
Closing statement
Cloud on title
Commission
Common law covenants
Consideration
Contractual capacity
Conveyancing
Covenant
Covenant against encumbrances
Covenant of further assurances
Covenant of right to convey
Covenant of seizin
Covenant of quiet enjoyment
Covenant of warranty
Damages
Deed
Deposit
Doctrine of equitable conversion
Donee
Donor
Down payment
Earnest money
Encumbrance
Equitable mortgage
Equitable redemption
Escrow
Estoppel by deed
Exclusive listing
Exclusive right to sell
Execution
Foreclosure
Foreclosure by advertisement
General warranty deed

Grantee
Grantor-grantee index
Installment sale
Insurable title
Judicial foreclosure
Lien
Listing agreement
Marketable title
Mechanic's lien
Metes and bounds description
Mortgage
Mortgagee
Mortgagor
Mortgage insurance
Note
Notice
Offer
Offeree
Offeror
Open listing
Plat book
Plat description
Principal meridian
Quitclaim deed
Race
Race-notice
Recording act
Rectangular survey description
Redemption
Redemption in equity
Settlement
Special warranty deed
Specific performance
Statutory redemption
Subject to the mortgage
Survey
Time is of the essence
Title insurance
Title search
Tract index
Usual covenants
Vendor and Purchaser Risk Act
Warranty

Exercises

1. Search the title to your residence at the county recorder's office.
2. Determine which type of recording act is in effect in your state.
3. Analyze the provisions of mortgage agreement to determine the type of information that will be required of the borrower.
4. Obtain a sample land sales contract and analyze its provisions.
5. Discuss the circumstances under which a person might be willing to accept a quitclaim deed. What could be done to protect this person's interest?

Situational Analysis

A real estate agent induces a couple to buy a house by stating that several famous people have owned and stayed in the house. After the sale, the couple learn that no famous person ever resided or visited the house. What, if anything, can the couple do?

Edited Cases

Many legal problems are the result of contractual conflicts. *Kipahulu Investment Co. v. Seltzer Partnership* concerns the breach of a land sales contract, and *Stambovsky v. Ackley* discusses a real estate broker's obligation with respect to the sale of realty.

Kipahulu Investment Company v. Seltzer Partnership
4 Haw. App. 625, 675 P.2d 778 (1983)

Plaintiff Kipahulu Investment Company (Kipahulu), a Hawaii general partnership, appeals the judgment denying its claim against defendants Seltzer Partnership (Seltzer), a Pennsylvania general partnership, and its partners for damages for breach of a land sale contract.

Kipahulu and its partners appeal the $34,552.04 judgment against them in favor of Seltzer and its partners for breach of the same contract. We affirm.

In July 1973 Kipahulu purchased two parcels of land in Kipahulu, Maui: parcel 8-B-1 (217.83 acres) and a forest reserve parcel (140 acres) (subject parcels). Notwithstanding breaks in the chains of record title of Kipahulu, Title Guaranty of Hawaii, Inc. (Title Guaranty), as agent, issued a clean (no title defects) policy of title insurance from Title Insurance and Trust Company (Title Insurance) to Kipahulu's mortgagee upon Kipahulu's agreeing to pursue quiet title proceedings and to indemnify and hold

Title Guaranty and Title Insurance harmless from any claims against the policy.

In January 1977 Kipahulu informed Allen Stack (Stack), counsel for Seltzer, a prospective buyer of the subject parcels, that there were some breaks in the chains of record title. However, Kipahulu gave Stack a copy of Title Insurance's clean title insurance policy in favor of Kipahulu's mortgagee without telling him of Kipahulu's agreements to indemnify and quiet title.

On November 25, 1977 Seltzer offered to purchase the subject parcels for $1,200,000. Kipahulu accepted the offer on December 1, 1977. The agreement required that Kipahulu convey marketable title on or before 2:00 p.m., on January 3, 1978. About December 20, 1977 Stack found out about the seriousness of the defects in Kipahulu's record title and of Kipahulu's promises to indemnify and quiet title. Thereupon, Kipahulu advised Seltzer of its willingness at its expense to bring, in Seltzer's name, an action to quiet title. Concluding that such an action would be bad public relations, Seltzer declined the offer. On December 29, 1977, at Kipahulu's request, Title Guaranty released Kipahulu from its obligation to pursue quiet title proceedings.

On January 3, 1978 Seltzer refused to close. On February 14, 1978 Kipahulu commenced an action to quiet title to parcel 8-B-1. The forest reserve parcel was not included because it had not been legally subdivided from adjoining forest reserve land, and although Seltzer had not waived the parcel's title defects, it had waived such lack of subdivision. As of the April 10, 1978 return date in the action, the only substantial claim was the state's claim to a jeep trail easement across parcel 8-B-1. The state filed a disclaimer on October 12, 1978. A judgment quieting title in Kipahulu was filed on November 6, 1978.

On June 13, 1978 Kipahulu sued Seltzer and its two partners seeking specific performance or damages for breach of the agreement. Seltzer and its two partners counterclaimed against Kipahulu and filed a third-party complaint against Kipahulu's partners for damages for breach of the agreement. Subsequently, Kipahulu dismissed its claim for specific performance. The trial was jury waived.

In their appeal Kipahulu and its partners assert that the trial court made the following errors:

I. The trial court erred in concluding that under the agreement title insurance did not satisfy the requirements of marketable title.

II. The trial court erred in concluding that the breaks in Kipahulu's chains of record title to parcel 8-B-1 made Kipahulu's title unmarketable. It also erred in concluding that Kipahulu did not prove that it had marketable title by adverse possession.

III. The trial court erred in concluding that time was of the essence under the agreement. Since time was not of the essence, (1) Kipahulu had a reasonable time within which to perform; (2) the lack of substantial claims against parcel 8-B-1 as of the April 10, 1978 return date in the quiet title action proved marketability by adverse possession as of that date; (3) that date was within a reasonable time; and (4) consequently, Seltzer was required to close on April 10, 1978.

I.

Under the agreement, Kipahulu was required to deliver to Seltzer at closing (1) "a warranty deed conveying title to the property in fee simple absolute, free and clear of all encumbrances, except as specifically set forth in the property description attached" and "further" (2) "an owner's extended coverage policy of title insurance in the amount of the full purchase price . . . insuring [Seltzer] to have marketable title to the property[.]"

Marketable title and insurable title are not generally synonymous. R. Powell & P. Rohan, Powell on Real Property Sec. 1044 (1982). See *Hebb v. Severson*, 32 Wash. 2d 159, 168, 201 P.2d 156, 160 (1948). Here, the lower court concluded, as do we, that under the agreement Seltzer was entitled to both marketable title and title insurance and the existence of title insurance did not satisfy the requirement of marketable title. See *New York Investors, Inc. v. Manhattan Beach Bathing Parks Corp.*, 229 A.D. 593, 243 N.Y.S. 548 (1930), *aff'd* 256 N.Y. 162, 176 N.E. 6 (1931).

II.

"A marketable title is a title which is free from encumbrances and any reasonable doubt as to its validity, and such as a reasonably intelligent person, who is well informed as to the facts and their legal bearings, and ready and willing to perform his contract, would be willing to accept in the exercise of ordinary business prudence." *Clarke v. Title Guaranty Co.*, 44 Haw. 261, 269, 353 P.2d 1002, 1007 (1960) (quoting *Sinclair v. Weber*, 204 Md. 324, 104 A.2d 561, 565 (1954)).

The lower court found that "the defects or breaks in title to parcel 8-B-1 . . . constituted a rational or substantial doubt which caused an uncertainty to the title of said parcel" and "constituted a reasonable doubt as to the marketability of said title[.]" Those findings of fact, which are mislabelled as conclusions of law, are not clearly erroneous and provide adequate support for the lower court's conclusion of law that Kipahulu's record title was not marketable. In fact, one of Kipahulu's managing general partners testified that its "title was essentially based upon adverse possession." Consequently, Kipahulu's real contention is that notwithstanding the defects in its record title, it proved that it had marketable title through adverse possession.

The level of Kipahulu's burden to prove that notwithstanding the lack of a judgment quieting title it had marketable title by adverse possession is debatable. See 77 Am. Jur. 2d, Vendor and Purchaser, Sec. 178 (1975). We need not decide that question because we hold that under all possibly applicable standards Kipahulu failed to meet its burden.

Adverse possession involves (1) intent, (2) fact, and (3) notice. *In re Keamo*, 3 Haw. App. 360, 650 P.2d 1365 (1982). With respect to (3), if the person claiming adverse possession knows or has "reason to suspect" that a cotenancy exists, the statutory period does not begin to run against his cotenant until the cotenant has actual notice that he is claiming adversely to the cotenant's title or until he makes "a good faith, reasonable effort to notify" his cotenant that he is claiming adversely to his cotenant's title. *City & County v. Bennett*, 57 Haw. 195, 209, 552 P.2d 1380, 1390 (1976).

Kipahulu's record title to parcel 8-B-1 derives from thirteen separate chains of title. Seltzer's expert testified that eleven of the chains were broken and in nine Kipahulu had record title to less than a 100% interest. Its record title to the forest reserve parcel derived from one of the eleven but not one of the nine. The breaks in Kipahulu's chains of record title provided "reason to suspect" the existence of one or more cotenancies. The fact that Kipahulu had assured itself that it and its predecessors in interest had occupied the land for at least 50 years and there were no known claimants nor any likelihood of potential claimants to the property including possible tenants in common does not satisfy Bennett's notice requirements. See *Hana Ranch, Inc. v. Kanakaole*, 1 Haw. App. 573, 578-580, 623 P.2d 885, 888-889 (1981) (Hana Ranch apparently assured itself that there were no known claimants nor any likelihood of potential claimants, but at the quiet title action claimant Flores asserted a serious claim to a fractional cotenancy interest). *Bennett* requires Kipahulu and its predecessors to have made "a good faith, reasonable effort to notify the [reasonably suspected] cotenants" that Kipahulu and its predecessors were claiming adversely to the cotenants' title. There is no evidence in the record of such effort by Kipahulu and its predecessors in interest. Kipahulu failed to prove compliance with the *Bennett* requirements for adverse possession against reasonably suspected cotenants and, consequently, did not meet its burden of proving marketable title by adverse possession.

III.

Time is of the essence under an agreement if made so expressly or where such intention is clearly manifested from the agreement as a whole, construed in the light of the surrounding facts. *Lum v. Stevens, Adm'r'x Soffra Est.*, 42 Haw. 286 (1958). Although *Lum v. Stevens* was an action in equity, we deem its rule as to time equally applicable in actions at law. See 17 Am. Jur. 2d Contracts Sec. 332 (1964).

Here, the agreement stated in relevant part:

> 5. Closing.   The closing of this transaction shall occur on or before January 3, 1978, in Honolulu, Hawaii, at the offices of Carlsmith, Carlsmith, Wichman & Case, at 2:00 p.m. . . .
> 8. Construction of Offer and Acceptance. . . .
> (f) Time.   Time is of the essence of this offer.

The agreement did not expressly make time of the essence as to its performance. However, one of the lower court's conclusions of law was that "[t]ime was of the essence of the letter agreement."

We have stated that "[t]he construction and the legal effect to be given a contract is a question of law. . . . Consequently, an appellate court is not bound by a trial court's construction of a contract based solely upon the terms of a written instrument without the aid of extrinsic evidence. . . . In such circumstances, the appellate court must make its own independent determination." *American Security Bank v. Read Realty, Inc.*, 1 Haw. App. 161, 165-66, 616 P.2d 237, 241 (1980) (citations omitted).

Here the question is, what is the standard where the trial court's construction is based upon the terms of a written instrument with the aid of extrinsic evidence? The lower court's decision in such a case mixes fact and law. See 5A Moore's Federal Practice para. 52.05[1] (1982); Wright & Miller, Federal Practice and Procedure: Civil Sec. 2589 (1971).

Generally, the lower court's findings of fact are subject to Hawaii Rules of Civil Procedure (HRCP), Rule 52(a)'s clearly erroneous standard of review and its conclusions of law from those findings are subject to the right/wrong standard of review explained in *Davis v. Davis*, 3 Haw. App. 501, 506, 653 P.2d 1167, 1171, n.5 (1982).

When the lower court is deciding what the extrinsic or surrounding facts are, it is making findings of fact which we review under the clearly erroneous standard. Rule 52, HRCP. When it is construing the agreement as a whole in light of those surrounding facts, it is making conclusions of law which we review under the right/wrong standard. See *State v. Miller*, 4 Haw. App. 603, 671 P.2d 1037 (1983).

Although the lower court did not specifically find these facts, the extrinsic evidence clearly indicates that the parties specifically negotiated the closing date and each was anxious to close the transaction on or before that date. Thus, the lower court's implicit finding of fact that the parties intended time to be of the essence under the agreement is not clearly erroneous and its conclusion of law that "[t]ime was of the essence of the letter agreement" is right.

The fact that after January 3, 1978 Seltzer continued to negotiate for the acquisition of the subject parcels did not constitute a waiver of its right to insist on performance of the November 25, 1977 agreement on January 3, 1978. When Kipahulu was unable to perform its obligations under the November 25, 1977 agreement as required on January 3, 1978, Seltzer was entitled to lawfully terminate that agreement without prejudice to its right to negotiate a new agreement containing different terms.

This is an action at law for damages, not an action for equitable relief. Consequently, *Jenkins v. Wise*, 58 Haw. 592, 574 P.2d 1337 (1978), as clarified in *Kaiman Realty, Inc. v. Carmichael*, 2 Haw. App. 499, 634 P.2d 603 (1981), *rev'd in part*, 65 Haw. 637, 655 P.2d 872 (1982), *supp'd on reconsideration*, 66 Haw. 103, 659 P.2d 63 (1983), and their progeny are inapplicable.

Affirmed.

Case Questions

1. How does the court distinguish between marketable title and insurable title?

2. What factors caused the court to conclude that Kipahulu did not acquire title by adverse possession?

Stambovsky v. Ackley
169 A.D.2d 254, 572 N.Y.S.2d 672 (1991)

Plaintiff, to his horror, discovered that the house he had recently contracted to purchase was widely reputed to be possessed by poltergeists, reportedly seen by defendant seller and members of her family on numerous occasions over the last nine years. Plaintiff promptly commenced this action seeking rescission of the contract of sale. Supreme Court reluctantly dismissed the complaint, holding that plaintiff has no remedy at law in this jurisdiction.

The unusual facts of this case, as disclosed by the record, clearly warrant a grant of equitable relief to the buyer who, as a resident of New York City, cannot be expected to have any familiarity with the folklore of the Village of Nyack. Not being a "local," plaintiff could not readily learn that the home he had contracted to purchase is haunted. Whether the source of the spectral apparitions seen by defendant seller are parapsychic or psychogenic, having reported their presence in both a national publication (Readers' Digest) and the local press (in 1977 and 1982, respectively), defendant is estopped to deny their existence and, as a matter of law, the house is haunted. More to the point, however, no divination is required to conclude that it is defendant's promotional efforts in publicizing her close encounters with these spirits which fostered the home's reputation in the community. In 1989, the house was included in a five-home walking tour of Nyack and described in a November 27th newspaper article as "a riverfront Victorian (with ghost)." The impact of the reputation thus created goes to the very essence of the bargain between the parties, greatly impairing both the value of the property and its potential for resale. The extent of this impairment may be presumed for the purpose of reviewing the disposition of this motion to dismiss the cause of action for rescission (*Harris v. City of New York*, 147 A.D.2d 186, 188-189) and represents merely an issue of fact for resolution at trial.

While I agree with Supreme Court that the real estate broker, as agent for the seller, is under no duty to disclose to a potential buyer the phantasmal reputation of the premises and that, in his pursuit of a legal remedy for fraudulent misrepresentation against the seller, plaintiff hasn't a ghost of a chance, I am nevertheless moved by the spirit of equity to allow the buyer to seek rescission of the contract of sale and recovery of his down payment. New York law fails to recognize any remedy for damages incurred as a result of the seller's mere silence, applying instead the strict rule of caveat emptor. Therefore, the theoretical basis for granting relief, even under the extraordinary facts of this case, is elusive if not ephemeral.

"Pity me not but lend thy serious hearing to what I shall unfold" (William Shakespeare, Hamlet, Act I, Scene V [Ghost]).

From the perspective of a person in the position of plaintiff herein, a very practical problem arises with respect to the discovery of a paranormal phenomenon: "Who you gonna' call?" as a title song to the movie "Ghostbusters" asks. Applying the strict rule of caveat emptor to a contract involving a house possessed by poltergeists conjures up visions of a psychic or medium routinely accompanying the structural engineer and Terminix man on an inspection of every home subject to a contract of sale. It portends that the prudent attorney will establish an escrow account lest the subject of the transaction come back to haunt him and his client — or pray that his malpractice insurance coverage extends to supernatural disasters. In the interest of avoiding such untenable consequences, the notion that a haunting is a condition which can and should be ascertained upon reasonable inspection of the premises is a hobgoblin which should be exorcised from the body of legal precedent and laid quietly to rest.

It has been suggested by a leading authority that the ancient rule which holds that mere nondisclosure does not constitute actionable misrepresentation "finds proper application in cases where the fact undisclosed is patent, or the plaintiff has equal opportunities for obtaining information which he may be expected to utilize, or the defendant has no reason to think that he is acting under any misapprehension" (Prosser, Torts Sec. 106, at 696 [4th ed 1971]). However, with respect to transactions in real estate, New York adheres to the doctrine of caveat emptor and imposes no duty upon the vendor to disclose any information concerning the premises (*London v. Courduff*, 141 A.D.2d 803) unless there is a confidential or fiduciary relationship between the parties (*Moser v. Spizzirro*, 31 A.D.2d 537, aff'd 25 N.Y.2d 941; *IBM Credit Fin. Corp. v. Mazda Motor Mfg. [USA] Corp.*, 152 A.D.2d 451) or some conduct on the part of the seller which constitutes "active concealment" (see *17 E. 80th Realty Corp. v. 68th Assocs.*, A.D.2d [1st Dept., May 9, 1991] [dummy ventilation system constructed by seller]; *Haberman v. Greenspan*, 82 Misc. 2d 263 [foundation cracks covered by seller]). Normally, some affirmative misrepresentation (e.g., *Tahini Invs. v. Bobrowsky*, 99 A.D.2d 489 [industrial waste on land allegedly used only as farm]; *Jansen v. Kelly*, 11 A.D.2d 587 [land containing valuable minerals allegedly acquired for use as campsite]) or partial disclosure (*Junius Constr. Corp. v. Cohen*, 257 N.Y. 393 [existence of third unopened street concealed]; *Noved Realty Corp. v. A.A.P. Co.*, 250 App. Div. 1 [escrow agreements securing lien concealed]) is required to impose upon the seller a duty to communicate undisclosed conditions affecting the premises (contra, *Young v. Keith*, 112 A.D.2d 625 [defective water and sewer systems concealed]).

Caveat emptor is not so all-encompassing a doctrine of common law as to render every act of nondisclosure immune from redress, whether legal or equitable.

> In regard to the necessity of giving information which has not been asked, the rule differs somewhat at law and in equity, and while the law courts would permit no recovery of damages against a vendor, because of mere concealment of facts under certain circumstances, yet if the vendee refused to complete the contract because of the concealment of a material fact on the part of the other, equity would refuse to compel him so to do, because equity only compels the specific perfor-

mance of a contract which is fair and open, and in regard to which all material matters known to each have been communicated to the other.

(*Rothmiller v. Stein*, 143 N.Y. 581, 591-592. Even as a principle of law, long before exceptions were embodied in statute law (see, e.g., UCC 2-312, 2-313, 2-314, 2-315; 3-417[2][e]), the doctrine was held inapplicable to contagion among animals, adulteration of food, and insolvency of a maker of a promissory note and of a tenant substituted for another under a lease (see *Rothmiller v. Stein*, supra, at 592-593, and cases cited therein). Common law is not moribund. Ex facto jus oritur (law arises out of facts). Where fairness and common sense dictate that an exception should be created, the evolution of the law should not be stifled by rigid application of a legal maxim.

The doctrine of caveat emptor requires that a buyer act prudently to assess the fitness and value of his purchase and operates to bar the purchaser who fails to exercise due care from seeking the equitable remedy of rescission (see, e.g., *Rodas v. Manitaras*, 159 A.D.2d 341). For the purposes of the instant motion to dismiss the action pursuant to CPLR 3211(a)(7), plaintiff is entitled to every favorable inference which may reasonably be drawn from the pleadings (*Arrington v. New York Times Co.*, 55 N.Y.2d 433, 442; *Rovello v. Orofino Realty Co.*, 40 N.Y.2d 633, 634), specifically, in this instance, that he met his obligation to conduct an inspection of the premises and a search of available public records with respect to title. It should be apparent, however, that the most meticulous inspection and the search would not reveal the presence of poltergeists at the premises or unearth the property's ghoulish reputation in the community. Therefore, there is no sound policy reason to deny plaintiff relief for failing to discover a state of affairs which the most prudent purchaser would not be expected to even contemplate (see *Da Silva v. Musso*, 53 N.Y.2d 543, 551).

The case law in this jurisdiction dealing with the duty of a vendor of real property to disclose information to the buyer is distinguishable from the matter under review. The most salient distinction is that existing cases invariably deal with the physical condition of the premises (e.g., *London v. Courduff*, supra [use as a landfill]; *Perin v. Mardine Realty Co.*, 5 A.D.2d 685, *aff'd* 6 N.Y.2d 920 [sewer line crossing adjoining property without owner's consent]); defects in title (e.g., *Sands v. Kissane*, 282 App. Div. 140 [remainderman]); liens against the property (e.g., *Noved Realty Corp. v. A.A.P. Co.*, supra); expenses or income (e.g., *Rodas v. Manitaras*, supra [gross receipts]) and other factors affecting its operation. No case has been brought to this court's attention in which the property value was impaired as the result of the reputation created by information disseminated to the public by the seller (or, for that matter, as a result of possession by poltergeists).

Where a condition which has been created by the seller materially impairs the value of the contract and is peculiarly within the knowledge of the seller or unlikely to be discovered by a prudent purchaser exercising due care with respect to the subject transaction, nondisclosure constitutes a basis for rescission as a matter of equity. Any other outcome places upon the buyer not merely the obligation to exercise care in his purchase but rather to be omniscient with respect to any fact which may affect the bargain. No practical purpose is served by imposing such a burden upon a purchaser. To the contrary, it encourages predatory business practice and offends the principle that equity will suffer no wrong to be without a remedy.

Defendant's contention that the contract of sale, particularly the merger or "as is" clause, bars recovery of the buyer's deposit is unavailing. Even an express disclaimer will not be given effect where the facts are peculiarly within the knowledge of the party invoking it (*Danann Realty Corp. v. Harris,* 5 N.Y.2d 317, 322; *Tahini Invs. v. Bobrowsky,* supra). Moreover, a fair reading of the merger clause reveals that it expressly disclaims only representations made with respect to the physical condition of the premises and merely makes general reference to representations concerning "any other matter or things affecting or relating to the aforesaid premises." As broad as this language may be, a reasonable interpretation is that its effect is limited to tangible or physical matters and does not extend to paranormal phenomena. Finally, if the language of the contract is to be construed as broadly as defendant urges to encompass the presence of poltergeists in the house, it cannot be said that she has delivered the premises "vacant" in accordance with her obligation under the provisions of the contract rider.

To the extent New York law may be said to require something more than "mere concealment" to apply even the equitable remedy of rescission, the case of *Junius Constr. Corp. v. Cohen* (257 N.Y. 393, supra), while not precisely on point, provides some guidance. In that case, the seller disclosed that an official map indicated two as yet unopened streets which were planned for construction at the edges of the parcel. What was not disclosed was that the same map indicated a third street which, if opened, would divide the plot in half. The court held that, while the seller was under no duty to mention the planned streets at all, having undertaken to disclose two of them, he was obliged to reveal the third (see also *Rosenschein v. McNally,* 17 A.D.2d 834).

In the case at bar, defendant seller deliberately fostered the public belief that her home was possessed. Having undertaken to inform the public-at-large, to whom she has no legal relationship, about the supernatural occurrences on her property, she may be said to owe no less a duty to her contract vendee. It has been remarked that the occasional modern cases which permit a seller to take unfair advantage of a buyer's ignorance so long as he is not actively misled are "singularly unappetizing" (Prosser, Torts Sec. 106, at 696 [4th ed. 1971]). Where, as here, the seller not only takes unfair advantage of the buyer's ignorance but has created and perpetuated a condition about which he is unlikely to even inquire, enforcement of the contract (in whole or in part) is offensive to the court's sense of equity. Application of the remedy of rescission, within the bounds of the narrow exception to the doctrine of caveat emptor set forth herein, is entirely appropriate to relieve the unwitting purchaser from the consequences of a most unnatural bargain.

Accordingly, the judgment of the Supreme Court, New York County (Edward H. Lehner, J.), entered April 9, 1990, which dismissed the complaint pursuant to CPLR 3211(a)(7), should be modified, on the law and the facts, and in the exercise of discretion, and the first cause of action seeking rescission of the contract reinstated, without costs.

Case Questions

1. What does the court conclude are the obligations of the real estate agent?

2. How does the court interpret the vendor's duty to disclose in this case?

Exhibit 4.3: Contract of Sale

Agreement made this   day of

A.D. 19   between

of the first part, and

of the second part.

The party of the first part hereinafter referred to as the SELLER hereby agrees to sell and the
party of the second part hereinafter referred to as the BUYER agrees to purchase a certain estate
situated

and bounded and described as follows:

Included in this sale as a part of said premises are the usual Landlord's fixtures belonging to
the SELLER and used in connection therewith including, if any, all furnaces, heaters, stoves, ranges,
oil and gas burners and fixtures appurtenant thereto, hot water heaters, electric, gas refrigerators, air
conditioning apparatus, mantels, electric and other lighting fixtures, venetian blinds and window shades,
screens, screen doors, storm or other detached windows and doors, blinds, awnings, bathroom fixtures,
television antennas, fences, gates, garbage disposers, dishwashers, washing machines, driers and hardy
shrubs and other fixtures, in so far as the same are or can by agreement of the parties be made a part
of the realty.

Exhibit 4.3: *(Continued)*

Said premises are to be conveyed on or before   by a
good and sufficient   deed of the SELLER, conveying a good and
clear title to the same, free from all encumbrances, except:

- (a) Provisions of local zoning laws, if any;
- (b) Existing rights created by instruments of record in party or partition walls (if any);
- (c) Such taxes for the current year as are not due and payable on the date of the delivery of such deed, and any liens for municipal betterments assessed after the date of this agreement.

To enable the SELLER to make conveyance as herein provided, the SELLER may, if the SELLER so desires, at the time of the delivery of the deed, use the purchase money or any portion thereof to clear the title of any or all encumbrances or interests; all instruments so procured to be recorded simultaneously with the delivery of said deed.

and for such deed and conveyance the BUYER is to pay the sum of

                                                                                                    dollars
of which   dollars
have been paid this day,   dollars
are to be paid in cash upon the delivery of said deed, and the remainder is to be paid by the note of
the BUYER, dated
bearing interest at   per cent per annum, payable
and secured by a power of sale mortgage, in the usual form, upon the said premises, such note to be
payable

Full possession of the said premises, free of all tenants

                                                is to be delivered to the BUYER at the
time of the delivery of the deed, the said premises to be then in the same condition in which they now
are reasonable use and wear of the buildings thereon, and damage by fire or other unavoidable casualty
excepted.

Exhibit 4.3: *(Continued)*

The buildings on said premises shall, until the full performance of this agreement, be kept insured in the sum of
by the SELLER in offices satisfactory to the BUYER, and, in case of any loss, all sums recovered or recoverable on account of said insurance shall be paid over or assigned, on delivery of the deed, to the BUYER, unless the premises shall previously have been restored to their former condition by the SELLER.

Rents, Insurance Premiums, Water Rates, and Taxes, shall be apportioned as of the day of delivery of the deed, and the taxes assessed for the year 19   shall be paid by

The deed is to be delivered and the consideration paid, if the purchaser so requires, at the Registry of Deeds in which the deed should by law be recorded, on   19
at   M. unless some other place and time should be mutually agreed upon.

If the SELLER shall be unable to give title or to make conveyance as above stipulated, any payments made under this agreement shall be refunded, and all other obligations of either party hereunto shall cease, but the acceptance of a deed and possession by the BUYER shall be deemed to be a full performance and discharge hereof.

In consideration of the above,   , wife of the
said   , hereby agrees to join in the said deed
to be made as aforesaid, and to release and convey to the BUYER all statutory and other rights and interests in said premises.

IT IS UNDERSTOOD THAT A BROKER'S COMMISSION OF   per cent
on the said sale is to be paid to   ,
by the said SELLER.

The contracting parties agree that this contract contains all the terms and conditions of this sale. It is mutually agreed that any oral representation made by either party prior to the signing of this agreement is null and void.

In witness whereof,   the said parties hereto, and to another instrument of like tenor, set their hands and seals on the day and year first above written.

Signed and sealed in presence of

....

....

....

Extension

The time for the performance of the foregoing agreement is extended until

Witness our hands and seals this   day of   19

....

....

Exhibit 4.3: *(Continued)*

with

Agreement
[REAL ESTATE]

From the office of

(Please print or type)

RETURN TO ➡

HOBBS & WARREN, INC.
Publishers Standard Legal Forms
Boston - Mass.
FORM 223
Revised 1970

Exhibit 4.4: Rider to a Residential Contract of Sale

RIDER TO CONTRACT OF SALE
between

_____ (the "Seller")

and

_____ (the "Purchaser")

for the Sale of

_____ (the "Premises")

1. <u>CONFLICT</u>: In the event of a conflict between the terms of the printed portion of the Contract and the terms of this Rider, the terms of this Rider shall control, govern and prevail and the contradicted and/or inconsistent provisions of the printed portion of the Contract shall be deemed amended and superseded accordingly.

2. <u>TITLE</u>: Purchaser agrees to order a title report within ten (10) days after the date hereof, and to deliver or make sure that the title insurance company delivers to Seller's attorney, copies of the title insurance company's report, including the exception sheets, tax searches, property description, departmental searches and, if ordered, survey and survey reading, when issued. Since Purchaser is currently an owner of the Premises, Seller shall not be obligated to take any action to clear title and to cure any other violations under this Contract, and shall not be required to bring any action or proceeding or make any expenditure.

3. <u>INSPECTION, CONDITION OF PREMISES</u>: Purchaser acknowledges and represents to Seller that Purchaser has inspected or has had inspected by an inspector of Purchaser's choice, the Premises and all items of personal and real property included in the sale of the Premises, and is fully familiar with and satisfied with the physical nature and condition of same and will accept the Premises and all items of personal and real property included in the sale of the Premises "AS IS." On advance notice to Seller and reasonable appointment within 24 hours prior to closing, Purchaser shall be given the opportunity to reinspect the Premises, only for the purpose of determining whether the Premises are in the condition required by this Contract.

4. <u>REPRESENTATIONS, NON-SURVIVAL</u>: Purchaser expressly acknowledges, agrees and represents that no broker, representative, agent, employee, or attorney of Seller previously did nor does now make, and Purchaser is not relying upon, and has not been induced to enter into this Contract on the basis of, any warranties, representations, information, broker setups, inducements, or other statements (expressed or implied) as to the past, present or future physical condition of the Premises, the status

Exhibit 4.4: *(Continued)*

of any termite infestation, or of any material or chemical, the expenses, taxes, operation, or maintenance, the school district, the quantity, quality or condition of the articles of personal property, fixtures, utilities and equipment agreed to be sold with the Premises, or as to the Premises, except as and only to the extent in this Contract specifically set forth. Acceptance by Purchaser of the deed at closing shall be and be deemed to be full compliance, performance and discharge of every agreement, representation and obligation expressed or implied (other than as required by law) on the part of Seller contained anywhere in this Contract. No representation, warranty or guarantee of Seller shall be deemed to survive the earlier of closing or possession by Purchaser or be the basis of any claim against Seller unless specifically and expressly stated in this Contract to survive.

5. <u>NOTICE:</u> _____ is the attorney for Purchaser, and _____ are the attorneys for Seller. The aforesaid addresses are the respective addresses for notices to said attorneys pursuant to this Contract. Notices shall be deemed valid and effective when received by the notified party's attorney, at the above address, and mailed to the party to be notified, addressed to the party at the party's address stated at the beginning of this Contract; or to such other address as the party or attorney may hereafter designate by notice as herein provided. Any and all notice, demands or requests required or permitted to be given by any of the provisions of this Contract must be in writing and shall be validly given or made and effective the date when delivered personally against receipt, or actually received, or three (3) days after mailing with postage prepaid by either U.S. certified mail, return receipt requested, or by regular mail receipt of which is acknowledged by the receiving party or attorney. The attorneys are hereby expressly authorized, on behalf of their respective clients, to serve, and/or receive any written notice, whenever such notice is permitted to be given under the terms and conditions of this Contract; and to extend any of the time limitations as provided in this Contract; any such notice and/or extension, if any, shall be in writing and duly signed by said party or said party's attorney.

6. <u>MISCELLANEOUS:</u>
a. <u>No Recording:</u> This Contract or any memorandum of notice of same shall not be recorded or tendered for recording by or on behalf of Purchaser and any attempt to record the same by or on behalf of Purchaser shall be deemed a default by Purchaser; and thereupon, at Seller's election, this Contract shall be deemed canceled and Seller shall have any and all remedies for a default by Purchaser provided for herein and by law. If Purchaser files a notice of pendency of action or any other notice or memorandum in any court or land records department and either fails to commence a court action against Seller, or does not obtain judgment against Seller based on said court action, Purchaser agrees to pay Seller interest

Exhibit 4.4: *(Continued)*

at the prime rate plus 1% as published in the New York Times on the unpaid balance of the purchase price commencing on date of filing the notice and ending when the notice is removed, together with reasonable legal, bonding and other costs and expenses, including attorneys fees, incurred by Seller in the defense of said action and as to removal of said notice.

      b. <u>No Offer</u>: The transmittal of this document or any written or oral communication by Seller or of any attorney, broker or agent shall not be deemed a binding or continuing offer to sell or a meeting of the minds of the prospective parties on material terms and conditions, nor shall it be deemed a consummation of a contract or an accepted offer. The subject Premises are subject to prior sale, price change and/or withdrawal from sale and there shall be no binding contract unless and until Seller executes and delivers to Purchaser a fully executed Contract.

      c. <u>Assessments</u>: Seller represents to Purchaser that Seller is not aware of any assessments affecting the Premises either pending or threatened. If at the time of closing, the Premises are affected by an assessment or assessments which are or may become payable in annual installments, the assessments payable after closing of the title shall be payable by Purchaser and by the owner of the Premises if payable on the date of or prior to closing of title.

      d. <u>Fire, Other Major Casualty</u>: If prior to closing there shall be any fire, flood, explosion or other casualty, or condemnation affecting the Premises or any of the property to be conveyed in connection therewith, the New York General Obligations Law, Section 5-1311 shall apply, except that there shall be no abatement of purchase price.

      e. <u>Liens at Closing</u>: If there be a mortgage or other lien on the Premises, the Premises shall be conveyed subject to said mortgage or other lien. The existence of said mortgage or other lien shall not constitute an objection to title if Purchaser's title insurance company omits such mortgage or other lien as an exception to title.

      7. <u>DOWN PAYMENT, ESCROW</u>: The down payment shall be deemed paid to Seller on account of the purchase price, but shall be paid by check to the Seller's attorney, who shall also act as Escrow Agent. Purchaser's check payable to P.C. ("Escrow Agent"), is to be deposited in escrow by the Escrow Agent subject to clearance and the funds held in escrow in accordance with the provisions of this Contract. The escrow deposit may be delivered to or for Seller, on the stated closing date unless (1) upon Purchaser's default, to Seller, or (2) if Purchaser shall sooner be entitled to a refund thereof pursuant to this Contract, in which case shall be paid to Purchaser, or (3) if Seller shall default or cannot give title as required by this Contract, the escrow deposit shall be repaid to Purchaser. Interest accrued on the down payment will be paid to the party to whom the down payment is paid or refunded.

Exhibit 4.4: *(Continued)*

If the Escrow Agent is notified by a party of an escrow dispute, the Escrow Agent may (i) retain the funds in escrow until receipt by Escrow Agent of a written agreement and authorization from Seller and Purchaser directing the disposition of the funds; or (ii) at any time deposit the escrow funds with the Clerk of the Court, County, or by direction of any Court having jurisdiction over the parties, and thereby be released and discharged by the parties for any and all costs, responsibilities, obligations and liabilities as to the escrow fund; and the Escrow Agent shall be compensated as to any expenses by the losing party. The Escrow Agent shall not be liable for any error, omission or action taken unless resulting from the Escrow Agent's gross negligence or willful breach of the terms of this section. By signing this Rider, who is Seller's agent as to receipt of the funds, agrees to act as the Escrow Agent for the down payment subject to the terms of this Section. In case of a dispute or any threatened or actual litigation, notwithstanding acting as the Escrow Agent, may represent Seller. If Purchaser's down payment check is dishonored for any reason by the bank upon which it is drawn, then Seller, in addition to any other rights and remedies Seller may have, may, at Seller's option, declare this Contract null and void and at an end and thereupon Seller shall be relieved and released from all obligations hereunder.

_____

Seller

_____

Seller

_____

Purchaser

By: _____

Exhibit 4.5: Deed

M 297— Statutory Form F.
Referee's Deed in Foreclosure. 11-98.

DISTRIBUTED BY **Blumberg**Excelsior Inc.
NYC 10013

This Deed

Made the   *day of*

Between   *Referee*

duly appointed in the action hereinafter mentioned, Grantor

And

                                     Grantee:

Witnesseth, *that the Grantor, the Referee appointed in an action between*

                                 plaintiff(s),

and

                                 defendant(s),

foreclosing a mortgage recorded on   *in the office of the*

of the County of   *in liber*   *of mortgages,*

at page

in pursuance of a judgment entered at a special term of the

on   *and in consideration of*

                             Dollars paid by the Grantee,

being the highest sum bid at the sale under said judgment does hereby grant and convey unto the Grantee, all the

right, title and interest of the defendants

in and to

Exhibit 4.5: *(Continued)*

All

Exhibit 4.5: *(Continued)*

To have and to hold   *the premises herein granted unto the Grantee*

and assigns forever.

Whenever the text hereof requires, the singular number as used herein shall include the plural and all genders.

In Witness Whereof,   *the Grantor has hereunto set his hand and seal, the date first above written.*

--- {L. S.}
                                                    Referee

In Presence of:

State of New York

County of   } ss.:   ACKNOWLEDGMENT RPL 309-a (Do not use outside New York State.)

On   before me, personally appeared

personally known to me or proved to me on the basis of satisfactory evidence to be the individual(s) whose name(s) is (are) subscribed to the within instrument and acknowledged to me that he/she/they executed the same in his/her/their capacity(ies), and that by his/her/their signature(s) on the instrument, the individual(s), or the person upon behalf of which the individual(s) acted, executed the instrument.

(signature and office of individual taking acknowledgment)

Exhibit 4.5: *(Continued)*

𝔇𝔢𝔢𝔡

REFEREE'S DEED IN FORECLOSURE

TO

Dated,

STATE OF NEW YORK

County of_____**ss.**

RECORDED ON THE

............*day of*..

at.............*o'clock*........... *M.*

in Liber.....................*of Deeds*

at Page......................*and examined*

....
                                                                    CLERK

PLEASE RECORD AND RETURN TO:

Reserve this space for use of Recording Office.

Exhibit 4.6: Quitclam Deed

MASSACHUSETTS QUITCLAIM DEED INDIVIDUAL (LONG FORM) 882

of   County, Massachusetts,

being unmarried, for consideration paid, and in full consideration of

grant to   *

of   with **quitclaim covenants**

the land in

[Description and encumbrances, if any]

(*Individual — Joint Tenants — Tenants in Common.)

Exhibit 4.6: *(Continued)*

𝕎𝕚𝕥𝕟𝕖𝕤𝕤 _____ hand   and seal   this _____ day of _____ , 19____

_____   _____
_____   _____
_____   _____

The Commonwealth of Massachusetts

            ss.   19

Then personally appeared the above named

and acknowledged the foregoing instrument to be   free act and deed, before me

_____
                                    Notary Public — Justice of the Peace

My commission expires   19

CHAPTER 183 SEC. 6 AS AMENDED BY CHAPTER 497 of 1969
Every deed presented for record shall contain or have endorsed upon it the full name, residence and post office address of the grantee and a recital of the amount of the full consideration thereof in dollars or the nature of the other consideration therefor, if not delivered for a specific monetary sum. The full consideration shall mean the total price for the conveyance without deduction for any liens or encumbrances assumed by the grantee or remaining thereon. All such endorsements and recitals shall be recorded as part of the deed. Failure to comply with this section shall not affect the validity of any deed. No register of deeds shall accept a deed for recording unless it is in compliance with the requirements of this section.

Exhibit 4.6: *(Continued)*

MASSACHUSETTS

𝔖tatute 𝔉orm of

𝔔uitclaim 𝔇eed

(INDIVIDUAL)

TO

_____ 19____

at _____ o'clock and _____ minutes _____ m.

Received and entered with _____

_____ Deeds

Book _____ Page _____ .

Attest:

_____
Register

FROM THE OFFICE OF

(Please print or type)

RETURN TO ➜

FORM 882

REVISED CHAPTER 497-1969 – 727-1980

(H&W) HOBBS & WARREN ™

BOSTON

Exhibit 4.7: Uniform Residential Loan Application

UNIFORM RESIDENTIAL LOAN APPLICATION
(Complete this form for Full Documentation Loans)

This application is designed to be completed by the applicant(s) with the lender's assistance. Applicants should complete this form as "Borrower" or "Co-Borrower," as applicable. Co-Borrower information must also be provided (and the appropriate box checked) when ☐ the income or assets of a person other than the "Borrower" (including the Borrower's spouse) will be used as a basis for loan qualification or ☐ the income or assets of the Borrower's spouse will not be used as a basis for loan qualification, but his or her liabilities must be considered because the Borrower resides in a community property state, the security property is located in a community property state, or the Borrower is relying on other property located in a community property state as a basis for repayment of the loan.

I. TYPE OF MORTGAGE AND TERMS OF LOAN						
Mortgage Applied for:	☐ Conventional		☐ Other:		Agency Case Number	Lender Case Number
Amount $	Interest Rate %	No. of Months	Amortization Type:	☐ Fixed Rate ☐ GPM	☐ Other (explain): ☐ ARM (type):	

II. PROPERTY INFORMATION AND PURPOSE OF LOAN	
Subject Property Address (street, city, state, zip)	No. of Units
Legal Description of Subject Property (attached description if necessary)	Year Built

Purpose of Loan:	☐ Purchase ☐ Refinance	☐ Construction ☐ Construction-Permanent	☐ Other (explain):	Property will be: ☐ Primary Residence ☐ Secondary Residence ☐ Investment

Complete this line if construction or construction-permanent loan.

Year Lot Acquired	Original Cost $	Amount Existing Liens $	(a) Present Value of Lot $	(b) Cost of Improvements $	Total (a + b) $

Complete this line if this is a refinance loan.

Year Acquired	Original Cost $	Amount Existing Liens $	Purpose of Refinance	Describe Improvements ☐ Made ☐ To Be Made Cost: $

Title Will Be Held In What Name(s)	Manner in Which Title Will Be Held	Estate Will Be Held In: ☐ Fee Simple
Source of Down Payment, Settlement Charges and/or Subordinate Financing (explain)		☐ Leasehold (show expiration date)

III. BORROWER INFORMATION	CO-BORROWER INFORMATION
Borrower's Name (include Jr. or Sr. if applicable)	Co-Borrower's Name (include Jr. or Sr. if applicable)

Social Security Number	Home Phone ( )	Age	Yrs. School	Social Security Number	Home Phone ( )	Age	Yrs. School
☐ Married ☐ Unmarried (include ☐ Separated single, divorced, widowed)		Dependents (not listed by Co-Borrower) no. ages		☐ Married ☐ Unmarried (include ☐ Separated single, divorced, widowed)		Dependents (not listed by Borrower) no. ages	
Present Address (street, city, state, zip) ☐ Own ☐ Rent No. Yrs. ___				Present Address (street, city, state, zip) ☐ Own ☐ Rent No. Yrs. ___			

If residing at present address for less than two years, complete the following:

Former Address (street, city, state, zip) ☐ Own ☐ Rent No. Yrs. ___	Former Address (street, city, state, zip) ☐ Own ☐ Rent No. Yrs. ___
Former Address (street, city, state, zip) ☐ Own ☐ Rent No. Yrs. ___	Former Address (street, city, state, zip) ☐ Own ☐ Rent No. Yrs. ___

IV. EMPLOYMENT INFORMATION BORROWER	EMPLOYMENT INFORMATION CO-BORROWER
Name & Address of Employer ☐ Self Employed	Yrs. on this job ___ Yrs. employed in this line of work/profession ___	Name & Address of Employer ☐ Self Employed	Yrs. on this job ___ Yrs. employed in this line of work/profession ___
Position/Title/Type of Business	Business Phone ( )	Position/Title/Type of Business	Business Phone ( )

If employed in current position for less than two years or if currently employed in more than one position, complete the following:

Exhibit 4.7: *(Continued)*

V. MONTHLY INCOME AND COMBINED HOUSING EXPENSE INFORMATION						
Gross Monthly Income	Borrower	Co-Borrower	Total	Combined Monthly Housing Expense	Present	Proposed
Base Empl. Income*	$	$	$	Rent	$	$
Overtime				First Mortgage (P&I)		
Bonuses				Other Financing (P&I)		
Commissions				Hazard Insurance		
Dividends/Interest				Real Estate Taxes		
Net Rental Income				Mortgage Insurance		
Other *(before completing see the notice in "describe other income," below)*				Homeowner Assn. Dues		
				Other:		
Total	$	$	$	Total	$	$

*Self Employed Borrower(s) may be required to provide additional documentation such as tax returns and financial statements.

B/C	Describe Other Income *Notice:* Alimony, child support, or separate maintenance income need not be revealed if the Borrower (B) or Co-Borrower (C) does not choose to have it considered for repaying this loan.	Monthly Amount
		$

VI. ASSETS AND LIABILITIES

This Statement and any applicable supporting schedules may be completed jointly by both married and unmarried Co-Borrowers if their assets and liabilities are sufficiently joined so that the Statement can be meaningfully and fairly presented on a combined basis; otherwise separate Statements and Schedules are required. If the Co-Borrower section was completed about a spouse, this Statement and supporting schedules must be completed about that spouse also.

Completed: ☐ Jointly   ☐ Not Jointly

Assets Description	Cash or Market Value	Liabilities and Pledged Assets. List the creditor's name, address and account number for all outstanding debts, including automobile loans, revolving charge accounts, real estate loans, alimony, child support, stock pledges, etc. Use continuation sheet, if necessary. Indicate by (*) those liabilities which will be satisfied upon sale of real estate owned or upon refinancing of the subject property.		
Cash deposit toward purchase held by:	$	Liabilities	Monthly Pmt. & Mos. Left to Pay	Unpaid Balance
		Name and Address of Company	$ Pmt./Mos.	$
List checking and savings accounts below				
Name and Address of Bank, S&L, or Credit Union				
		Acct. No.		
		Name and Address of Company	$ Pmt./Mos.	$
Acct. No.	$			
Name and Address of Bank, S&L, or Credit Union				
		Acct. No.		
		Name and Address of Company	$ Pmt./Mos.	$
Acct. No.	$			
Name and Address of Bank, S&L, or Credit Union				
		Acct. No.		
		Name and Address of Company	$ Pmt./Mos.	$
Acct. No.	$			
Name and Address of Bank, S&L, or Credit Union				
		Acct. No.		
		Name and Address of Company	$ Pmt./Mos.	$
Acct. No.	$			
Stocks & Bonds *(Company name/number & description)*	$			
		Acct. No.		
		Name and Address of Company	$ Pmt./Mos.	$
Life insurance net cash value	$			
Face amount: $				
Subtotal Liquid Assets	$	Acct. No.		
Real estate owned *(enter market value from schedule of real estate owned)*	$	Name and Address of Company	$ Pmt./Mos.	$
Vested interest in retirement fund	$			
Net worth of business(es) owned	$	Acct. No.		

Exhibit 4.7: *(Continued)*

VI. ASSETS AND LIABILITIES (cont'd)

Schedule of Real Estate Owned *(If additional properties are owned, use continuation sheet.)*

Property Address (enter S if sold, PS if pending sale or R if rental being held for income) --------➤	Type of Property	Present Market Value	Amount of Mortgages & Liens	Gross Rental Income	Mortgage Payments	Insurance, Maintenance, Taxes & Misc.	Net Rental Income
		$	$	$	$	$	$
		$	$	$	$	$	$

List any additional names under which credit has previously been received and indicate appropriate creditor name(s) and account number(s):

Alternate Name	Creditor Name	Account Number

VII. DETAILS OF TRANSACTION

a. Purchase price	$
b. Alterations, improvements, repairs	
c. Land *(if acquired separately)*	
d. Refinance *(incl. debts to be paid off)*	
e. Estimated prepaid items	
f. Estimated closing costs	
g. PMI, MIP, Funding Fee	
h. Discount *(if Borrower will pay)*	
i. Total Costs (add items a through h)	
j. Subordinate financing	
k. Borrower's closing costs paid by Seller	
l. Other Credits *(explain)*	
m. Loan amount *(exclude PMI, MIP, Funding Fee financed)*	
n. PMI, MIP, Funding Fee financed	
o. Loan amount (add m & n)	
p. Cash from/to Borrower *(subtract j, k, l & o from i)*	

VIII. DECLARATIONS

If you answer "Yes" to any questions a through i, please use continuation sheet for explanation.

	Borrower Yes	No	Co-Borrower Yes	No
a. Are there any outstanding judgments against you?	☐	☐	☐	☐
b. Have you been declared bankrupt within the past 7 years?	☐	☐	☐	☐
c. Have you had property foreclosed upon or given title or deed in lieu thereof in the last 7 years?	☐	☐	☐	☐
d. Are you a party to a lawsuit?	☐	☐	☐	☐
e. Have you directly or indirectly been obligated on any loan which resulted in foreclosure, transfer of title in lieu of foreclosure, or judgment? (This would include such loans as home mortgage, loans, SBA loans, home improvement loans, educational loans, manufactured (mobile) home loans, any mortgage, financial obligation, bond, or loan guarantee. If "Yes," provide details, including date, name and address of Lender, FHA or V.A. case number, if any, and reasons for the action.)	☐	☐	☐	☐
f. Are you presently delinquent or in default on any Federal debt or any other loan, mortgage, financial obligation, bond, or loan guarantee? If "Yes," give details as described in the preceding question.	☐	☐	☐	☐
g. Are you obligated to pay alimony, child support, or separate maintenance?	☐	☐	☐	☐
h. Is any part of the down payment borrowed?	☐	☐	☐	☐
i. Are you a co-maker or endorser on a note?	☐	☐	☐	☐
j. Are you a U.S. citizen?	☐	☐	☐	☐
k. Are you a permanent resident alien?	☐	☐	☐	☐
l. Do you intend to occupy the property as your primary residence? If "Yes," complete question m below	☐	☐	☐	☐
m. Have you had an ownership interest in a property in the last three years?	☐	☐	☐	☐
(1) What type of property did you own — principal residence (PR), second home (SH), or investment property (IP)?				
(2) How did you hold title to the home — solely by yourself (S), jointly with your spouse (SP), or jointly with another person (O)?				

IX. ACKNOWLEDGMENT AND AGREEMENT

The undersigned specifically acknowledge(s) and agree(s) that: (1) the loan requested by this application will be secured by a first mortgage or deed of trust on the property described herein; (2) the property will not be used for any illegal or prohibited purpose or use; (3) all statements made in this application are made for the purpose of obtaining the loan indicated herein; (4) occupation of the property will be as indicated above; (5) verification or reverification of any information contained in the application may be made at any time by the Lender, its agents, successors and assigns, either directly or through a credit reporting agency, from any source named in this application, and the original copy of this application will be retained by the Lender, even if the loan is not approved; (6) the Lender, its agents, successors and assigns will rely on the information contained in the application and I/we have a continuing obligation to amend and/or supplement the information provided in this application if any of the material facts which I/we have represented herein should change prior to closing; (7) in the event my/our payments on the loan indicated in this application become delinquent, the Lender, its agents, successors and assigns, may, in addition to all their other rights and remedies, report my/our name(s) and account information to a credit reporting agency; (8) ownership of the loan may be transferred to successor or assign of the Lender without notice to me and/or the administration of the loan account may be transferred to an agent, successor or assign of the Lender with prior notice to me; (9) the Lender, its agents, successors and assigns make no representations or warranties, express or implied, to the Borrower(s) regarding the property, the condition of the property, or the value of the property.

Certification: I/We certify that the information provided in this application is true and correct as of the date set forth opposite my/our signature(s) on this application and acknowledge my/our understanding that any intentional or negligent misrepresentation(s) of the information contained in this application may result in civil liability and/or criminal penalties including, but not limited to, fine or imprisonment or both under the provisions of Title 18, United States Code, Section 1001, et seq. and liability for monetary damages to the Lender, its agents, successors and assigns, insurers and any other person who may suffer any loss due to reliance upon any misrepresentation which I/we have made on this application.

Borrower's Signature	Date	Co-Borrower's Signature	Date
X		X	

X. INFORMATION FOR GOVERNMENT MONITORING PURPOSES

The following information is requested by the Federal Government for certain types of loans related to a dwelling, in order to monitor the Lender's compliance with equal credit opportunity, fair housing and home mortgage disclosure laws. You are not required to furnish this information, but are encouraged to do so. The law provides that a Lender may neither discriminate on the basis of this information, nor on whether you choose to furnish it. However, if you choose not to furnish it, under Federal regulations this Lender is required to note race and sex on the basis of visual observation or surname. If you do not wish to furnish the above information, please check the box below. (Lender must review the above material to assure that the disclosures satisfy all requirements to which the Lender is subject under applicable state law for the particular type of loan applied for.)

Borrower   ☐ I do not wish to furnish this information   **Co-Borrower**

Exhibit 4.7: *(Continued)*

CONTINUATION SHEET/RESIDENTIAL LOAN APPLICATION		
Use this continuation sheet if you need more space to complete the Residential Loan Application. Mark B for Borrower or C for Co-Borrower	Borrower:	Agency Case Number:
	Co-Borrower:	Lender Case Number:

I/We fully understand that it is a Federal crime punishable by fine or imprisonment, or both, to knowingly make any false statements concerning any of the above facts as applicable under the provisions of Title 18, United States Code, Section 1001 et seq.

Borrower's Signature:	Date	Co-Borrower's Signature:	Date
X		X	

Exhibit 4.7: *(Continued)*

INTEREST RATE ELECTION AGREEMENT

☐ NEW LOAN	☐ EXISTING LOAN--->>☐ Lock-In ☐ (Product) Change ☐ Relock/Extension
Rate Sheet # ____	Loan #_____ Rate Sheet # _____

BORROWERS MUST MAKE AN INTEREST RATE ELECTION AT TIME OF APPLICATION.
(TO BE COMPLETED BY MORTGAGE CONSULTANT)

BORROWER NAME: _____   **SUBJECT PROPERTY:**_____

CO-BORROWER NAME:_____   _____

                                                        _____

LOAN INFORMATION:

LOAN AMOUNT: _____

PRODUCT (code_____): ☐ Fixed   Variable: ☐ 1YR   ☐ 3/1   ☐ 5/1   ☐ 7/1   ☐ 10/1

TERM: ☐ 15 YR   ☐ 30 YR   ☐ Other_____

PROGRAM :   ☐ Full Doc+   ☐ Hi Q   ☐ Hi Q+   ☐ Agency   ☐ Investor

INITIAL INTEREST RATE: _____   **POINTS:**_____   **MARGIN:**_____

INITIAL MONTHLY PRINCIPAL & INTEREST PAYMENT:_____

ESCROW WAIVED: Tax , Homeowner's, & Flood (if applicable) Insurance. ☐ NO ☐ YES   T & I__ I ONLY__

FEES: Application: $_____   Credit Report*: $_____   Appraisal*: $_____
                Lock-In (1% of the loan amount): $_____   Other (specify): $_____
                * Good faith estimate

INTEREST RATE ELECTION

I may elect to lock-in an interest rate and points, in which event these terms will be guaranteed, provided the Loan closes on or before the lock expiration date recited herein. Otherwise, I may elect to have the interest rate and points float with the market until a later date, at which time I may then lock-in an interest rate and points. The locked-in interest rate and points are valid only for the loan product for which I have applied.

☐ **I HAVE ELECTED NOT TO LOCK-IN INTEREST RATE AND DISCOUNT POINTS AT TIME OF APPLICATION**

A. I have elected to allow the interest rate and points to float until such time as I contact Emigrant Mortgage Company, Inc. ("Lender") to lock-in the interest rate and points and execute a Revised Interest Rate Election Agreement in connection herewith. By selecting this option, the Lender does not guarantee a specific interest rate, points or the continued availability of the loan program.

B. I may contact the Lender between the hours of 12:00 P.M. and 5:00 P.M. EST on any business day either to obtain current information on the interest rate and points for the Loan or to lock-in such terms. If locking-in, I must execute a Revised Interest Rate Election Agreement which specifies the interest rate and points applicable to the Loan. I UNDERSTAND I MUST LOCK-IN THE INTEREST RATE AND POINTS AT LEAST THREE (3) BUSINESS DAYS PRIOR TO CLOSING. IF I DO NOT LOCK-IN, MY LOAN WILL AUTOMATICALLY BE LOCKED AS OF THE LATER OF THREE (3) BUSINESS DAYS PRIOR TO CLOSING OR THE DATE ON WHICH THE CLOSING DOCUMENTS ARE DRAWN BY EMIGRANT BASED UPON EMIGRANT'S CURRENT INTEREST RATE ON THAT DATE WITH SIMILAR TERMS.

_____   _____   _____   _____
BORROWER   DATE   CO-BORROWER   DATE

☐ **I HAVE ELECTED TO LOCK-IN INTEREST RATE AND DISCOUNT POINTS.**

A. If the Loan does not close on or before the lock Expiration date stated below, the interest rate and points may change. I will be required to execute a Revised Interest Rate Election Agreement and pay the higher of (i) the interest rate and discount points indicated above, or (ii) the interest rate and discount points prevailing at the time I execute the Revised Interest Rate Election Agreement, as determined by Lender. In any event, the Lender reserves the right to re-qualify me at the new interest rate and discount points. I MUST RE-LOCK THE INTEREST RATE AND POINTS AT LEAST THREE (3) BUSINESS DAYS PRIOR TO CLOSING OR MY LOAN WILL AUTOMATICALLY BE LOCKED AS OF THE LATER OF THREE (3) BUSINESS DAYS PRIOR TO CLOSING OR THE DATE ON WHICH THE CLOSING DOCUMENTS ARE DRAWN BY EMIGRANT BASED UPON EMIGRANT'S CURRENT INTEREST RATE ON THAT DATE WITH SIMILAR TERMS. THE LOCK IN FEE IS DUE UPON RETURN OF THIS SIGNED AGREEMENT TO LENDER.

   Lock-in Date: _____   Lock Period: _____   Lock Expiration Date: _____

Exhibit 4.7: *(Continued)*

NEW YORK PROPERTIES:
I must close on this subject property on or before the Lock Expiration Date to be guaranteed the Initial Interest Rate.

A. Monthly escrow payment of 1\12 of the annual real estate taxes and insurance premium may be required.

B. If the Interest Rate is variable, it will be adjusted periodically based on an Index, subject to caps on adjustment. The Index is the weekly average yield on U.S. Treasury Securities adjusted to a constant one year maturity, as published in the Federal Reserve Bulletin by the Federal Reserve Board, and made available each week in Statistical Release 11.15 (519). The new Interest Rate will be calculated by adding _____ Percentage Points to the Index with the result rounded to the nearest one-eighth of a percentage point.

C. The Lock-In Fee, points, deposits or portion thereof paid to the Emigrant Mortgage Company, Inc. ("Lender") upon execution of this Agreement or otherwise prior to issuance of a conditional commitment by the Lender to the Borrower ("Commitment"), shall be refundable only (1) if the Property appraisal report is not favorable for the Loan, (2) if the Borrower has provided complete and correct credit information as required by the Lender's application form for the Loan, and the Lender determines that the Borrower does not qualify as creditworthy for the Loan, or (3) as required by law. If my loan does close, the Lock-In Fee will be applied to any points or closing costs payable at closing.

D. Upon the issuance of the Commitment and my acceptance of such, a Commitment Fee of $ _____ will be required as per the terms of said Commitment. This deposit will be retainable by the Lender, subject to the terms of the Commitment if my loan does not close. If my loan does close, the Commitment Fee plus any Lock-In Fees will be applicable to any closing costs or points payable at closing.

E. This Agreement does not constitute a commitment or agreement by the Lender to make the Loan or any other loan under any terms and conditions to me or to any other person, or an agreement to issue a commitment for the Loan or a commitment for any other loan, or the acceptance of sufficiency or accuracy of any information furnished by me herewith or in or with the Loan application. The Lender expressly reserves the right to decline to issue the Commitment in the event the application form, the Property appraisal, or credit or other information required by the Lender is not furnished to the Lender or is deemed incorrect, incomplete, unverified or otherwise unsatisfactory to the Lender.

F. This Agreement sets forth the terms and conditions for the Lender's agreement to lock in the Initial Interest Rate currently offered by the Lender for the Loan during the Lock-In Term. This Agreement will be otherwise superseded in full by the terms of the Commitment upon issuance of the Commitment. The Commitment will contain additional terms and conditions of the Loan, and requirements for closing of the Loan not set forth in this Agreement. In the event of any discrepancy between the Commitment and this Agreement, the Commitment shall prevail.

G. A loan exceeding 80% loan-to-value (sales price or appraised value, whichever is lower), may require insurance by a private mortgage insurance ("PMI") company of Lender's choice at an additional cost to me. The premium and renewal cost of such insurance is determined by the insurance company. PMI is no longer required when my loan principal balance no longer exceeds 75% of the original appraised value, provided I have not been in default of any payment due on the loan during the preceeding twelve (12) months, or such earlier time as applies under the then current policies and procedures of an investor which has purchased my loan, if applicable.

II. Based on the information I have provided to Lender and should my loan application be accepted, the following property-related documents and conditions are typically required to be satisfied by the borrower in order to close a mortgage loan:

For 1-4 family houses \ condominiums:

(a) title report and insurance;

(b) property survey;

(c) copy of certificate of occupancy for use;

(d) satisfactory final inspection (if new construction);

(e) evidence of appropriate hazard insurance;

(f) evidence of flood insurance as appropriate;

(g) master policy insurance certificate (if applicable in the case of condominiums);

(h) termite inspection report (if required in Commitment);

(i) radon test report;

(j) well water test report;

(k) septic inspection report;

(l) An appraisal of the premises in form and substance satisfactory to Lender. The appraisal must comply in form and substance with Title XI of the Federal Financial Institutions Reform, Recovery, and Enforcement Act of 1989 ("FIRREA") and Part 323 of the Regulations of the Federal Deposit Insurance Corporation. In addition, the Loan is subject to analysis by Lender of the projected future value of the premises as providing adequate security for the loan for the five years following closing. The Loan may be rejected or reduced based upon Lender's review of the appraisal or Lender's analysis of projected future value; and

(m) All prior liens, if any, must be fully satisfied.

For co-operative unit loans:

(a) proprietary lease;

(b) recognition agreement;

(c) pledge of share of stock;

(d) warranty and representation that no outstanding claims against the proprietary lease or stock will exist at closing; and

(e) copy of certificate of occupancy and title policy for the entire building if conversion has occurred within the last six months.

Other conditions which are not foreseeable at this time may be required to be satisfied before the closing of a mortgage loan.

I. In the event the Lock-In Term shall expire prior to the closing of the Loan, the Lender's obligation to lock in the Initial Interest Rate and maintain will expire.

5 Real Estate Closing Procedures

CHAPTER OVERVIEW

Chapter 4, Conveyancing, provided an introduction to the concept of the real estate closing. The purpose of this chapter is to detail the formalities of the closing procedure, including aspects of the pre- and post-closing process. For the legal professional working in a general and real estate practice, the closing is one of the mainstays of the office.

Prior to the actual closing, the day on which the title to the property passes from the seller to the buyer, certain information must be gathered to assure that the parties are appropriately protected. Many of these items have already been addressed in Chapter 4 in the discussion of the real estate sales contract; however, certain other items must be included as well. Before entering into the sales contract, the buyer must be aware of all the costs that will be involved in the sale. These costs include not only the actual purchase price of the property, but also the financing costs and overall fees associated with purchasing the realty. Generally, the following items are included in the final closing costs:

(a) attorneys' fees, which include the preparation of all legal documents involved in the sale as well as out-of-pocket expenses;
(b) the cost of a title search and the premiums on title insurance if such is deemed advisable with respect to the property (also, many financial institutions require a borrower to acquire title insurance as a condition of granting a mortgage);
(c) surveys;
(d) recording costs — the cost of recording the deed in the county recorder's office;

(e) if the sale involves the purchase of a condominium or cooperative, there may be special assessments that are paid to the homeowners' association, but the specifics vary with each such purchase;

(f) inspection fees for examining the property for safety and code
provisions; and

(g) certain costs that are involved in obtaining mortgage loan financing, which may include:
- application fee
- credit check
- financing fee
- loan decision fee
- processing fee
- appraisal fee
- inspection fee
- lender's attorney's fee
- escrow fee
- document preparation fee
- any other fees, including fees for interim loans.

As can be seen, the costs involved in the sale of real estate can far
exceed the base purchase price, and many people discover to their chagrin
that they can afford the purchase price but not the additional costs involved in the closing. Consequently, all of these financial considerations
must be addressed prior to the parties' actually entering into the contract
for sale.

This chapter analyzes the procedures involved in three separate time
frames: the period between the contract and the closing date, the actual
closing, and the period following the closing.

Between the Contract of Sale and the Closing Date

The responsibilities of the parties between the signing of the contract and
the transfer of title at the closing vary depending on whether one is the
purchaser or the seller.

The Purchaser

After the contract has been entered into, it is the responsibility of the
buyer to make sure that any contingencies or conditions in the contract
that are her responsibilities are fulfilled. One of the most common of these
preliminary steps is to contract for the services of various experts who are
responsible for making the many inspection reports that are necessary
prior to consummating the sale. Generally, before a financial institution is

willing to lend money to the purchaser of realty it wants to make sure that there are no internal problems with the property, and the institution uses these experts' reports to make that decision.

The result of these reports may give rise to a claim that the property contains a defect. A **defect** can be any adverse impact of a physical or structural nature that would cause a significant reduction in the value of the property. If such a condition is discovered as a result of the inspection, the purchaser may be able to seek a reduction in the purchase price or to require the seller to remedy the defect prior to the closing.

If the property passes the inspection satisfactorily, or any discovered defect is cured, the buyer typically submits an application to a financial institution to obtain a mortgage loan. As a rule of thumb, if the purchaser is putting down less than 30 percent of the total purchase price, the lender requires the purchaser to obtain mortgage insurance. **Mortgage insurance** operates to discharge the loan obligation if the insured borrower dies or meets any other condition specified in the contract to trigger the obligation of the insurer. This insurance protects both the lender who is guaranteed repayment of the loan and the borrower who is protected from having the property foreclosed on (see Chapter 4).

Once financing has been arranged, the buyer and the seller agree on the date for the closing, which typically occurs between 30 and 90 days after the signing of the contract or the buyer obtains financing, whichever occurs first.

Many sellers of realty who have covenanted for title will acquire **title insurance** to protect them against claims of ownership to the property. To acquire the insurance, a title search must be conducted to determine the current status of the title, and the cost of the insurance may be borne by either party to the sale, depending on the terms of the sales contract. The title search alerts the purchaser to any encumbrances on the property that might render it unmarketable, and if it is unmarketable, the buyer may avoid the contract (see Chapter 4) if the encumbrance is not removed by the seller by the closing date. As discussed in previous chapters, examples of encumbrances would be existing mortgages, judgments on the property, liens for taxes and other government charges, and mechanics' liens.

During the period between the contract and the closing, the purchaser will conduct a survey of the property to make sure that the property being conveyed corresponds to the terms of the contract for sale. Not only could this have an effect on the sales contract, if the realty turns out to be more or less than described in the contract, but the financial institution providing the funds for the purchase may require the survey prior to approving the loan.

Finally, pursuant to the **Real Estate Settlement Procedure Act,** the federal statute governing all federally guaranteed mortgage loans, a **settlement statement** must be prepared. This form is prepared by the United States Department of Housing and Urban Development, and is usually referred to as the **HUD-1 Uniform Settlement Statement.** This is the standard form used in most real estate transactions, even if no federal mortgage loans are involved. The HUD-1 specifies all items of closing costs,

Exhibit 5.1: HUD-1 Settlement Statement

HUD-1 Settlement Statement

A. U. S. DEPARTMENT OF HOUSING AND URBAN DEVELOPMENT	SETTLEMENT STATEMENT

B. TYPE OF LOAN	6. File Number	7. Loan Number
1. ☐ FHA 2. ☐ FmHA		
3. ☐ CONV. UNINS. 4. ☐ VA 5. ☐ CONV. INS.	8. Mortgage Insurance Case Number	

C. Note: This for is furnished to give you a statement of actual settlement costs. Amounts paid to and by the settlement agent are shown. Items marked "(p.o.c.)" were paid outside the closing; they are shown here for informational purposes and are not included in the totals.

D. NAME AND ADDRESS OF BORROWER:	E. NAME AND ADDRESS OF SELLER:	F. NAME AND ADDRESS OF LENDER:

G. PROPERTY LOCATION:	H. SETTLEMENT AGENT: NAME AND ADDRESS	
	PLACE OF SETTLEMENT:	I. SETTLEMENT DATE:

J. SUMMARY OF BORROWER'S TRANSACTION		K. SUMMARY OF SELLER'S TRANSACTION	
100. GROSS AMOUNT DUE FROM BORROWER:		400. GROSS AMOUNT DUE TO SELLER:	
101. Contract sales price		401. Contract sales price	
102. Personal property		402. Personal property	
103. Settlement charges to borrower (line 1400)		403.	
104.		404.	
105.		405.	
Adjustments for items paid by seller in advance		*Adjustments for items paid by seller in advance*	
106. City/town taxes to		406. City/town taxes to	
107. County taxes to		407. County taxes to	
108. Assessments to		408. Assessments to	
109.		409.	
110.		410.	
111.		411.	
112.		412.	
120. GROSS AMOUNT DUE FROM BORROWER		420. GROSS AMOUNT DUE TO SELLER	
200. AMOUNTS PAID BY OR IN BEHALF OF BORROWER		500. REDUCTIONS IN AMOUNT DUE TO SELLER:	
201. Deposit of earnest money		501. Excess deposit (see instructions)	
202. Principal amount of new loan(s)		502. Settlement charges to seller (line 1400)	
203. Existing loan(s) taken subject to		503. Existing loan(s) taken subject to	
204.		504. Payoff of first mortgage loan	
205.		505. Payoff of second mortgage loan	
206.		506.	
207.		507.	
208.		508.	
209.		509.	
Adjustments for items unpaid by seller		*Adjustments for items unpaid by seller*	
210. City/town taxes to		510. City/town taxes to	
211. County taxes to		511. County taxes to	
212. Assessments to		512. Assessments to	
213.		513.	
214.		514.	
215.		515.	
216.		516.	
217.		517.	
218.		518.	
219.		519.	
220. TOTAL PAID BY/FOR BORROWER		520. TOTAL REDUCTION AMOUNT DUE SELLER	
300. CASH AT SETTLEMENT FROM/TO BORROWER		600. CASH AT SETTLEMENT TO/FROM SELLER	
301. Gross amount due from borrower (line 120)		601. Gross amount due to seller (line 420)	
302. Less amounts paid by/for borrower (line 220)		602. Less reductions in amount due seller (line 520)	
303. CASH (☒ FROM) (☐ TO) BORROWER			

and serves two specific purposes: to reflect the amount to be paid by the seller and to specify the amount to be paid by the purchaser to close the sale. (See Exhibit 5.1. This form can also be accessed online at www.hud.gov.)

The Seller

Between the contract and the closing, the seller has fewer obligations to perform than the purchaser. Generally, the responsibilities of the seller

Exhibit 5.1: *(Continued)*

L. SETTLEMENT CHARGES			PAID FROM BORROWER'S FUNDS AT SETTLEMENT	PAID FROM SELLER'S FUNDS AT SETTLEMENT
700. TOTAL SALES/BROKER'S COMMISSION based on price $ @ % =				
Division of Commission (line 700) as follows:				
701. $	to			
702. $	to			
703. Commission paid at Settlement				
704.				
800. ITEMS PAYABLE IN CONNECTION WITH LOAN				
801. Loan Origination Fee	%			
802. Loan Discount	%			
803. Appraisal Fee	to			
804. Credit Report	to			
805. Lender's Inspection Fee				
806. Mortgage Insurance Application Fee	to			
807. Assumption Fee				
808.				
809.				
810.				
811.				
900. ITEMS REQUIRED BY LENDER TO BE PAID IN ADVANCE				
901. Interest from to @ $	/day			
902. Mortgage Insurance Premium for	months to			
903. Hazard Insurance Premium for	years to			
904.	years to			
905.				
1000. RESERVES DEPOSITED WITH LENDER				
1001. Hazard Insurance	months @ $	per month		
1002. Mortgage Insurance	months @ $	per month		
1003. City property taxes	months @ $	per month		
1004. County property taxes	months @ $	per month		
1005. Annual assessments	months @ $	per month		
1006.	months @ $	per month		
1007.	months @ $	per month		
1008. Aggregate Adjustment	months @ $	per month		
1100. TITLE CHARGES				
1101. Settlement or closing fee	to			
1102. Abstract or title search	to			
1103. Title examination	to			
1104. Title insurance binder	to			
1105. Document preparation	to			
1106. Notary fees	to			
1107. Attorney's fees	to			
(includes above items numbers:)				
1108. Title insurance	to			
(includes above items numbers:)				
1109. Lender's coverage	$			
1110. Owner's coverage	$			
1111.				
1112.				
1113.				
1200. GOVERNMENT RECORDING AND TRANSFER CHARGES				
1201. Recording fees: Deed $; Mortgage $; Releases $				
1202. City/county tax/stamps: Deed $; Mortgage $				
1203. State tax/stamps: Deed $; Mortgage $				
1204.				
1205.				
1300. ADDITIONAL SETTLEMENT CHARGES				
1301. Survey	to			
1302. Pest inspection	to			
1303.				
1304.				
1305.				
1400. TOTAL SETTLEMENT CHARGES (enter on lines 103, Section J and 502, section K)				

during this period can be summed up as making sure that he or she can transfer a marketable title on the closing date.

Certain local governments require that a seller produce a **certificate of occupancy** if the property has buildings on it. This certificate is the result of a general inspection of the premises to ascertain that the building is fit to be occupied. If such certificate is required and not provided, the purchaser may avoid the sale.

If the seller utilized the services of a real estate broker to make the sale, the seller must make sure that all commissions owed to the broker are paid prior to the closing, and the seller should obtain a receipt to document the payment. As a general rule, the seller's commission for the seller's broker is simply deducted from the purchase price that is received at the closing.

If any cloud appears on the title to the property, it is the seller's responsibility to see that such cloud is removed pursuant to the provisions of the deed that has been contracted to be conveyed (see Chapter 4).

Finally, during this period the seller must prepare all the documents that he is required to present at the closing. These documents include the following:

- The deed: The deed must conform to the nature of the title that has been agreed to in the sales contract (see Chapter 4).
- Affidavit of title: This is a separate document made by the seller that specifies his title to the property and indicates all improvements made on the property since the seller first acquired the title.
- **Form 1099-S:** This is an IRS form that must be filed for real estate transactions, except for the following:

  Gifts
  Refinancings
  Commercial property

  (See Exhibit 5.2.)
- **Certificate of non-foreign status:** The IRS also requires this form if the parties are U.S. citizens; foreign nationals are required to make certain payments pursuant to section 1445 of the Internal Revenue Code. (See Exhibit 5.3.)
- Survey affidavit, if the seller agrees to provide one to the buyer.
- Settlement statement (discussed above).
- All documents relating to the seller's mortgage.
- **Notice to attorn:** This document applies to property that has been leased to a tenant not a party to the sale. This notice alerts the tenant of the transfer of ownership of the property.
- The seller is usually required to pay a **realty transfer fee** mandated by the government.
- **Payoff amount:** this reflects the amount that is still outstanding on the seller's mortgage and is used by the purchaser to make sure that this encumbrance is discharged by the date of the closing (typically, a portion of the buyer's loan is used to discharge this obligation).
- The seller should have all utility companies provide a final reading of all charges due by the date of the closing so that such charges are allocated between the parties.
- Any other document affecting the right to the property, such as foreclosure papers if the property was acquired by means of a foreclose sale, or estate papers if the property was inherited.

Exhibit 5.2: Form 1099-S

7575 ☐ VOID ☐ CORRECTED

FILER'S name, street address, city, state, ZIP code, and telephone no.		**1** Date of closing	OMB No. 1545-0997	
		2 Gross proceeds	**2001**	**Proceeds From Real Estate Transactions**
		$	Form **1099-S**	
FILER'S Federal identification number	TRANSFEROR'S identification number	**3** Address or legal description (including city, state, and ZIP code)		**Copy A**
TRANSFEROR'S name				**For Internal Revenue Service Center** File with Form 1096.
Street address (including apt. no.)				For Privacy Act and Paperwork Reduction Act Notice, see the **2001 General Instructions for Forms 1099, 1098, 5498, and W-2G.**
City, state, and ZIP code		**4** Check here if the transferor received or will receive property or services as part of the consideration. ▶ ☐		
Account number (optional)		**5** Buyer's part of real estate tax $		

Form **1099-S** Cat. No. 64292E Department of the Treasury - Internal Revenue Service

☐ CORRECTED (if checked)

FILER'S name, street address, city, state, ZIP code, and telephone no.		**1** Date of closing	OMB No. 1545-0997	
		2 Gross proceeds	**2001**	**Proceeds From Real Estate Transactions**
		$	Form **1099-S**	
FILER'S Federal identification number	TRANSFEROR'S identification number	**3** Address or legal description		**Copy B**
TRANSFEROR'S name				**For Transferor** This is important tax information and is being furnished to the Internal Revenue Service. If you
Street address (including apt. no.)				are required to file a return, a negligence penalty or other sanction may be
City, state, and ZIP code		**4** Transferor received or will receive property or services as part of the consideration (if checked). ▶ ☐		imposed on you if this item is required to be
Account number (optional)		**5** Buyer's part of real estate tax $		reported and the IRS determines that it has not been reported.

Form **1099-S** (Keep for your records.) Department of the Treasury - Internal Revenue Service

☐ VOID ☐ CORRECTED

FILER'S name, street address, city, state, ZIP code, and telephone no.		**1** Date of closing	OMB No. 1545-0997	
		2 Gross proceeds	**2001**	**Proceeds From Real Estate Transactions**
		$	Form **1099-S**	
FILER'S Federal identification number	TRANSFEROR'S identification number	**3** Address or legal description (including city, state, and ZIP code)		**Copy C**
TRANSFEROR'S name				**For Filer**
Street address (including apt. no.)				For Privacy Act and Paperwork Reduction Act Notice, see the **2001 General Instructions for Forms 1099, 1098, 5498, and W-2G.**
City, state, and ZIP code		**4** Check here if the transferor received or will receive property or services as part of the consideration. ▶ ☐		
Account number (optional)		**5** Buyer's part of real estate tax $		

Form **1099-S** Department of the Treasury - Internal Revenue Service

Exhibit 5.3: F.I.R.P.T.A. Non-Foreign Certification by Individual Transferor

1. Section 1445 of the Internal Revenue Code provides that a transferee of a United States real property interest must withhold tax if the transferor is a foreign person.

2. In order to inform the transferee that witholding of tax is not required upon the disposition by [name of transferor(s)] of the United States real property described as follows:

   the undersigned transferor certifies and declares by means of this certification, the following

   a. I (we) am (are) not non-resident alien(s) for purposes of United States income taxation and,

   b. My United States taxpayer identifying number (Social Security number) is

NAME   SOCIAL SECURITY NUMBER

_____   _____

_____   _____

   c. My home address is _____

                          _____

   d. There are not other persons who have an ownership interest in the above described property other than those persons set forth above in subparagraph b.

3. The undersigned hereby further certified and declares

   a. I (we) understand that the purchaser of the above described property intends to rely on the foregoing representations in connection with the United States Foreign Investment in Real Property Tax Act. (94 Stat 2682 as amended)

   b. I (we) understand this certification may be disclosed to the Internal Revenue Service by transferee and that any false statement contained in this certification may be punished by fine, imprisonment or both.

   Under penalties of perjury I (we) declare I (we) have examined carefully this certification and it is true, correct and complete.

Date: _____

                             _____

_____

Exhibit 5.3: F.I.R.P.T.A. (Foreign Investment in Real Property Tax) Affidavit of Facts Relating to the Withholding of Tax Upon the Disposition of United States Real Property Interests Pursuant to 26 U.S.C. 1445(B)(2)

STATE OF NEW YORK)

)   SS.:

COUNTY OF)

The Undersigned, being duly sworn, deposes and says:

1. that the Undersigned are/is the owner(s) of the premises known as _____

being conveyed this date to _____

2. That the Undersigned are/is not a foreign person(s) as defined at 26 U.S.C. 1445 (f)(3).

3. That the Undersigned's United States Taxpayer Identification Number appears following his/her signature below.

Sworn to before me this _____
day of _____ 199_

_____
Notary Public

The Closing

The actual closing usually occurs at the office of the buyer's attorney, but may occur at any mutually agreed-upon location. Generally, the attorneys for the buyer and the seller attend, along with the parties and a representative of the financial institution providing the mortgage loan.

    The purchaser usually contacts the title company 24 to 48 hours before the day of the closing to make sure that the title is still free of all clouds and encumbrances. At this point the purchaser will **mark up** the title instrument, meaning that he or she will tick off any item specified in the contract — grantor, grantee, liens, mortgages, judgments, etc. — to indicate that the title is marketable.

When all of the foregoing has taken place, the buyer and the seller transfer all documents and the deed is given to the buyer. In many instances the seller does not appear in person but is represented by an attorney.

The typical closing can be completed in less than two hours.

Post-Closing Procedures

Once the actual closing has taken place, there still remain many items to complete to protect the transferee. The most important of these is to record all the documents necessary to provide a clear chain of title. This includes recording the deed and any mortgage with the county recorder's office.

The financial institution that provides the funds for the purchase will usually create a packet of closing instruments for the borrower, and all the requirements specified in this packet must be completed by the mortgagor. If the purchase includes paying off an existing mortgage, the purchaser must make sure that this encumbrance is discharged and must receive a release from the mortgagee to clear any potential problem with respect to any encumbrance on the property.

Following the purchase of a newly constructed cooperative or condominium, the purchaser can create a **punch list** of items that still require attention, for example, a problem with the flooring. The developer has a specified period of time in which to correct these problems.

Finally, all professionals involved in the transaction must be paid.

Practical Tips

- Be sure to make a complete file of all necessary documents, such as title searches, financing papers, and the parties' information sheets.
- Make a summary of all of the contract information.
- Make sure all contract contingencies have been met.
- Check local rules to determine what searches may be required.
- It is safer to deliver all title documents by hand to minimize the risk of loss or delay.
- Check local statutes to determine what affidavits may be required.
- Check with the local court to determine if there are any special requirements for completing the closing.
- Prepare a log of all important dates and information.
- Prepare the IRS Form 1099-S.

Chapter Review

The process of closing a real estate transaction is a fairly formalized affair that follows set procedures and formats. During the period between the contract and the closing date, most of the burden is on the purchaser to make sure that no problem exists with regard to the property being purchased. No one wants to buy a potential lawsuit.

For the most part, during the pre-closing period the seller is merely required to see that he or she is in a position to provide a marketable title at the closing date.

The closing itself is generally a simple, straightforward, and quick affair in which all documents are signed and transferred, the purchase price is paid, and any existing encumbrances on the property are discharged. After the closing, the purchaser must see that all documents are properly recorded to protect his or her title, and must complete any other documents required by the institution financing the purchase.

Ethical Concern

Once a person is represented by counsel it is unethical for the opposing side to have direct contact with that party. All communication must be made through the attorney. In a real estate closing, because so much information and documents must be gathered, it is tempting to contact the parties directly. Do not do so when the party is represented by counsel.

Key Terms

Certificate of non-foreign status
Certificate of occupancy
Defect
Form 1099-S
HUD-1 Uniform Settlement
  Statement
Mark up
Mortgage insurance

Notice to attorn
Payoff amount
Punch list
Real Estate Settlement Procedure
  Act
Realty transfer fee
Settlement statement
Title insurance

Exercises

1. What are some of the reasons a person would acquire mortgage insurance?
2. What is the benefit of title insurance?

3. Prepare a closing packet based on the documents discussed in this chapter.
4. Indicate the problems that would permit a purchaser to avoid a real estate contract.
5. Analyze the provisions of the HUD-1 statement included in this chapter.

Situational Analysis

Your office represents the buyer of a residential house. The day before the closing you discover that the seller still has not fulfilled all the contract obligations. What are the steps you would take to protect your client's interests?

Edited Cases

The following two cases discuss various problems associated with real estate closings. The first decision, *Windell v. Miller,* concerns the breach of a warranty deed, and the second opinion, although fairly lengthy, provides an important discussion of the unauthorized practice of law as it relates to real estate settlements and the details of closing procedures.

Windell v. Miller
687 N.E.2d 585 (Ind. App. 1997)

Statement of the Case

Jerry B. Windell ("Jerry") appeals from the trial court's judgment that found him liable for breach of a Warranty Deed. Jerry and his former wife, Debra L. Windell ("Debra"), owned real estate as tenants in common which they conveyed to Tommye Opal (England) Daniel ("Daniel"), now deceased. Robert C. Miller, Jr. ("Miller"), the Executor of Daniel's estate, discovered that three judgment liens against Debra's undivided one-half interest in the real estate had been recorded prior to the sale. Miller paid $11,500 for release of the liens and then filed a complaint against both Jerry and Debra. After a bench trial, the trial court found Jerry and Debra jointly and severally liable. The sole issue presented for our review is whether Jerry is liable as a tenant in common for breach of the covenant that the real estate was free from all encumbrances.

We reverse.

Facts

Jerry and Debra purchased a marital residence in 1976. During the marriage, Jerry and Debra owned the real estate as tenants by the entirety.

The couple divorced in 1991, and they then owned the real estate as tenants in common. Debra continued to occupy the residence after the divorce and remained responsible for the mortgage. When Debra experienced financial difficulties, Jerry's mother, Betty, paid the $6,957.48 balance owed on the mortgage in order to prevent a foreclosure.

In August of 1993, Jerry and Debra sold the real estate to Daniel for $30,000 in cash. At the closing attorney Samuel Vogt ("Vogt") represented Jerry and Debra. Daniel was not represented by counsel. Vogt prepared a closing statement which distributed the proceeds from the sale among Jerry, Debra and Betty. At the time of the sale, Jerry and Debra also executed a warranty deed which included a provision that each was conveying and warranting his respective undivided one-half interest in the real estate. Daniel signed a statement prepared by Vogt which acknowledged that Vogt had not examined the title to the real estate and that he had not made any representations to her about the title.

After Daniel's death in 1994, Miller discovered that three judgment liens had attached to the real estate prior to the sale. The judgments had been entered and the liens had been recorded against Debra individually and not against Jerry. After paying a total of $11,500 for release of the liens, Miller filed a complaint against Jerry and Debra in June of 1995 for breach of the warranty deed alleging that when they sold the property to Daniel the title was not free and clear but was encumbered by the judgment liens. After a bench trial, the trial court entered judgment against Jerry and Debra jointly and severally. Debra's obligation was discharged in bankruptcy. Jerry now appeals.

Discussion and Decision

Jerry argues that the provision in the deed limited his warranty to his undivided one-half interest in the property and, therefore, that he cannot be liable for the breach which resulted from judgment liens recorded against Debra. Miller counters that Jerry and Debra held an undivided interest in the whole property and, therefore, that the liens against Debra encumbered the entire title. Thus, Miller contends that Jerry and Debra are jointly liable on the warranty deed.

Standard of Review [omitted]

Tenancy in Common

We begin our review by considering the nature of a tenancy in common. A tenancy in common is property held by two or more persons by several and distinct titles. 27 I.L.E. Tenancy in Common Sec. 1 (1960). Tenants in common are united only by their right to possession of the property. 86 C.J.S. Tenancy in Common Sec. 3 (1997). The rights and interests of tenants in common are several, and there is no unity of title between them. Id. Sec. 40. There is no implied agency on the part of one cotenant in common to bind the interest of another cotenant. *Mann v. Schnarr*, 228 Ind. 654, 668-69, 95 N.E.2d 138, 144 (1950).

Judgment Lien

We next consider the operation of a judgment lien and how a lien against one cotenant affects the interest of another cotenant. A judgment is a lien only on the debtor's interest in the land. See *Wright v. Jones*, 105 Ind. 17, 28, 4 N.E. 281, 287 (1886) ("the interest which the lien of a judgment affects is the actual interest which the debtor has in [the] property."). Since cotenants do not act as agents, the rights of one cotenant in the common estate cannot be impaired by liens against the other without his consent. *Foltz v. Wert*, 103 Ind. 404, 409, 2 N.E. 950, 954 (1885). It follows that creditors of one tenant in common can only enforce their claims against their debtor's interest in the common estate subject to all the equitable interests of the other tenants therein. *Peck v. Williams*, 113 Ind. 256, 258, 15 N.E. 270, 272 (1888). Here, the three judgment liens were only against Debra and were not against Jerry. Because Jerry's undivided interest could not be encumbered by the liens against Debra, and Debra's creditors could not have enforced their claims against Jerry, his interest in the property was not liable to execution to satisfy Debra's liens.

Covenants of Title

We must also consider whether Jerry, whose interest in the property was unencumbered, could limit his warranty to his undivided one-half interest. There are various methods by which a grantor can modify the covenants of title in a general warranty deed. A warranty deed is a deed in which the grantor warrants good clear title. 10 I.L.E. Deeds Sec. 2 (1983). The usual covenants of title are warranties of seisen, quiet enjoyment, right to convey, freedom from encumbrances, and defense of title as to all claims. Id. If the extent of the warranty is limited, it is known as a "special warranty deed" or a "limited warranty deed." 2 Rufford G. Patton, L.L.B. & Carroll G. Patton, L.L.B., Patton on Land Titles, Sec. 331 (2d ed. 1957).

Under Indiana Code Sec. 32-1-2-12, the words "convey and warrant" comprehend and express all the covenants of title as fully as if they were written out at length in the deed. *Jackson v. Green*, 112 Ind. 341, 342, 14 N.E. 89, 90 (1887). As previously stated, one of these covenants is the grantor's guarantee that the real estate is "free from all encumbrances." *McClaskey v. Bumb & Mueller Farms Inc.*, 547 N.E.2d 302, 304 (1989), *trans. denied*. However, the covenants of title may be modified by additional terms contained within the text of the deed providing for exceptions, reservations, conditions or other covenants.

In the present case, the warranty deed states, in relevant part: The grantors Jerry B. Windell and Debra L. Windell, by their execution of this Deed, are each conveying and warranting their [sic] respective undivided one-half interests in and to the above-described real estate. Record at 168. Jerry argues that this provision effectively limits his warranty to his undivided one-half interest, thereby creating several liability. Miller counters that the provision merely advises the grantee that Jerry and Debra are conveying the property as tenants in common.

In *Ragle v. Dedman*, 50 Ind. App. 359, 98 N.E. 367 (1912), we considered whether the covenants of title in a warranty deed from tenants in common were joint or several. In that case, although only one of the tenants in common had a valid judgment lien against him prior to the conveyance, the grantees brought suit against all of the cotenants for breach of the covenant against encumbrances. Id. The trial court found that the tenant with the encumbered interest was solely liable for the breach, and the issue on appeal was whether the covenant in the deed was to be construed as joint or several. Id.

The *Ragle* court reasoned that "the rights of the parties must be measured by their agreement as expressed in the deed." Id. at 362, 98 N.E. 368. This court then recognized the principle that "in the case of parties demising or granting the separate interest of each in an estate, the covenant shall be considered co-extensive with the interest granted; and, therefore, these shall be several, where a several interest is granted; and joint, if a joint interest is granted." Id. (citing *Evans v. Sanders*, 49 Ky. 291, 292 (1850)). We concluded that "where an obligation is created by two or more, the general presumption is that it is joint, and words of severance are required in order to confine the liability of the covenantor to his own acts." Id. at 363, 98 N.E. 368 (citations omitted). This comports with the general rule that with respect to third persons, the entire tenancy constitutes a joint estate and a single entity in all dealings affecting it as a whole. See 86 C.J.S. Tenancy in Common Sec. 3 (1997).

"Words of Severance"

The deed in *Ragle* contained no provision limiting the broad scope of the covenant against all encumbrances. Id. at 361, 98 N.E. 368. We found no indication that the covenant was intended to be limited to the separate interests but that the wording of the deed imported a joint obligation. Id. at 363, 98 N.E. 368. Thus, we held that absent "words of severance," a warranty deed executed by tenants in common will bind the cotenants jointly in the event a breach occurs.

Here, we must determine whether the warranty deed contains "words of severance" that limit Jerry's covenants of title to his undivided one-half interest. Id. There are several rules of construction to be used when construing the meaning of a particular deed. The object of deed construction is to ascertain the intent of the parties. *Brown v. Penn. Cent. Corp.*, 510 N.E.2d 641, 643 (Ind. 1987). Where there is no ambiguity in the deed, the intention of the parties must be determined from the language of the deed alone. Id. Where ambiguous language exists in a deed that was prepared by the grantor, that language should be construed against the grantor and in favor of the grantee. 10 I.L.E. Deeds Sec. 99.

The warranty deed states that "[t]he grantors Jerry B. Windell and Debra L. Windell . . . are each conveying and warranting their [sic] respec-

tive undivided one-half interest in and to the above-described real estate."
Record at 168. The significant term within this provision is "respective."
The plain meaning of the word respective is "relating to particular persons
or things; particular; several; as, their respective homes." Black's Law Dic-
tionary 1311 (6th ed. 1990). The provision in the deed not only notifies
Daniel that Jerry and Debra were tenants in common but also clearly states
their intent to convey and warrant their own particular or several interests.
As we stated in *Ragle*, "The contract, as expressed in the deed, must be
enforced as made. . . ." *Ragle*, 50 Ind. App. at 363, 98 N.E. 368 (citations
omitted). Unlike the parties in *Ragle*, the deed executed by Jerry and Debra
includes "words of severance" that confine the liability of each to his own
particular acts and, thus, limit Jerry's warranty to his undivided one-half
interest.

Conclusion

As tenants in common, Jerry and Debra conveyed the property as a
common estate to Daniel. The three judgment liens against Debra that had
been recorded prior to the sale encumbered only Debra's interest in the
property and did not affect Jerry's interest. The provision inserted in the
warranty deed contains "words of severance" that limit Jerry's warranty
to his undivided one-half interest in the common estate. Accordingly, the
judgment that Jerry and Debra were jointly liable for breach of the warranty deed was clearly erroneous. We hold that because only Debra's interest in the common property was encumbered and liable to execution, and
Jerry limited his warranty to his own interest, Jerry cannot be held responsible for breach of the covenant that the real estate was free from all encumbrances. We reverse the trial court's judgment that Jerry was liable for
Miller's damages.

Reversed.

Case Questions

1. What covenants were included in this warranty deed?
2. What did the court decide about the impact of a judgment lien
against one cotenant on the other cotenant? Why?

In Re Opinion No. 26 of the Committee on the Unauthorized
Practice of Law
139 N.J. 323, 654 A.2d 1344 (1995)

We again confront another long-simmering dispute between realtors
and attorneys concerning the unauthorized practice of law. See *New Jersey
State Bar Ass'n v. New Jersey Ass'n of Realtor Bds.*, 93 N.J. 470, 461 A.2d 1112
(1983). Title companies are also involved. Our resolution of the dispute
turns on the identification of the public interest. Since our decision today
permits sellers and buyers in real estate transactions involving the sale of

a home to proceed without counsel, we find it necessary to state the Court's view of the matter at the outset. The Court strongly believes that both parties should retain counsel for their own protection and that the savings in lawyers fees are not worth the risks involved in proceeding without counsel. All that we decide is that the public interest does not require that the parties be deprived of the right to choose to proceed without a lawyer.

The question before us is whether brokers and title company officers, who guide, control and handle all aspects of residential real estate transactions where neither seller nor buyer is represented by counsel, are engaged in the unauthorized practice of law. That many aspects of such transactions constitute the practice of law we have no doubt, including some of the activities of these brokers and title officers. Our power to prohibit those activities is clear. We have concluded, however, that the public interest does not require such a prohibition. Sellers and buyers, to the extent they are informed of the true interests of the broker and title officer, sometimes in conflict with their own interests, and of the risks of not having their own attorney, should be allowed to proceed without counsel. The South Jersey practice, for it is in that part of the state where sellers and buyers are most often unrepresented by counsel in residential real estate transactions, may continue subject to the conditions set forth in this opinion. By virtue of this decision, those participating in such transactions shall not be deemed guilty of the unauthorized practice of law so long as those conditions are met. Our decision in all respects applies not only to South Jersey, but to the entire state.

Under our Constitution, this Court's power over the practice of law is complete. N.J. Const. art. 6, Sec. 2, P 3. We are given the power to permit the practice of law and to prohibit its unauthorized practice. We have exercised that latter power in numerous cases. *In re Application of N.J. Soc'y of Certified Public Accountants,* 102 N.J. 231, 507 A.2d 711 (1986); *New Jersey State Bar Ass'n v. New Jersey Ass'n of Realtor Bds.,* 93 N.J. 470, 461 A.2d 1112 (1983); *Cape May County Bar Ass'n v. Ludlam,* 45 N.J. 121, 211 A.2d 780 (1965); *New Jersey State Bar Ass'n v. Northern N.J. Mortgage Assocs.,* 22 N.J. 184 (1956); *In re Baker,* 8 N.J. 321, 85 A.2d 505 (1951); *Stack v. P.G. Garage,* 7 N.J. 118, 80 A.2d 545 (1951).

The question of what constitutes the unauthorized practice of law involves more than an academic analysis of the function of lawyers, more than a determination of what they are uniquely qualified to do. It also involves a determination of whether non-lawyers should be allowed, in the public interest, to engage in activities that may constitute the practice of law. As noted later, the conclusion in these cases that parties need not retain counsel to perform limited activities that constitute the practice of law and that others may perform them does not imply that the public interest is thereby advanced, but rather that the public interest does not require that those parties be deprived of their right to proceed without counsel. We reach that conclusion today given the unusual history and experience of the South Jersey practice as developed in the record before us.

We determine the ultimate touchstone — the public interest — through the balancing of the factors involved in the case, namely, the risks and benefits to the public of allowing or disallowing such activities. In other words, like all of our powers, this power over the practice of law must be exercised in the public interest; more specifically, it is not a power given to us in order to protect lawyers, but in order to protect the public, in this instance by preserving its right to proceed without counsel. We believe that parties to the sale of a family home, both seller and buyer, would be better served if each were represented by counsel from the beginning to the end of the transaction, from contract signing through closing. We are persuaded, however, that they should continue to have the right to choose not to be represented. They should, of course, be informed of the risks. The record fails to demonstrate that the public interest has been disserved by the South Jersey practice over the many years it has been in existence. While the risks of non-representation are many and serious, the record contains little proof of actual damage to either buyer or seller. Moreover, the record does not contain proof that, in the aggregate, the damage that has occurred in South Jersey exceeds that experienced elsewhere. In this case, the absence of proof is particularly impressive, for the dispute between the realtors and the bar is of long duration, with the parties and their counsel singularly able and highly motivated to supply such proof as may exist. The South Jersey practice also appears to save money. For the record demonstrates what is obvious, that sellers and buyers without counsel save counsel fees. We believe, given this record, that the parties must continue to have the right to decide whether those savings are worth the risks of not having lawyers to advise them in what is almost always the most important transaction they will ever undertake. We realize this conclusion means that throughout the transaction, sellers and buyers may not have the benefit of their own counsel but will look to brokers and title officers, often with conflicting interests, for practical guidance and advice.

I

Proceedings Below

Opinion No. 26 of the Committee on the Unauthorized Practice of Law, 130 N.J.L.J. 882 (March 16, 1992), was issued in response to an inquiry, one of many, from the New Jersey State Bar Association. The inquiry sought a determination of whether the South Jersey practice constituted the unauthorized practice of law. That practice, described in detail later, concerns the sale of a home generally financed by a purchase money mortgage. The essence of the South Jersey practice is that from the beginning of the transaction to the end, neither seller nor buyer is represented by counsel. Every aspect of the transaction is handled by others, every document drafted by others, including the contract of sale, affidavit of title, bond and mortgage. The Committee on the Unauthorized Practice of Law (the Committee), relying largely on our decisions in *New Jersey State Bar Association v. New Jersey Association of Realtor Boards*, 93 N.J. 470, 461 A.2d 1112

(1983); *Cape May County Bar Association v. Ludlam,* 45 N.J. 121, 211 A.2d 780 (1965); *New Jersey State Bar Association v. Northern New Jersey Mortgage Associates,* 32 N.J. 430, 161 A.2d 257 (1960), and its own prior determination in Opinion No. 11 of the Committee on the Unauthorized Practice of Law, 95 N.J.L.J. 1345 (December 28, 1972), ruled that the ordering of a title search by the broker, the preparation of conveyancing and other documents by title officers, their clearing of title questions, and indeed the activities of both broker and title officers at the closing itself, where neither buyer nor seller was represented by counsel, that all of these activities constituted the unauthorized practice of law. The decision was interpreted widely as prohibiting the South Jersey practice, in effect prohibiting a seller and buyer from proceeding with the sale of a home without counsel.

On July 20, 1992, the Committee issued a notice to the bar and the public, clarifying its opinion. 131 N.J.L.J. 910 (July 20, 1992). The Committee explained that it did not intend to prohibit a seller or a buyer from proceeding in these matters without counsel. But at the same time the Committee adhered to its determination concerning what constituted the unauthorized practice of law in these matters, without in any way changing that determination. The result, it appeared to many, was that the right of seller and buyer to proceed without counsel was theoretical, for those whose help they would inevitably require to go through with the transaction seemed, by virtue of the Committee's opinion, to be able to give such help only by engaging in the unauthorized practice of law. Given the concerns of both potential sellers and buyers, as well as those of brokers and title officers, and given the fact that the South Jersey practice had continued for so long, we stayed the effect of Opinion No. 26 pending review by this Court.

Following briefing and oral argument by those interested in the matter — the organized bar, brokers, title officers — we remanded the matter to develop a fuller record, referring it to Judge Edward S. Miller, as Special Master, for that purpose. After sixteen days of hearing, Judge Miller rendered his report to us. While personally strongly favoring a requirement that sellers and buyers be represented by counsel, Judge Miller recommended essentially that we allow the South Jersey practice to continue subject to certain conditions.

The hearing conducted by Judge Miller, leading to his findings and recommendations, is critical to our decision. It was directed not only at determining the extent of the practice of law engaged in by non-lawyers, a circumstance generally known and relatively uncomplicated, but more so at the consequences and implications of the practice. The purpose of the remand was to examine in depth the many factors that would enable this Court to determine whether and to what extent allowing parties to proceed without counsel in such transactions disserved the public interest. That remand was similar to the action taken by this Court in other unauthorized practice of law cases described later, although the depth and detail of both our inquiry and Judge Miller's hearing and report went beyond most such remands. We asked that the scope of the remand include not only all of the factual aspects of the South Jersey practice, but also its impact on buyers and sellers including both costs and risks; the knowledge of the parties of those risks, and of the conflicting interests of brokers and title officers; the frequency of transactions in which neither party is represented by counsel; comparable advantages and disadvantages to consumers in South Jersey transactions as compared to transactions where both are represented by counsel; the actual incidence of problems in both cases; remedies available to both buyers and sellers for damage caused by brokers or title officers; consumer satisfaction; and other matters. Judge Miller responded to all of our inquiries, and his recommendations covered the issues posed as well as some that arose during the hearings.

Judge Miller found that there had been no proof of actual damage resulting from the South Jersey practice, or more accurately that whatever problems existed did not in the aggregate exceed those in matters where the parties were represented by counsel, that many of the activities undertaken by brokers and title officers, taken in isolation, did not involve the practice of law in any sense, and that, if informed of the risks, and of the interests of those who might otherwise be thought to represent them — including the conflicting interests of the brokers and title officers — sellers and buyers should have the right to decide whether or not to have counsel.

Judge Miller found that when both buyer and seller are represented by counsel, the fees in South Jersey are lower than those in North Jersey. Although he made no explicit finding on the point, implicit in all of his findings is the obvious fact that the unrepresented buyers and sellers in the South Jersey practice save the entire counsel fee they would otherwise have to pay, a fairly substantial sum. He was strongly of the opinion that those savings were not worth the risk that inevitably existed where either seller or buyer went unrepresented. Given this Court's prior decisions on related matters, however, he concluded that the judiciary could not, or would not, mandate representation, but rather that all of the foregoing circumstances called for a determination allowing the continuation of the South Jersey practice subject to various conditions. He recommended that the Court allow brokers to order title reports, contrary to the opinion of the Committee; that only attorneys be allowed to draft the bargain and sale deed, but where that drafting was not accompanied by true representation and advice of counsel, it could be done by others only through the explicit request in writing of the seller; that any other similar conveyancing documents, presumably the bond and mortgage, could be drafted by lawyers representing the title company, again only at the specific written request of either the buyer or mortgagee; that neither the broker nor the title officers present at the closing, or at any other time, could render legal advice; that while the title company could attempt to resolve certain kinds of problems affecting the title, such as arranging to pay off prior mortgages and judgment liens, it could not attempt to resolve others, or presumably give any advice concerning others, such as restrictions on use, easements, and rights of way. Finally, he recommended that the practice, especially the South Jersey practice, of title companies conducting settlements where both buyer and seller are unrepresented be allowed, thereby disagreeing with the Committee's conclusion that such conduct constituted the unauthorized practice of law. He agreed with the Committee's condemnation of conduct that encourages the parties not to retain counsel.

Judge Miller so ruled even though it was his opinion that practically every aspect of a real estate transaction involving the sale of a home constituted the practice of law. As he put it, if he thought he had the power, he would require that both seller and buyer be represented by counsel.

While technically the matter now before us is the review of the opinion of the Committee, R. 1:22-7(b) and R. 1:19-8, we now have the benefit of a full hearing, along with the findings of fact and recommendations that are part of the Special Master's report. The subsequent oral argument and briefing by the parties who participated in that hearing, the New Jersey State Bar Association, the New Jersey Association of Realtors and the New Jersey Land Title Association, focused on both Opinion No. 26 and Judge Miller's report. Our decision today, substantially in accord with Judge Miller's recommendations, affirms portions of Opinion No. 26 and reverses others. Specifically, we rule as follows: a real estate broker may order a title search and abstract; an attorney retained by a title company or a real estate broker may not prepare conveyance documents for a real estate transaction except at the specific written request of the party on whose behalf the document is to be prepared; a title company may not participate in the clearing of certain legal objections to title, see infra at 58; and the practice of conducting closings or settlements without the presence of attorneys shall not constitute the unauthorized practice of law. We hold further, however, that unless the broker conforms to the conditions set forth later in this opinion, all participants at the closing who have reason to believe those conditions have not been complied with will be engaged in the unauthorized practice of law, and any attorney with similar knowledge so participating in such a transaction will have committed unethical conduct.

II

The South Jersey Practice

Although the variations are numerous, the South Jersey practice complained of typically involves residential real estate closings in which neither buyer nor seller is represented by counsel, and contrasts most sharply with the North Jersey practice if one assumes both parties are represented there. Obviously, that is not always the case: the record shows that about sixty percent of the buyers and about sixty-five percent of the sellers in South Jersey are not represented by counsel. In North Jersey, only one half of one percent of buyers, and fourteen percent of sellers, proceed without counsel.

In North Jersey, when both seller and buyer are represented by counsel, they sign nothing, agree to nothing, expend nothing, without the advice of competent counsel. If, initially without counsel, they sign a contract of sale prepared by the broker, they ordinarily then retain counsel who can revoke that contract in accordance with the three-day attorney review clause. They are protected, and they pay for that protection. The seller in North Jersey spends on average $750 in attorney fees, and the buyer in North Jersey spends on average $1,000. The buyer in South Jersey who chooses to proceed without representation spends nothing. The South Jersey seller whose attorney does no more than prepare the deed and affidavit of title, usually without even consulting with the seller, spends about $90. South Jersey buyers and sellers who are represented throughout the process, including closing, pay an average of $650 and $350, respectively. Savings obviously do not determine the outcome of this case; they are but one factor in the mix of competing considerations.

The typical South Jersey transaction starts with the seller engaging a broker who is ordinarily a member of the multiple listing system. The first broker to find an apparently willing buyer gets in touch with the seller and ultimately negotiates a sale price agreeable to both. The potential buyer requires financing arrangements which are often made by the broker. Before the execution of any sales contract the broker puts the buyer in touch with a mortgage company to determine if the buyer qualifies for the needed loan.

At this preliminary stage, no legal obligations of any kind are likely to have been created, except for those that arise from the brokerage relationship itself.

Assuming the preliminary understanding between the seller and buyer remains in effect, the broker will present the seller with the standard form of contract used in that area (usually a New Jersey Association of Realtors Standard Form of Real Estate Contract). That form includes, pursuant to our opinion in *New Jersey State Bar Association v. New Jersey Association of Realtor Boards*, 93 N.J. 470, 461 A.2d 1112 (1983), notice that the attorney for either party can cancel the contract within three business days. If the seller signs the contract, and does not within three days retain counsel, the seller will have become legally bound to perform numerous obligations without the benefit of any legal advice whatsoever, some of which may turn out to be onerous, some costly, some requiring unanticipated expense, and some beyond the power of the seller to perform, with the potential of substantial liability for such nonperformance. Many sellers will not understand just what those obligations are, and just what the risks are. Not only has the seller not retained a lawyer, the only person qualified to explain those risks. Worse yet, the only one the seller has had any contact with in the matter is the broker, whose commission depends entirely on consummation of the transaction, and whose interest is primarily — in some cases it is fair to say exclusively — to get the contract signed and the deal closed.

After the seller signs the contract, the broker delivers it to the buyer for execution. The buyer may not know if the description of the property is precisely that assumed to be the subject of the purchase. The buyer may have no idea if the title described in the contract is that with which he would be satisfied, no sound understanding of what the numerous obligations on the part of the seller mean, and no fair comprehension of whether all of the possible and practical concerns of a buyer have been addressed by the contract. No lawyer is present to advise or inform the buyer; indeed, there is no one who has the buyer's interest at heart, only the broker, whose interests are generally in conflict with the buyer's. Although the record does not dispose of the issue, and although Judge Miller explicitly left it undecided, he noted concern that the broker, through his or her actions, may lead the buyer to believe that the broker is looking out for the buyer's interests. Therefore, without independent advice, the buyer signs the contract. If no attorney is retained within three days, the buyer is bound by all of its terms.

For both seller and buyer, it is that contract that substantially determines all of their rights and duties. Neither one of them can be regarded as adequately informed of the import of what they signed or indeed of its importance. At that point the broker, who represents only the seller and clearly has an interest in conflict with that of the buyer (the broker's interest is in consummation of the sale, the buyer's in making certain that the sale does not close unless the buyer is fully protected) performs a series of acts on behalf of the buyer, and is the only person available as a practical matter to explain their significance to the buyer. The broker orders a binder for title insurance, or a title commitment to make sure that the buyer is going to get good title. The buyer has no idea, and hopefully never will have, whether the broker ordered the right kind of title search, a fairly esoteric question that only an experienced attorney can determine.

The broker also orders numerous inspection and other reports, all primarily of interest to the buyer, to make certain that not only is the title good, but that there are no other problems affecting the premises, the house and their use. Those reports can have substantial legal consequences for both seller and buyer. For example, at what threshold dollar amount of required repairs should the seller (or the buyer) be able to cancel the contract? At what dollar amount should the buyer ignore the repairs? At what dollar amount should the buyer be able to compel the seller to make the repairs, and within what time frame? At this stage of the transaction the help of a lawyer could be invaluable, and the advice of a broker problematic.

The seller in the meantime is happy to hear from no one, for it suggests there are no problems. Eventually, the seller is told that a deed will be arriving drafted by an attorney selected by the broker, the instrument that our decisions clearly require may be drafted only by the seller's attorney. *Cape May County Bar Ass'n v. Ludlam*, 45 N.J. 121, 211 A.2d 780 (1965). Of course, the purpose of that ruling was to assure competent counsel in the drafting of such a uniquely legal document, but "competent" always meant counsel who understood the entire transaction. In South Jersey, the attorney selected by the broker, while theoretically representing the seller, may be primarily interested in the broker, the source of the attorney's "client" and the likely source of future "clients," and consequently primarily interested in completing the sale. That attorney is likely to prepare a deed satisfactory to the title company — in fact that attorney often does not even contact the seller. He or she may have no idea of anything in the contract of sale other than the description of the land and the fact that a certain kind of deed is required. No advice on the substance of the transaction comes from such an attorney even though the seller may get the impression that, since an attorney drafted the deed, the seller's interests are somehow being protected. In fact, the only protection those interests ever received, other than those that happened to appear in the form contract, is in the numbers inserted in that contract, the total purchase price, the down payment, and the closing date, for those are probably the only terms of that contract fully understood by the seller.

The buyer's position is even worse when the closing occurs. The seller will at least know that he or she got paid. Legal training is not required for that fact, even though there is no practical assurance that the seller will not thereafter be sued. The buyer, on the other hand, wants something that is largely incomprehensible to almost all buyers, good and marketable title, one that will not result in problems in the future. What the buyer gets before closing is a "title binder," a piece of paper that may suggest something about the quality of the seller's title, but that is very much in need of explanation for any substantial understanding of its meaning. The title company is required to mail to the unrepresented buyer notice of any exceptions or conditions associated with the title insurance policy. N.J.S.A. 17:46B-9. This notice, which must be sent five days prior to the closing, must also notify the buyer of the right to review the title commitment with an attorney. Ibid. If the buyer chooses not to retain an attorney, there is no one to give the buyer that understanding other than the broker and the title agent. The broker's knowledge will often be inadequate, and the conflicting interest apparent. The title company similarly has a conflicting interest, for it too is interested in completion of the transaction, the sine qua non of its title premium. But the title company is also interested in good title, for it is guaranteeing that to the mortgage company, as well as to the buyer. "Good title," however, may be one on which the title company and the mortgagee are willing to take a risk, but one on which a buyer might or should not be willing to, if the buyer knew what the risk was. Again, there is no one to tell the buyer what those risks are, and in some cases the explicit exceptions found in a title policy, those matters that the title company will not guarantee, are of the greatest importance. The significance of those matters is conceded by all to be something that only attorneys can give advice on, and it is contended by all that they never give such advice. Yet such exceptions exist, and title still closes, and the buyer is totally unrepresented by counsel. One must assume that somewhere, somehow, the buyer is satisfied that there is nothing to worry about, leading to the inescapable conclusion that either the broker or the title officer provides some modicum of assurance or explanation.

The day for closing arrives and everyone meets, usually at the offices of the title company. Seller and buyer are there, each without an attorney; the broker is there, and the title officer is there, representing both the title company and the mortgagee. The funds are there. And the critical legal documents are also on hand: the mortgage and the note, usually prepared by the mortgagee; the deed, along with the affidavit of title, prepared by the attorney selected by the broker or by the title company; the settlement statement, usually prepared by the title company, indicating how much is owed, what deductions should be made for taxes and other costs and what credits are due; and the final marked-up title binder, which evidences the obligation of the title company to issue a title policy to the buyer, and which at that point is probably practically meaningless to the buyer. All are executed and delivered, along with other documents, and the funds are delivered or held in escrow until the title company arranges to pay off prior mortgages and liens.

It would take a volume to describe each and every risk to which the seller and buyer have exposed themselves without adequate knowledge. But it takes a very short sentence to describe what apparently occurs: the deal closes, satisfactory to buyer and seller in practically all cases, satisfactory both at the closing and thereafter.

III

The Unauthorized Practice of Law

As noted above, this transaction in its entirety, the sale of real estate, especially real estate with a home on it, is one that cannot be handled competently except by those trained in the law. The most important parts of it, without which it could not be accomplished, are quintessentially the practice of law. The contract of sale, the obligations of the contract, the ordering of a title search, the analysis of the search, the significance of the title search, the quality of title, the risks that surround both the contract and the title, the extent of those risks, the probability of damage, the obligation to close or not to close, the closing itself, the settlement, the documents there exchanged, each and every one of these, to be properly understood must be explained by an attorney. And the documents themselves to be properly drafted, must be drafted by an attorney. Mixed in with these activities are many others that clearly do not require an attorney's knowledge, such as the ordering of inspection and other reports, and the price negotiation. But after that, even though arguably much can be accomplished by others, practically all else, to be done with full understanding, requires the advice of counsel.

Practically all of the cases in this area are relatively recent. They consistently reflect the conclusion that the determination of whether someone should be permitted to engage in conduct that is arguably the practice of law is governed not by attempting to apply some definition of what constitutes that practice, but rather by asking whether the public interest is disserved by permitting such conduct. The resolution of the question is determined by practical, not theoretical, considerations; the public interest is weighed by analyzing the competing policies and interests that may be involved in the case; the conduct, if permitted, is often conditioned by requirements designed to assure that the public interest is indeed not disserved.

In *Auerbacher v. Wood*, 142 N.J. Eq. 484, 59 A.2d 863 (E. & A. 1948), our then highest court held that someone who performs the usual functions of a labor relations consultant is not guilty of the unauthorized practice of law. The court noted that the issue could not be determined by reference to any satisfactory definition. "What constitutes the practice of law does not lend itself to precise and all inclusive definition. There is no definitive formula which automatically classifies every case." Id. at 485. The court noted that in drawing the line between that which is and is not permitted, "guidance is to be found in the consideration that the licensing of law practitioners is not designed to give rise to a professional monopoly, but rather to serve the public right to protection against unlearned and unskilled advice and service in matters relating to the science of the law." Id. at 486. In *In re Baker*, 8 N.J. 321, 334, 85 A.2d 505 (1951), this Court, holding respondents in contempt for their unauthorized practice of law, similarly observed that "the reason for prohibiting the unauthorized practice of the law by laymen is not to aid the legal profession but to safeguard the public from the disastrous results that are bound to flow from the activities of untrained and incompetent individuals," those not only lacking the many years of preparation, but also the high standards of professional conduct imposed on members of the bar and enforced by the Court.

In a case involving some of the same questions now before us, *New Jersey State Bar Association v. Northern New Jersey Mortgage Associates*, 22 N.J. 184, 123 A.2d 498 (1956), an appeal was taken from the trial court's dismissal of a suit alleging unauthorized practice of law, the trial court concluding that the Supreme Court had exclusive jurisdiction over such matters. The action had been brought by the New Jersey State Bar Association and five individual attorneys. The practice complained of was quite similar to that found in South Jersey, although in fact the business was conducted in North Jersey. The defendants, in the business of searching titles, acting as agents for title companies, and handling the closing of transactions involving sellers, buyers, and mortgagees, admitted that they prepared bonds, mortgages and other instruments connected with titles and mortgage loans, and that the services performed incidental to closing included the giving of legal advice in connection with those transactions. Id. at 190-92.

We ruled that our exclusive power over the practice of law did not divest a court of chancery (the trial court) of its jurisdiction to enjoin the unauthorized practice of law. Id. at 193. We further ruled that the individual plaintiffs could maintain the action only if they could show irreparable damage to their own individual financial interests, and since they could not, the dismissal of the action as to them was affirmed. Id. at 196, 199. The Bar Association, however, was placed on a different footing, for in its attempts to enjoin the unauthorized practice of law it sought to protect the public interest, for the protection of which an injunction could be granted. Id. at 194, 196. In that respect the action was deemed to be "on behalf of the public." Id. at 194.

In analyzing the Bar Association's claim to represent the public interest, we noted that, concerning the nature of the right to practice law, the more recent attitude in New Jersey has been "that admission to our bar is a privilege granted in the interest of the public to those who are morally fit and mentally qualified, solely for the purpose of protecting the unwary and the ignorant from injury at the hands of persons unskilled or unlearned in the law" and that "attorneys enjoy rights peculiar to themselves, not enjoyed by those outside the profession, but only as an incident to the public welfare." Id. at 195. We further noted that the licensing of attorneys " 'is not designed to give rise to a professional monopoly, but rather to serve the public right to protection against unlearned and unskilled advice and service in matters relating to the science of the law.' " Ibid. (quoting *Auerbacher v. Wood*, supra, 142 N.J. Eq. at 486).

The case was remanded to the Chancery Division to develop a more complete record, similar to the remand in this case to the Special Master. The host of issues set forth by the Court on which further evidence was required before a determination could be made are similar to those in this matter on which we sought further information, at least in the sense that they asked more than questions obviously directed at specific conduct that might constitute the practice of law: the questions sought to know more about the business that was going on, the relationships between the parties, the possibility that independent counsel was being discouraged, the charges made, the exact fee and compensation arrangements, and the percentage of occasions when parties were represented by counsel, id. at 199, all obviously for the purpose of enabling the Court to make a sound decision based on the public interest rather than one premised on some abstract definition of the practice of law.

After remand and plenary hearing, this Court again certified the appeal, on its own motion, from the trial court's dismissal of the charge that defendants were engaged in the unauthorized practice of law. *New Jersey State Bar Ass'n v. Northern N.J. Mortgage Assocs.*, 32 N.J. 430 (1960). In passing on the issues the Court repeated again that the restrictions against the practice of law by non-lawyers "are designed to serve the public interest by protecting 'the unwary and the ignorant from injury at the hands of persons unskilled or unlearned in the law.' " Id. at 436 (citation omitted). Noting that "the line between such activities and permissible business and professional activities by non-lawyers is indistinct," id. at 437, and that some fields may in some areas properly overlap the law, we went on to observe that "each individual set of circumstances must be passed upon 'in a common-sense way which will protect primarily the interest of the public and not hamper or burden that interest with impractical and technical restrictions which have no reasonable justification.' " Ibid. (quoting *Gardner v. Conway*, 234 Minn. 468, 48 N.W.2d 788, 797 (Minn. 1951)).

The message is clear: not only is the public interest the criterion for determining what is the unauthorized practice of law, but in making that determination practical considerations and common sense will prevail, not impractical and technical restrictions that may hamper or burden the public interest with no reasonable justification. That language is from a court that previously had remanded the case to get the full record that would give it all of the facts that would enable it to determine that public interest. The title company, the company that had succeeded to the interests of defendants in the prior case, claimed that on the basis of the entire record its activities did not constitute the unauthorized practice of the law. By then the measuring rod was clear, for the title company's contention was that "the public policy of this State" compelled that conclusion. Id. at 447. The Court disagreed, but not with the standard against which the issue would be determined, for it found that by enjoining the practices involved in the case "the public interest will not be disserved but on the contrary will be significantly advanced." Ibid. There, the public interest consisted of removing "unwarranted charges imposed by the Title Company on purchasers" and encouraging "parties to obtain the important protection of independent counsel." Ibid.

In *State v. Bander*, 56 N.J. 196, 265 A.2d 671 (1970), we sounded the same theme, although in a different context. There we held that the disorderly persons act definition of the unauthorized practice of law did not cover a broker who had prepared a contract for the sale of land even though that conduct, as implied by the decision, clearly constituted the practice of law. We concluded that even if it was the unauthorized practice of law, the broker not being an attorney, the Legislature was free to exclude it (as it did) from its criminal sanctions without offending this Court's exclusive power to determine what constitutes the unauthorized practice of law: in other words, while we may have that exclusive power, it does not prevent the Legislature from criminalizing only certain conduct that constitutes the unauthorized practice of law, leaving others unaffected by the criminal law, although still vulnerable to such prohibitions and remedies as this Court may devise outside of the criminal law. As a result of that conclusion, we noted that we did not have to reach the question "whether defendant's actions constituted an unauthorized practice of law." Id. at 202. The significance of the case, insofar as the present issue is concerned, was in our subsequent discussion of that issue, which "was partially explored at the oral argument" of the case. Ibid.

    It developed that the problem has so many ramifications that it could not be intelligently considered on the present record. As to that issue it is suggested that an answer might be obtained in a separate suit for an injunction against the type of acts undertaken by defendant or for a declaratory judgment. In this manner a complete and detailed record could be made disclosing, inter alia, the extent, length of existence, effect and result of the performance of similar acts by real estate brokers generally and the public need for such service. This Court could then give a valued and intelligent reply to such an inquiry. [Id. at 202-203.]

    That opinion, commenting on an activity that clearly involved the practice of law — the drafting of a contract for the sale of land by a non-lawyer — suggested our approach to the public interest standard that governed determinations of what constituted the unauthorized practice of law. It was an interest to be determined not by any abstract definition, but by a "complete and detailed record," including "the extent, length of existence, effect and result of the performance of similar acts by real estate brokers," and ultimately a record that would show "the public need for such service." That is, of course, precisely the record developed thereafter in order to determine that specific issue, the public interest in the right of parties to decline legal representation in the drafting of real estate sales contracts. *New Jersey Ass'n of Realtor Bds.,* supra.

Although the public interest standard for determination of the issue of unauthorized practice of law remained intact, Opinion No. 11 of the Committee on the Unauthorized Practice of Law, 95 N.J.L.J. 1345 (Dec. 28, 1972), reached a conclusion on it different from what we have determined in this case. The issue there was practically identical to that now before us. What was involved was the South Jersey practice. The Committee decided, contrary to our decision today, and based largely on the decision in *Northern New Jersey Mortgage Associates,* supra, 32 N.J. at 430, that title companies are engaged in the unauthorized practice of law when they issue a title search or policy or abstract at the request of a broker and that they are similarly guilty when they conduct real estate settlements on their premises without the presence of an attorney for any of the parties to the transaction. While the facts in the case were somewhat different from those here (the Committee finding that the parties to the transaction were discouraged by brokers from retaining counsel, that this practice was encouraged when title companies paid rebates to referring brokers for their business, and that apparently practically all documents were drafted by the title company) their similarity is remarkable. Indeed, if that opinion were to be followed we would be obliged to declare the acts challenged before us the unauthorized practice of law. The critical difference, of course, is that there was no showing in that case before the Committee similar to that found in the record before us of the impact on the public interest in allowing the South Jersey practice to continue. Apparently, all that the Committee had before it was an unadorned description of what occurs prior to and during the closing, without any evaluation of its benefits and detriments, without any evaluation of the advantages and disadvantages to the public. For present purposes, however, Opinion No. 11 is of note in its firm adherence to the standards set by the prior cases. In determining the issue the Committee said, "the measuring rod is the public interest," 95 N.J.L.J. at 1345, and asked, "Does this practice serve the public interest?" Id. at 1360. Its conclusion was that it did not. In support of its ultimate conclusion prohibiting settlements without the presence of attorneys, the Committee said, "Since the practice does constitute the practice of law and such practice by a lay corporation or person is not in the public interest, it constitutes the unauthorized practice of law." Ibid. It is of course remarkable that despite Opinion No. 11 the South Jersey practice flourished, leading ultimately to Opinion No. 26, the matter before us today. The approach we take in this case, the imposition of conditions to assure the public interest is not disserved, as well as that taken in the important cases involving the preparation of real estate contracts by brokers, *New Jersey Association of Realtor Boards,* supra, and inheritance tax returns by accountants, *In re Application of New Jersey Society of Certified Public Accountants,* 102 N.J. 231, 507 A.2d 711 (1986).

In what is undoubtedly the clearest example of the dominating influence of the public interest in this area, we decided in *New Jersey Association of Realtor Boards,* supra, that real estate brokers may draft contracts for the sale of residential property if the contract contains a prominent clause informing the parties of their right, through counsel, to cancel it within three days. While our decision took the form of the approval of a settlement reached between the brokers and the bar, our approval was explicitly based on a finding by Justice Sullivan, sitting as the trial judge, that the settlement was in the public interest, a finding with which we concurred. The initially proposed settlement of the matter had previously been submitted to us and subjected to a public hearing, but after being informed that the settlement had unraveled, we remanded the matter for trial to Justice Sullivan. At that trial a new settlement was arrived at and again subjected to a public hearing before the trial court.

Noting the position of those who objected to the settlement in its entirety, Justice Sullivan concisely summed up the entire law in this area with the observation that "the basic question is how is the public interest best served." *New Jersey State Bar Ass'n v. New Jersey Ass'n of Realtor Bds.,* 186 N.J. Super. 391, 396, 452 A.2d 1323 (Ch. Div. 1982). He concluded that "the settlement is in the public interest" and that the three-day cancellation clause "affords adequate protection to purchasers and sellers of residential real estate or lessors and lessees thereof." Id. at 398. In so concluding, he noted that it had been asserted "without contradiction that 'no State in the Country has prohibited Brokers from completing form contracts in connection with residential property sales.'" Id. at 396. The record in this case also demonstrates that the conduct in question is permitted in many other states. . . .

Our holding today, therefore, accords with the Court's consistent treatment of this issue. Although technically we have overruled the holding of *Northern New Jersey Mortgage Associates,* supra, 32 N.J. 430, that case applied precisely the same standard in passing on the challenged conduct before it — the public interest. As we view it, the real difference is found in the differing records before the Court in the two cases, for in that case the public interest in allowing the challenged practices to continue was apparently nowhere demonstrated, and certainly not with the force of the record before us. Indeed, since the practice challenged apparently related solely to one firm located in North Jersey, and not to the South Jersey practice, it may have seemed that such showing would be irrelevant. More than that, at the time of our decision in that case, we had not yet ruled that brokers could prepare contracts of sale, a change which has affected the entire landscape in this area.

In this case, the record clearly shows that the South Jersey practice has been conducted without any demonstrable harm to sellers or buyers, that it apparently saves money, and that those who participate in it do so of their own free will presumably with some knowledge of the risk; as Judge Miller found, the record fails to demonstrate that brokers are discouraging the parties from retaining counsel, or that the conflict of interest that pervades the practice has caused material damage to the sellers and buyers who participate in it. Given that record, and subject to the conditions mentioned hereafter, we find that the public interest will not be compromised by allowing the practice to continue. We note again that our prior decisions and those of the Committee on this issue did not have the benefit of such a record and were premised on the irrefutable finding that the activities of the non-lawyers in the South Jersey practice constituted the practice of law. That they do, but with the benefit of the record before us it is equally clear that the practice does not disserve the public interest.

Of decisive weight in our determination is the value we place on the right of parties to a transaction to decide whether or not they will retain counsel. We should not force them to do so absent persuasive reasons. Given the importance in our decision of the assumption that the parties have chosen not to retain counsel, and without coercion have made that decision, we have attached a condition to the conclusion that the South Jersey practice does not constitute the unauthorized practice of law. The condition is designed to assure that the decision is an informed one. If that condition is not met, the brokers (and title officers, if aware of the fact) are engaged in the unauthorized practice of law, and attorneys with knowledge of that fact who participate are guilty of ethical misconduct. That ruling is similar to the clear implication in the brokers' and accountants' cases that unless those professions conform to the conditions mentioned in those decisions, they will be guilty of the unauthorized practice of law. *New Jersey Ass'n of Realtor Bds.*, supra, 93 N.J. at 472 ("Licensed real estate brokers and salespersons shall be permitted to prepare certain types of residential sales and lease agreements if these agreements contain specified provisions."); *In re Application of N.J. Soc'y of Certified Public Accountants*, supra, 102 N.J. at 242 (permitting certified public accountants to prepare and file inheritance tax returns "subject to the condition" that client be notified in writing that review by counsel may be desirable).

The public needs protection in these matters. The Legislature has recognized such need and afforded statutory protection for both buyers and sellers at various stages of the real estate transaction. N.J.S.A. 46:3B-1 to -20 (New Home Warranty and Builders' Registration Act); N.J.S.A. 45:15-1 to -42 (Real Estate Broker Regulations); N.J.S.A. 45:22A-1 to -20 (Retirement Community Full Disclosure Act); N.J.S.A. 45:22A-21 to -56 (Planned Real Estate Development Full Disclosure Act); N.J.S.A. 17:46B-1 to -62 (Title Insurance Act); N.J.S.A. 46:10A-6 ("closed shop law" providing that mortgage lenders cannot require borrowers to employ their attorney or to pay lenders' attorney fees and that lenders must also disclose that their attorney works for them and that borrowers should retain their own attorney). In addition, Congress has recognized the need for uniformity in consumer real estate transactions. 12 U.S.C.A. Secs. 2601-2617 (Real Estate Settlement Procedures Act); 15 U.S.C.A. Secs. 1601-1693 (Truth in Lending Act); see Gerald S. Meisel, RESPA: Federal Control of Residential Real Estate, 98 N.J.L.J. 713 (August 21, 1975).

We do not here adopt a "consumerism" that invariably requires that services be made available at the lowest price no matter how great the risk. The record suggests that despite their conflict of interest, brokers' ethical standards have resulted in some diminishment of those risks. Unlike prior cases, there is no finding here, for instance, that brokers are discouraging retention of counsel, no suggestion that title companies are paying rebates to referring brokers. Today's public, furthermore, not only has the benefit of the attorney review clause, but is presumably better educated about the need for counsel, the function of attorneys, and the legal aspects of the sale of the home. The public continues, in South Jersey, to choose not to be represented. We assume that the public has simply concluded that the perceived advantages are worth those risks.

We do not adopt a rule, however, that so long as informed consent from the parties is obtained, any conduct that might otherwise constitute the unauthorized practice of law is permitted. Most of the practices restricted to attorneys can be performed, and may be performed, only by them regardless of the informed consent of the parties and regardless of the lower cost of using non-attorneys. All we decide is that in this case, concerning this practice, the record demonstrates that the public interest will not be compromised by allowing what would otherwise be the unauthorized practice of law if the parties are adequately informed of the conflicting interests of brokers and title officers and of the risks involved in proceeding without counsel.

We emphasize the nature of the public interest standard applied in this case. It is the same as in the cases allowing brokers to prepare real estate sales contracts and certified public accountants to prepare inheritance tax returns. No suggestion was made or implied in those cases that the public was better served if they used brokers and certified public accountants rather than lawyers for the services involved. On the contrary, the conditions imposed by this Court in both — requiring that the parties be informed in advance of their right to retain counsel — reflect our judgment that the parties would be well advised to obtain counsel. We decided only that the protection that lawyers provide and parties need — the basic rationale for prohibiting the unauthorized practice of law — was sufficiently addressed in those cases by assuring that the parties knowingly rejected it; we decided only that the public interest in those cases did not require depriving parties of their right to proceed without counsel, did not require the protection of counsel against their will. That is all we decide here today. We do not conclude that the public is better off without lawyers in the South Jersey practice. As stated several times above, we firmly believe the parties should retain counsel. We decide only that given the history and experience of the South Jersey practice, the public interest will not be disserved by allowing the parties, after advance written notice of their right to retain counsel and the risk of not doing so, to choose to proceed without a lawyer; we decide only that the public interest does not require that the protection of counsel be forced upon the parties against their will. Our required disclosure notice goes beyond that of other cases, reflecting our determination to assure that the parties who decide not to retain lawyers know the conflicting interests of others and know that there are risks of proceeding without one. . . .

IV

Conclusion and Conditions

We premise our holding on the condition that both buyer and seller be made aware of the conflicting interests of brokers and title companies in these matters and of the general risks involved in not being represented by counsel.

We shall ask the Civil Practice Committee to recommend to us practical methods for achieving those aims. Presumably, that Committee will want to form a subcommittee including those who have been involved with this problem for many years. Obviously, the best way to achieve the goal is to have a knowledgeable disinterested attorney sit down with both buyer and seller and carefully explain both the conflict factor and the risk factor, but we doubt if that would be practical. Pending the report of that Committee and our action on it, we have decided to adopt an interim notice requirement that the broker must comply with. If that notice is not given, the broker will be engaged in the unauthorized practice of law. Furthermore, anyone who participates in the transaction, other than buyer and seller, knowing that the notice has not been given when and as required, will also be engaged in the unauthorized practice of law. As for any attorney who, under the same circumstances, continues to participate in the transaction, that attorney will also be subject to discipline for unethical conduct. At the commencement of the closing or settlement, the title officer in charge shall inquire of both buyer and seller whether, how, and when, the notice was given, and shall make and keep a record of the inquiry and the responses at that time.

The interim notice that we require is attached as Appendix A. It is a written notice, and it shall be attached to the proposed contract of sale as its cover page. The notice may be appropriately revised if the broker represents the buyer or is a dual agent, one who represents both seller and buyer. Whenever a broker presents either buyer or seller with the proposed contract, that cover page shall be so attached, and the broker shall personally advise the buyer or seller at that point that he or she must read it before executing the contract. If the contract is not personally delivered by the broker to the buyer or seller, the broker must make certain, prior to such delivery, that buyer and seller have been so informed, and must do so by speaking to them personally or by phone.

Assuming such notice is given in accordance with the terms and conditions mentioned above, we hold that attendance and participation at the closing or settlement where neither party has been represented by counsel, or where one has not been so represented, does not constitute the unauthorized practice of law; that brokers may order abstracts, title binders, and title policies; that an attorney retained by the broker to draft a deed and/or affidavit of title for the seller may do so but only if the attorney personally consults with the seller; regardless of the prior restriction, any attorney retained by the broker for that purpose, or any attorney acting for the title company, may draft any of the documents involved in the transaction upon written request of the party, be it buyer, seller, lender, mortgagee, bank, or others; that the title company may participate in clearing up those minor objections which Judge Miller refers to as categories one and two: standard exceptions such as marital status and money liens customarily paid at closing, but not those classified as categories three and four: easements, covenants, or other serious legal objections to title.

Other equally important protections for buyer and seller should exist. Any broker participating in a transaction where buyer and seller are not represented should have the experience and knowledge required at least to identify a situation where independent counsel is needed. Under those circumstances the broker has a duty in accordance with the standards of that profession, to inform either seller or buyer of that fact. N.J.A.C.11:5-1.23(a), (f). Presumably, the same duty applies to any title officer, whether or not an attorney, but especially if an attorney, who becomes aware of the need of either party for independent counsel. In addition to whatever potential action might be taken by the bodies that regulate brokers and title officers, as well as by their own associations, their failure to inform exposes them to the risk of civil liability for resulting damages.

Our decision, while allowing continuation of the South Jersey practice, imposes new conditions on that practice and serious consequences for non-compliance. In order that brokers and others may adjust their practices to comply with those conditions, our decision will not become effective until sixty days from the date of this opinion and will apply to all real estate contracts subject to this opinion that are thereafter executed and to the transactions based on those contracts.

The decision of the Committee, Opinion No. 26, is affirmed in part, and reversed in part, and judgment entered declaring the rights of the participants in New Jersey residential real estate transactions in accordance with this opinion.

Case Questions

1. Why do you think the court spent so much time discussing the unauthorized practice of law? Do you believe such practices are commonplace? Explain.

2. What was the "unauthorized practice of law" discussed in this case?

6 Condominiums, Cooperatives, and Commercial Property

CHAPTER OVERVIEW

At this point it would be beneficial to examine, briefly, certain hybrid situations that are commonly encountered in a real estate law practice. These special situations include condominiums, cooperatives, and commercial property.

Condominiums and cooperatives first appeared over one hundred years ago, exclusively in urban settings. Land had become increasingly scarce with the growth of cities brought about by the Industrial Revolution. People who wanted to own their own homes had to share their houses with others because of escalating land values on limited space. Landowners began to construct taller buildings to increase the number of units that could be rented, further reducing the availability of land for single-family homes. Eventually, the owners of multi-story buildings decided to sell units rather than renting so that people could, in some way, own their own homes. The result was the condominium and the cooperative. This form of ownership is now popular in suburban and rural areas as well as the cities in which it began.

Although its title tracks the titles of all other property, commercial property involves several additional aspects with regard to its sale, basically because most commercial property involves leases with tenants in possession who have certain rights and obligations that must be taken into consideration when the property is sold.

This chapter briefly examines these three specific situations involving the sale of real property.

Condominiums

A **condominium** is a form of ownership of real property in which the condominium owners hold title outright to a specifically designated unit and, at the same time, hold title as joint tenants with all other condominium unit owners in the development for what are considered to be the "common areas." These common areas include hallways, entryways, roofs, stairways and elevators, and recreational areas such as a common swimming pool, tennis court, and health center. Basically, any area that is used by all of the unit owners may be deemed to be a common area.

 EXAMPLE:

A woman wants to retire to the Sun Belt and no longer wants to worry about maintaining her own home. She purchases a two-bedroom unit in a condominium development that has a golf course. The woman holds title to her unit (basically an apartment or a townhouse) as a tenant in severalty, and is a joint tenant with all other unit owners for the golf course and common walkways and areas.

The concept of a condominium did not exist under the common law, and consequently is a creature of statute. Every state has enacted laws that provide for the creation and regulation of condominiums (and cooperatives), and therefore each jurisdiction's statutes must be individually analyzed to determine particular rights and obligations. In addition to statutory regulation, the person who develops the condominium must also prepare a **condominium declaration** that is recorded with the deed to the land in the county recorder's office. This declaration details the specific rights and obligations of the unit owners (see Exhibit 6.1 at the end of this chapter for an example of a Sales Contract for a Condominium).

When creating a condominium, the developer must, usually by statutory mandate, establish rights and regulations for the governance of the condominium, and furthermore must prepare a plat description that shows the physical size and location of each of the units (see Chapter 4). Also, a **homeowners' association** must be formed to oversee the regulation of the condominium and to have authority to maintain the common areas. Before any units in the condominium can be sold, the condominium declaration, plat description, and homeowners' association must be established.

The homeowners' association, sometimes referred to as the **condominium association,** is formed as a non-profit corporation, and therefore, to be legally organized, is required to file **articles of incorporation** with the state secretary of state. These articles act as the association's creating document. The association must also adopt **bylaws** that detail the day-to-day operations of the association. The condominium unit owners elect some of the residents to act as members of the association's **board of directors** who manage the association for a stated period of time, at which point a new board will be elected by the unit owners. To maintain the condominium, the unit owners pay an **assessment** to cover the cost of maintaining and repairing the common areas.

 EXAMPLE:

> A condominium developer has filed all necessary papers to create a condominium, and has sold almost all the units. The developer has also filed a certificate of incorporation for the homeowners' association with the secretary of state. At this point the developer calls a meeting of the unit owners for the purpose of electing a board of directors. Five people are elected to the board. The board then has the unit owners pay the yearly assessment so that it can maintain the common areas.

With a condominium, each unit owner is liable for the maintenance and repair of his or her own individual unit, and is liable for any injuries that result from the failure to maintain the requisite standard of care associated with property ownership (see Chapter 4). The unit owner is also a joint tenant for the common areas and the owner is jointly liable for any injuries resulting from the failure of the homeowners' association to maintain the common areas in good repair.

Because the condominium represents individual ownership of the unit, the unit owner is free to sell, gift, devise, or rent his or her unit without restriction, *unless* there is some prohibition in the condominium declaration, which is rare. Condominium ownership typically provides for the free transferability of the property.

Cooperatives

A **cooperative** differs from a condominium. Cooperative ownership is considered to be ownership of personal property, not real property, because the owner purchases a share in a cooperative association, and the share entitles the holder to possess a specified unit that is owned by the cooperative. In other words, cooperative ownership is similar to ownership of a corporation. The shareholder owns a share that represents a percentage of corporation, and the share entitles the holder (with the cooperative) to possess, not own, a particular unit. Cooperatives are very popular on the East Coast of the United States.

Because the cooperative owner only holds a share, the shareholder has limited rights with respect to the transferability of that share. The cooperative is managed by a board that is responsible for the financial and physical well-being of the property. As a consequence, the board reviews all prospective purchasers for financial resources and personality, to determine whether the potential owner would be an appropriate tenant in the cooperative. Therefore, if an owner wishes to sell his or her share, the prospective buyer must be approved by the cooperative board. In the case of a stalemate, the cooperative agreement often provides that the cooperative will repurchase the shares from the owner, but the price is usually set at a rate below market value.

 EXAMPLE:

> The owner of a cooperative wants to move and has found a prospective buyer for his shares, a well-known rock musician. Although financially sound, the board refuses to approve the musician because they do not want "theatrical people" in the building. Therefore the board may block this potential sale.

Because the units are owned by the cooperative, not the shareholders, financing of the property is made by and through the cooperative, and each shareholder pays an assessment to the board to cover the financing. If a shareholder defaults, the other shareholders must make up the shortfall to maintain the property's financing.

Cooperatives, because of their restrictions on transferability, are usually less expensive than condominiums. See Exhibit 6.2 at the end of this chapter for an example of a Sales Contract for a Cooperative.

Commercial Property

The term "commercial property," as used in the context of this book, refers to real estate that has been developed for commercial use, such as office and apartment buildings and shopping centers, and consequently have tenants already in situ. Certain additional considerations must be addressed with any sale of this type of property:

- When the property is described in the contract for sale, items of personal property that are used in the operation of the commercial venture are also usually included, such as landscaping and snow removal equipment. If not included in the description of the property being transferred they must be specifically excluded if the items are not intended to be part of the sale.
- Purchasers of commercial property are entitled to a physical inspection of the property prior to the sale. This inspection can include

review of all contracts and financial documents associated with the property, and the buyer typically has the right to withdraw from the contract at this time if there are problems with the property that the seller refuses to remedy.

- In addition to the general covenants discussed in the previous chapter, if the sale involves commercial property, the seller is usually required to provide certain guarantees with respect to any leases that exist on the property, as well as all services and utilities in effect with respect to the property. The seller usually warrants that he or she will not enter into any new lease or contract before the closing date without the buyer's consent.
- If the property is leased to tenants at the time of the sale, the tenants may be required to sign an **estoppel letter,** which is a document that warrants the accuracy of the tenant's lease that is provided for the buyer by the seller. A copy of the purported lease is attached to the estoppel letter for this purpose.
- If the commercial property being sold is subject to a mortgage, and the buyer is taking title subject to the mortgage, the buyer will require the mortgagee to provide an **estoppel certificate** that details all the terms of the note and mortgage, indicating the amount of the outstanding balance and any amount in default as of the date of the signing of the estoppel certificate.
- For commercial property that is leased to tenants, the contract for sale will usually require a **proration** of the rent — a delineation of the amount of rent that will belong to the seller and the amount that will belong to the buyer. Furthermore, the contract must specify the taking over of any **security deposits** made by the tenants to the seller, which represent an amount that must be maintained in a trust account for the benefit of the property owner if the tenant defaults on the rent.
- Usually the buyer will require the seller to include an **indemnification** clause whereby the seller agrees to indemnify, or reimburse, the buyer for any cause of action on the property that was occasioned by events that occurred prior to the closing that are attributable to the seller's breach of a legal obligation.

See Exhibit 6.3 at the end of this chapter for a Land Description of a Commercial Property.

Practical Tips

- Make sure that all requirements of the co-op or condominium board have been met to effectuate a transfer.
- For commercial property, if dealing with an artificial entity, make sure that the entity has been lawfully formed; otherwise the transaction may be invalid.

- For commercial sales, make sure all tenants have received and/or prepared all necessary documents.

Chapter Review

Condominiums, cooperatives, and commercial property present special problems for anyone involved in the purchase and sale of realty.

The condominium represents a dual title to property: individual ownership for a given unit and a joint tenancy for the common areas. Condominiums are easy to transfer, but the unit owner has individual liability for his or her own unit and is jointly liable with the other unit owners for injuries resulting from poor maintenance of the common areas.

Cooperatives represent ownership in personal property of a share certificate that entitles the holder to possess, not own, a given unit. Liability for the cooperative owner is joint with all the other shareholders, and transferability of the share is difficult because alienation is restricted and subject to approval by the cooperative board.

Both condominiums and cooperatives are managed by boards pursuant to their certificates of incorporation.

The sale and purchase of commercial real estate, although following all the other categories of realty, require special attention for certain matters that apply only to property that is occupied by tenants who have rights and obligations with respect to the property. These considerations must be addressed in the contract for the sale of all commercial realty.

Ethical Concern

It is an unethical practice to represent both sides in a legal transaction unless both parties are aware of the representation and agree to it. This means that in a real estate transaction the same law office cannot represent the buyer and the seller, unless they both agree. Even if both sides agree, it still may be wise to decline such representations to avoid the appearance of impropriety.

Key Terms

Articles of incorporation	Cooperative
Assessment	Estoppel certificate
Board of directors	Estoppel letter
Bylaws	Homeowners' association
Condominium	Indemnification
Condominium association	Proration
Condominium declaration	Security deposit

Exercises

1. Review your state's statutes governing cooperatives and condominiums.
2. Briefly discuss the reasons a person might wish to purchase a cooperative rather than a condominium.
3. At the county recorder's office, search for an estoppel letter that appears with a deed to a commercial building.
4. Obtain from a local bank a copy of a mortgage application to purchase a cooperative and analyze its provisions.
5. Briefly discuss the additional factors that must be addressed with the purchase of commercial property.

Situational Analysis

A group of townhouses were constructed as a condominium. After several years the board decides that the exteriors of some of the houses need to be repainted, and it assesses all the unit owners, claiming that this is a common area. Your client is one of the unit owners so assessed whose house is not being painted and she claims this is not a common area. Argue both sides and decide the case.

Edited Cases

The following two cases underscore the power of a homeowners' association in attempting to bar children and dogs from the premises.

Board of Directors of 175 East Delaware Place Homeowners Association v. Hinojosa
287 Ill. App. 3d 886, 679 N.E.2d 407 (1997)

Plaintiff, board of directors of 175 East Delaware Place Homeowners Association (the Board), filed suit against defendants, Nancy Lee Carlson and Benjamin Tessler, Jorge and Donna Hinojosa, and Independence One Mortgage Corporation, seeking to foreclose on a statutory lien under the Condominium Property Act (the Act) (765 ILCS 605/9(h) (West 1994)). The trial court dismissed plaintiff's complaint. Plaintiff appeals, contending that the trial court erred in finding the Board's no-dog rule unreasonable. For the reasons that follow, we reverse.

Facts

175 East Delaware Place was organized as a condominium in 1973 by the recording of a declaration and bylaws. The property includes floors 45

through 92 of the John Hancock building and contains 705 condominium units. The declaration and bylaws were silent on the issue of pet ownership in the building. In 1976, the Board adopted a rule allowing owners to have pets, including dogs, only with the permission of the Board. On January 21, 1980, during a regular board meeting, the Board adopted a rule barring unit owners from bringing additional dogs onto the premises. In October of 1985, defendants Nancy Lee Carlson and Benjamin Tessler purchased a unit in the building. At this time, they signed a pet agreement acknowledging the no-dog rule. In February of 1993, while leasing out another one of their units, they signed the same agreement again. In March of 1993, the no-dog rule was reincluded in the Board's rules and regulations.

In June of 1993, defendants Carlson and Tessler acquired a dog. This same month, a group of owners brought suit against the Board challenging the no-dog rule. *Rodgers v. Board of Directors of 175 East Delaware Place Homeowners Ass'n*, No. 93 CH 5602. This suit was eventually abandoned and is not part of this appeal. In September of 1993, defendants Carlson and Tessler received notice of a hearing for their violation of the no-dog rule. The hearing was held on November 30, 1993, and the committee recommended to the Board that Carlson and Tessler be ordered to remove the dog within 30 days. If the dog remained on the premises after 30 days, defendants Carlson and Tessler should be assessed a fine of $100 per day for each day the dog remained. The Board adopted the committee's recommendation and on January 23, 1994, began assessing fines on defendants Carlson and Tessler. On April 20, 1994, after Carlson and Tessler failed to pay the fines, the Board recorded a notice and claim of statutory lien.

In August of 1994, defendants Carlson and Tessler sold the unit to defendants Jorge and Donna Hinojosa subject to the lien. In November of 1994, the Board filed the instant action seeking to foreclose on the lien. Defendants moved to dismiss the suit pursuant to section 2-619(a)(9) of the Code of Civil Procedure (735 ILCS 5/2-619(a)(9) (West 1994)), claiming the Board had no authority to adopt the no-dog rule because the rule conflicted with the declaration and bylaws. The trial court ruled that the Board had the power to promulgate the rule but held that the rule was unreasonable.

Analysis

A. Legal Background

Condominiums are creatures of statute and, thus, any action taken on behalf of the condominium must be authorized by statute. "When a controversy regarding the rights of a condominium unit owner in a condominium arises, we must examine any relevant provisions in the Act and the Declaration or bylaws and construe them as a whole." *Carney v. Donley*, 261 Ill. App. 3d 1002, 1008, 199 Ill. Dec. 219, 633 N.E.2d 1015 (1994).

A condominium is an interest in real estate created by statute that gives each owner an interest in an individual unit as well as an undivided interest in common elements. Administration and operation of the condominium are vested in the condominium association, which is comprised of all unit owners. The administration is exercised through the board of directors, which is elected by the owners. In addition to the Act, the operation and administration of the condominium are governed by three principal documents. These are the declaration, bylaws, and board rules and regulations. The declaration and bylaws form the basic framework of the administration, and the day-to-day operations are managed by board rules and regulations.

A condominium comes into being by the recording of a declaration. The declaration is prepared and recorded by either the developer or association. The Act defines the declaration as the "instrument by which the property is submitted to the provisions of [the] Act." 765 ILCS 605/2(a) (West 1994). Its primary function is to provide a constitution for the condominium — to guide the condominium development throughout the years. The declaration contains the property's legal description, defines the units and common elements, provides the percentage of ownership interests, establishes the rights and obligations of owners, and contains restrictions on the use of the property. R. Otto, Illinois Act in Condominium Titles, in Illinois Condominium Law Sec. 1.15, at 1-27 (Ill. Inst. for Cont. Legal Educ. 1994). All restrictions contained in the declaration are covenants that run with the land and bind each subsequent owner. They are given a strong presumption of validity. M. Kurtzon, Representing the Condominium Association, in Illinois Condominium Law Sec. 10.19, at 10-17 (Ill. Inst. for Cont. Legal Educ. 1994). Section 4 of the Act details what elements must be contained in the declaration. Paragraph (i) states: "Such other lawful provisions not inconsistent with the provisions of this Act as the owner or owners may deem desirable in order to promote and preserve the cooperative aspect of ownership of the property and to facilitate the proper administration thereof." 765 ILCS 605/4(i) (West 1994).

The second document is the bylaws, which deal with administration and procedural matters concerning the property. Bylaws may be embodied in the declaration or be a separate document. In either case, the bylaws must be recorded with the declaration. 765 ILCS 605/17(a) (West 1994). Should the bylaws conflict with the declaration, the declaration prevails. Section 18 of the Act sets forth certain provisions that shall be included in the bylaws. Relevant to the issue before us is paragraph (k), which states: "Restrictions on and requirements respecting the use and maintenance of the units and the use of the common elements, not set forth in the declaration, as are designed to prevent unreasonable interference with the use of their respective units and of the common elements by the several unit owners." 765 ILCS 605/18(k) (West 1994).

The third item governing condominium conduct is the board rules and regulations. Section 18.4 of the Act deals with powers and duties of the board and provides that the board may: "Adopt and amend rules and regulations covering the details of the operation and use of the property, after a meeting of the unit owners called for the specific purpose of discussing the proposed rules and regulations." 765 ILCS 605/18.4(h) (West 1994).

Under this rule, "a board of managers may not take any action that is beyond the authority granted it under the condominium instruments and the Condominium Property Act." 765 ILCS 605/18.4, Historical & Practice Notes, at 129 (West 1993). The board shall exercise for the association all powers, duties, and authority vested in the association by law or the condominium documents. It generally has broad powers and its rules govern the requirements of day-to-day living in the association. Board rules must be objective, evenhanded, nondiscriminatory, and applied uniformly. See J. Shifrin, Cooperative, Condominium, and Homeowners' Association Litigation, in Real Estate Litigation Sec. 11.20, at 11-17 (Ill. Inst. for Cont. Legal Educ. 1994).

B. *Power of the Board to Promulgate the No-Dog Rule*

As noted, pursuant to section 18.4 the Board has the power to adopt rules and regulations. Section 18(k) does discuss restrictions that shall be included in the bylaws. However, this provision merely gives the association the authority to include restrictions in the condominium instruments that will clothe the restrictions with a strong presumption of validity and make them less susceptible to attack. The provision does not state that if a restriction is not contained in the bylaws it will be unenforceable. We thus conclude that the Board's no-dog rule is not in conflict with the Act.

The 175 East Delaware Place declaration and bylaws do not make any reference to pet ownership or dogs, in particular. As to the Board's powers, the declaration provides:

> The Board may adopt such reasonable rules and regulations as it may deem advisable for the maintenance, conservation and beautification of the Property, and for the health, comfort, safety and general welfare of the Owners and Occupants of the Property. Written notice of such rules and regulations shall be given to all Owners and Occupants and the entire Property shall at all times be maintained subject to such rules and regulations.

The declaration clearly gives the Board authority to promulgate rules regarding use of and restrictions on the use of units. Because the Board is authorized to promulgate reasonable rules for the general welfare of the owners and the declaration is silent on the issue of dog ownership, the instant rule does not conflict with either the declaration or the bylaws.

Courts that have addressed the issue have held that dogs may be prohibited or restricted by provisions in the declaration or bylaws. See *Nahrstedt v. Lakeside Village Condominium Ass'n*, 8 Cal. 4th 361, 878 P.2d 1275, 33 Cal. Rptr. 2d 63 (1994) (restriction in recorded declaration barring all pets except fish and birds enforceable unless unreasonable); *Chateau Village North Condominium Ass'n v. Jordan*, 643 P.2d 791 (Colo. App. 1982) (rule barring all pets appended to bylaws and recorded enforceable); *Parkway Gardens Condominium Ass'n v. Kinser*, 536 So. 2d 1076 (Fla. App. 1988) (board rule barring pets unenforceable because declaration allowed them); *Zeskind v. Jockey Club Condominium Apartments, Unit II, Inc.*, 468 So. 2d 1021 (Fla. App. 1985) (no-pet rule in declaration enforceable); *Wilshire Condo-*

minium Ass'n v. Kohlbrand, 368 So. 2d 629 (Fla. App. 1979) (restriction in declaration barring replacement of lap dogs enforceable); *Johnson v. Keith,* 368 Mass. 316, 331 N.E.2d 879 (1975) (board rule barring all pets unenforceable; rule must be included in bylaws); *Noble v. Murphy,* 34 Mass. App. 452, 612 N.E.2d 266 (1993) (restriction barring all pets incorporated in original recorded documents enforceable); but see *Dulaney Towers Maintenance Corp. v. O'Brey,* 46 Md. App. 464, 418 A.2d 1233 (1980) (board rule limiting number of pets enforceable). The issue before us, however, is whether the Board may promulgate a rule restricting dog ownership. This issue has not been addressed in Illinois.

Apple II Condominium Ass'n v. Worth Bank & Trust Co., 277 Ill. App. 3d 345, 213 Ill. Dec. 463, 659 N.E.2d 93 (1995), addresses use restrictions under the Act. In *Apple II,* we set forth standards for evaluating such restrictions and adopted the analysis set forth in *Hidden Harbour Estates, Inc. v. Basso,* 393 So. 2d 637 (Fla. App. 1981). We differentiated use restrictions that are contained in the declaration or bylaws from those promulgated by board rule. The restrictions in the first category "are clothed in a very strong presumption of validity and will not be invalidated absent a showing that they are wholly arbitrary in their application, in violation of public policy, or that they abrogate some fundamental constitutional right. . . . 'Reasonableness' is not the appropriate test for such restrictions." *Apple II,* 277 Ill. App. 3d at 250-51. However, when the board promulgates a rule restricting the use of property, the second category, "the board must affirmatively show the use it wishes to prohibit or restrict is 'antagonistic to the legitimate objectives of the condominium association.'" *Apple II,* 277 Ill. App. 3d at 351, quoting *Basso,* 393 So. 2d at 640. Thus, "when such a rule [use restriction] is adopted by the board alone or requires the board to exercise discretion, we will scrutinize the restriction and uphold it only if it is affirmatively shown to be reasonable in its purpose and application." *Apple II,* 277 Ill. App. 3d at 352.

Based on the above, we conclude that the Board had the power to promulgate a reasonable no-dog rule.

C. Reasonableness of Rule

Because the rule was promulgated by the Board, it is not clothed with a strong presumption of validity. Thus, we must carefully scrutinize the rule to determine if it is reasonable in its purpose and application. Because the facts are not in dispute, the issue is one of law.

In *Dulaney Towers Maintenance Corp. v. O'Brey,* 46 Md. App. 464, 418 A.2d 1233 (1980), the court stated:

"The rationale for allowing the placing of restrictions in, or the barring of pets by way of, house rules is based on potentially offensive odors, noise, possible health hazards, clean-up and maintenance problems, and the fact that pets can and do defile hallways, elevators, and other common areas." *Dulaney Towers Maintenance,* 46 Md. App. at 466, 418 A.2d at 1235.

The above factors, in conjunction with the specific facts of this case, lead us to conclude the Board's no-dog rule is a reasonable exercise of the

Board's rule-making power. The John Hancock building is located in a very urban and densely populated area of the city where parks, grass, and other recreational areas for dogs are scarce. The 705 residences are located on the 45th through 92nd floors. In order to take a dog out, one must access elevators and descend anywhere from 45 to 92 floors.

The rule was adopted to prevent possible injury or harm. The original purpose for promulgating the rule was due to an incident in which one dog killed another dog in the building. The Board had tried less restrictive measures to regulate dogs in the past. However, these measures did not cure or alleviate what the Board reasonably perceived to be potential and real problems. It should also be noted that when the no-dog rule was adopted, owners were allowed to retain existing dogs. The rule only prohibited additional and/or replacement dogs.

Because the Board applied the rule to all owners and the purpose for the rule was rational, we conclude that the rule is reasonable under the specific facts of this case.

Conclusion

Based on the foregoing, we reverse the decision of the circuit court of Cook County and remand for further proceedings.

Reversed and remanded.

Case Questions

1. What is the court's conclusion with respect to the board's ability to make a no-dog rule?
2. How does the court determine "reasonableness?"

Pearlman v. Lake Dora Villas Management, Inc.
479 So. 2d 780 (Fla. App. 1985)

The Pearlmans (condominium unit owners) appeal from a summary judgment entered in favor of Lake Dora Villas Management, Inc. (a condominium association), which declared constitutional and enforceable against them a condominium declaration provision prohibiting all children under sixteen from permanent residence, except children of transferees from an institutional first mortgagee. They also challenge the trial court's award to the Association of $24,500.00 for attorney fees pursuant to section 718.303, Florida Statutes (1983). We reverse.

Lake Dora Villas Condominium Declaration provides, in relevant part: Every owner of an interest in one of the units shall (in addition to other obligations and duties set out herein):

(g) Not allow any children under sixteen (16) years of age to reside in permanent residence on the premises except as permitted under uniform regulations established from time to time by the Corporation. This sub-paragraph (g) shall not apply to transferees from an institutional first mortgagee.

The Pearlmans were in violation of this provision after the birth of their infant daughter, since she was a permanent resident of their unit, and they had not purchased the unit from an institutional first mortgagee or a transferee from a first mortgagee.

We agree with the Pearlmans that the provision on its face violates equal protection by its arbitrary creation and treatment of two classes of grantees.

Cases are legion upholding condominium age restrictions. *White Egret Condominium v. Franklin,* 379 So. 2d 346 (Fla. 1979); *Constellation Condominium Association, Inc. v. Harrington,* 467 So. 2d 378 (Fla. 2d DCA 1985); *Everglades Plaza Condominium Association, Inc. v. Buckner,* 462 So. 2d 835 (Fla. 4th DCA 1984); *De Slatopolsky v. Balmoral Condominium Association, Inc.,* 427 So. 2d 781 (Fla. 3d DCA 1983); *Star Lake North, Commodore Association, Inc. v. Parker,* 423 So. 2d 509 (Fla. 3d DCA 1982); *Pacheco v. Lincoln Palace Condominium, Inc.,* 410 So. 2d 573 (Fla. 3d DCA 1982). However, none of these cases have determined the validity of an age restriction containing an exception, such as the one involved in this case.

In *White Egret Condominium v. Franklin,* 379 So. 2d 346 (Fla. 1979), the seminal condominium age restrictions case in Florida, the court justified the provision as follows:

> The urbanization of this country requiring substantial portions of our population to live closer together coupled with the desire for varying types of family units and recreational activities have brought about new concepts in living accommodations. . . . We cannot ignore the fact that some housing complexes are specifically designed for certain age groups. In our view, age restrictions are a reasonable means to identify and categorize the varying desires of our population.

Id. at 351. The court cautioned against unreasonable uses of age restrictions, stating:

> We do recognize, however, that these age restrictions cannot be used to unreasonably or arbitrarily restrict certain classes of individuals from obtaining desirable housing. Whenever an age restriction is attacked on due process or equal protection grounds, we find the test is: (1) whether the restriction under the particular circumstances of the case is reasonable, and (2) whether it is discriminatory, arbitrary, or oppressive in its application.

Id. at 351.

The Association does not argue that children under the age of sixteen whose parents own a unit as transferees from an institutional first mortgagee are less intrusive than those children whose parents obtained title from another source. It speculates such a group may be smaller and the exception is required for financing purposes. However true that may be as a practical matter, the distinction between the two classes of children still remains arbitrary and discriminatory. Therefore, the exception cannot be justified under the rationale of *White Egret Condominium v. Franklin.*

Accordingly, we hold that the condominium declaration provision is unenforceable and we direct the trial court to enter summary judgment in the Pearlmans' favor. Because the Association is no longer the prevailing party, we reverse the award of attorney's fees.

Case Questions

1. How does the court determine that the equal protection clause has been violated?

2. How could a condominium validly create a "no children" rule?

Exhibit 6.1: Sales Contract for a Condominium

Blumbergs Law Products ® M 146-Contract of sale, condominium unit, 5-98
Prepared by the Committee on Real Property Law of the Association of the Bar of the City of New York.

DISTRIBUTED BY **Blumberg**Excelsior Inc.
NYC 10013

Note: This form is intended to deal with matters common to most transactions involving the sale of a condominium unit. Provisions should be added, altered or deleted to suit the circumstances of a particular transaction. No representation is made that this form of contract complies with Section 5-702 of the General Obligations Law ("Plain Language Law").

CONSULT YOUR LAWYER BEFORE SIGNING THIS AGREEMENT

Contract of Sale – Condominium Unit

Agreement made as of   between

residing at

and   ("Seller")

residing at

("Purchaser")

1. Unit: Seller agrees to sell and convey, and Purchaser agrees to purchase, Unit No.   ("Unit") in the building ("Building") known as   Condominium·("Condominium") and located at   , New York, together with a   percent undivided interest in the Common Elements (as defined in para. 6) appurtenant thereto, all upon and subject to the terms and conditions set forth herein. The Unit shall be as designated in the Declaration of Condominium Ownership (as the same may be amended from time to time, the "Declaration") of the Condominium, recorded in   County, New York or the By-Laws (as the same may be amended from time to time, the "By-Laws") of the Condominium.

2. Personal Property: (a) The sale includes all of Seller's right, title and interest, if any, in and to:

(i) the refrigerators, freezers, ranges, ovens, dishwashers, washing machines, clothes dryers, cabinets and counters, lighting and plumbing fixtures, air conditioning equipment, venetian blinds, shades, screens, storm windows and other window treatments, wall-to-wall carpeting, bookshelves, switchplates, door hardware, built-ins and articles of property and fixtures attached to or appurtenant to the Unit, except those listed in subpara. 2(b), all of which included property and fixtures are represented to be owned by Seller, free and clear of all liens and encumbrances other than those encumbrances ("Permitted Exceptions") set forth on Schedule A annexed hereto and made a part hereof *(strike out inapplicable items)*; and

(ii)

(b) Excluded from this sale are:

(i) furniture and furnishings (other than as specifically provided in this Contract); and
(ii)

(c) The property referred to in subpara. 2(a)(i) and (ii) may not be purchased if title to the Unit is not conveyed hereunder.

3. Purchase Price: (a) The purchase price ("Purchase Price") is $, payable as follows:

(i) $ ("Downpayment") on the signing of this Contract by check subject to collection, the receipt of which is hereby acknowledged, to be held in escrow pursuant to para. 16; and

(ii) $ constituting the balance of the Purchase Price, by certified check of Purchaser or official bank check (except as otherwise provided in this Contract) on the delivery of the deed as hereinafter provided.

(b) All checks in payment of the Purchase Price shall represent United States currency and be drawn on or issued by a bank or trust company authorized to accept deposits in New York State. All checks in payment of the Downpayment shall be payable to the order of Escrowee (as hereinafter defined). All checks in payment of the balance of the Purchase Price shall be payable to the order of Seller (or as Seller otherwise directs pursuant to subparas. 6(a)(ix) or 19(b)).

(c) Except for the Downpayment and checks aggregating not more than one-half of one percent of the Purchase Price, including payment for closing adjustments, all checks delivered by Purchaser shall be certified or official bank checks as hereinabove provided.

4. Closing of Title: The closing documents referred to in para. 6 shall be delivered, and payment of the balance of the Purchase Price shall be made, at the closing of title ("Closing"), to be held on   at   M., at the offices of

or at the office of Purchaser's lending institution or its counsel; provided, however, that such office is located in either the City or County in which either (a) Seller's attorney maintains an office or (b) the Unit is located.

5. Representations, Warranties and Covenants: Seller represents, warrants and covenants that:
(a) Seller is the sole owner of the Unit and the property referred to in subpara. 2(a), and Seller has the full right, power and authority to sell, covey and transfer the same;

(b) The common charges (excluding separately billed utility charges) for the Unit on the date hereof are $ per month;

(c) Seller has not received any written notice of any intended assessment or increase in common charges not reflected in subpara. 5(b). Purchaser acknowledges that it will not have the right to cancel this Contract in the event of the imposition of any assessment or increase in common charges after the date hereof of which Seller has not heretofore received written notice;

(d) The real estate taxes for the Unit for the fiscal year of   through   are $

(e) Seller is not a "sponsor" or a nominee of a "sponsor" under any plan of condominium organization affecting the Unit;

(f) All refrigerators, freezers, ranges, dishwashers, washing machines, clothes dryers and air conditioning equipment included in this sale will be in working order at the time of Closing;

(g) If a copy is attached to this Contract, the copy of the Certificate of Occupancy covering the Unit is a true and correct copy; and

(h) Seller is not a "foreign person" as defined in para. 18. *(If inapplicable, delete and provide for compliance with Code Withholding Section, as defined in para. 18.)*

6. Closing Documents: (a) At the Closing, Seller shall deliver to Purchaser the following:

(i) Bargain and sale deed with   covenant against grantor's acts ("Deed"), complying with RPL §339-0 and containing the covenant required by LL § 13(5), conveying to Purchaser title to the Unit, together with its undivided interest in the Common Elements (as such term is defined in the Declaration and which term shall be deemed to include Seller's right, title and interest in any limited common elements attributable to or used in connection with the Unit) appurtenant thereto, free and clear of all liens and encumbrances other than Permitted Exceptions. The Deed shall be executed and acknowledged by Seller and, if requested by the Condominium, executed and acknowledged by Purchaser, in proper statutory form for recording;

(ii) If a corporation and if required pursuant to BCL § 909, Seller shall deliver to Purchaser (1) a resolution of its board of directors authorizing the delivery of the Deed and (2) a certificate executed by an officer of such corporation certifying as to the adoption of such resolution and setting forth facts demonstrating that the delivery of the Deed is in conformity with the requirements of BCL § 909. The Deed shall also contain a recital sufficient to establish compliance with such law;

(iii) A waiver of right of first refusal of the board of managers of the Condominium ("Board") if required in accordance with para. 8;

(iv) A statement by the Condominium or its managing agent that the common charges and any assessments then due and a payable the Condominium have been paid to the date of the Closing;

(v) All keys to the doors of, and mailbox for, the Unit;

(vi) Such affidavits and/or other evidence as the title company ("Title Company") from which Purchaser has ordered a title insurance report and which is authorized to do business in New York State shall reasonably require in order to omit from its title insurance policy all exceptions for judgments, bankruptcies or other returns against Seller and persons or entities whose names are the same as or are similar to Seller's name;

(vii) Official New York State Real Property Transfer Gains Tax Tentative Assessment and Return (or, if applicable, Official Statement of No Tax Due) duly completed by the New York State Department of Taxation and Finance (or, if applicable, a duly executed and acknowledged affidavit of Seller in form required pursuant to the Gains Tax Law (as hereinafter defined) claiming exemption therefrom;

(viii) New York City Real Property Transfer Tax Return, if applicable, and combined Real Property Transfer Gains Tax Affidavits, prepared, executed and acknowledged by Seller in proper form for submission;

Exhibit 6.1: *(Continued)*

(ix) Checks in payment of all applicable real property transfer taxes except a transfer tax which by law is primarily imposed on the purchaser ("Purchaser Transfer Tax") and any New York State Real Property Transfer Gains Tax ("Gains Tax") due in connection with the sale. In lieu of delivery of such checks, Seller shall have the right, upon not less than 3 business days notice to Purchaser, to cause Purchaser to deliver said checks at the Closing and to credit the amount thereof against the balance of the Purchase Price. Seller shall pay the additional transfer taxes and Gains Taxes, if any, payable after the Closing by reason of the conveyance of the Unit, which obligation shall survive the Closing;

(x) Certification that Seller is not a foreign person pursuant to para. 18. *(If inapplicable, delete and provide for compliance with Code Section, as defined in para. 18.)*; and

(xi) Affidavit that a single station smoke detecting alarm device is installed pursuant to New York Executive Law §378(5).

(b) At the Closing, Purchaser shall deliver to Seller the following:

(i) Checks in payment of (y) the balance of the Purchase Price in accordance with subpara. 3(b) and (z) any Purchaser Transfer Tax;

(ii) If required by the Declaration or By-Laws, power of attorney to the Board, prepared by Seller, in the form required by the Condominium. The power of attorney shall be executed and acknowledged by Purchaser and, after being recorded, shall be sent to the Condominium;

(iii) New York City Real Property Transfer Tax Return executed and acknowledged by Purchaser and an Affidavit in Lieu of Registration pursuant to New York Multiple Dwelling Law, each in proper form for submission, if applicable, and combined Real Property Transfer Gains Tax Affidavits; and

(iv) If required, New York State Equalization Return executed and acknowledged by Purchaser in proper form for submission.

(c) It is a condition of Purchaser's obligation to close title hereunder that:

(i) All notes or notices of violations of law or governmental orders, ordinances or requirements affecting the Unit and noted or issued by any governmental department, agency or bureau having jurisdiction which were noted or issued on or prior to the date hereof shall have been cured by Seller;

(ii) Any written notice to Seller from the Condominium (or its duly authorized representative) that the Unit is in violation of the Declaration, By-Laws or rules and regulations of the Condominium shall have been cured; and

(iii) The Condominium is a valid condominium created pursuant to RPL Art. 9-B and the Title Company will so insure.

7. Closing Adjustments: (a) The following adjustments shall be made as of 11:59 P.M. of the day before the Closing:

(i) Real estate taxes and water charges and sewer rents, if separately assessed, on the basis of the fiscal period for which assessed, except that if there is a water meter with respect to the Unit, apportionment shall be based on the last available reading, subject to adjustment after the Closing, promptly after the next reading is available; provided, however, that in the event real estate taxes have not, as of the date of Closing, been separately assessed to the Unit, real estate taxes shall be apportioned on the same basis as provided in the Declaration or By-Laws or, in the absence of such provision, based upon the Unit's percentage interest in the Common Elements;

(ii) Common charges of the Condominium; and

(iii) If fuel is separately stored with respect to the Unit only, the value of fuel stored with respect to the Unit at the price then charged by Seller's supplier (as determined by a letter or certificate to be obtained by Seller from such supplier), including any sales taxes.

(b) If at the time of Closing the Unit is affected by an assessment which is or may become payable in installments, then, for the purposes of this Contract, only the unpaid installments which are then due shall be considered due and are to be paid by Seller at the Closing. All subsequent installments at the time of Closing shall be the obligation of Purchaser.

(c) Any errors or omissions in computing closing adjustments shall be corrected. This subpara. 7(c) shall survive the Closing.

(d) If the Unit is located in the City of New York, the "customs in respect to title closings" recommended by The Real Estate Board of New York, Inc., as amended and in effect on the date of Closing, shall apply to the adjustments and other matters therein mentioned, except as otherwise provided herein.

8. Right of First Refusal: If so provided in the Declaration or By-Laws, this sale is subject to and conditioned upon the waiver of a right of first refusal to purchase the Unit held by the Condominium and exercisable by the Board. Seller agrees to give notice promptly to the Board of the contemplated sale of the Unit to Purchaser, which notice shall be given in accordance with the terms of the Declaration and By-Laws, and Purchaser agrees to provide promptly all applications, information and references reasonably requested by the Board. If the Board shall exercise such right of first refusal, Seller shall promptly refund to Purchaser the Downpayment (which term, for all purposes of this Contract, shall be deemed to include interest, if any, earned thereon) and upon the making of such refund this Contract shall be deemed cancelled and of no further force or effect and neither party shall have any further rights against, or obligations or liabilities to, the other by reason of this Contract. If the Board shall fail to exercise such right of first refusal within the time and in the manner provided for in the Declaration or By-Laws or shall declare in writing its intention not to exercise such right of first refusal (a copy of which writing shall be delivered to Purchaser promptly following receipt thereof), the parties hereto shall proceed with this sale in accordance with the provisions of this Contract.

9. Processing Fee: Seller shall, at the Closing, pay all fees and charges payable to the Condominium (and/or its managing agent) in connection with this sale, including, without limitation, any processing fee, the legal fees, if any, of the Condominium's attorney in connection with this sale and, unless otherwise agreed to by Seller and Purchaser in writing, all "flip taxes," transfer or entrance fees or similar charges, if any, payable to or for the Condominium or otherwise for the benefit of the Condominium unit owners, which arise by reason of this sale.

10. No Other Representations: Purchaser has examined and is satisfied with the Declaration, By-Laws and rules and regulations of the Condominium, or has waived the examination thereof. Purchaser has inspected the Unit, its fixtures, appliances and equipment and the personal property, if any, included in this sale, as well as the Common Elements of the Condominium, and knows the condition thereof and, subject to subpara. 5(f), agrees to accept the same "as is," i.e., in the condition they are in on the date hereof, subject to normal use, wear and tear between the date hereof and the Closing. Purchaser has examined or waived examination of the last audited financial statements of the Condominium, and has considered or waived consideration of all other matters pertaining to this Contract and to the purchase to be made hereunder, and does not rely on any representations made by any broker or by Seller or anyone acting or purporting to act on behalf of Seller as to any matters which might influence or affect the decision to execute this Contract or to buy the Unit, or said personal property, except those representations and warranties which are specifically set forth in this Contract.

11. Possession: Seller shall, prior to the Closing, remove from the Unit all furniture, furnishings and other personal property not included in this sale, shall repair any damage caused by such removal, and shall deliver exclusive possession of the Unit at the Closing, vacant, broom-clean and free of tenancies or other rights of use or possession.

12. Access: Seller shall permit Purchaser and its architect, decorator or other authorized persons to have the right of access to the Unit between the date hereof and the Closing for the purpose of inspecting the same and taking measurements, at reasonable times and upon reasonable prior notice to Seller (by telephone or otherwise). Further, Purchaser shall have the right to inspect the Unit at a reasonable time during the 24-hour period immediately preceding the Closing.

13. Defaults and Remedies: (a) If Purchaser defaults hereunder, Seller's sole remedy shall be to retain the Downpayment as liquidated damages, it being agreed that Seller's damages in case of Purchaser's default might be impossible to ascertain and that the Downpayment constitutes a fair and reasonable amount of damages under the circumstances and is not a penalty.

(b) If Seller defaults hereunder, Purchaser shall have such remedies as Purchaser shall be entitled to at law or in equity, including, but not limited to, specific performance.

14. Notices: Any notice, request or other communication ("Notice") given or made hereunder (except for the notice required by para. 12), shall be in writing and either (a) sent by any of the parties hereto or their respective attorneys, by registered or certified mail, return receipt requested, postage prepaid, or (b) delivered in person or by overnight courier, with receipt acknowledged, to the address given at the beginning of this Contract for the party to whom the Notice is to be given, or to such other address for such party as said party shall hereafter designate by Notice given to the other party pursuant to this para. 14. Each Notice mailed shall be deemed given on the third business day following the date of mailing the same and each Notice delivered in person or by overnight courier shall be deemed given when delivered.

15. Purchaser's Lien: The Downpayment and all other sums paid on account of this Contract and the reasonable expenses of the examination of title to, and departmental violation searches in respect of, the Unit are hereby made a lien upon the Unit, but such lien shall not continue after default by Purchaser hereunder.

16. Downpayment in Escrow: (a) Seller's attorney ("Escrowee") shall hold the Downpayment for Seller's account in escrow in a segregated bank account at the depository identified at the end of this Contract until Closing or sooner termination of this Contract and shall pay over or apply the Downpayment in accordance with the terms of this para. 16. Escrowee shall *(not)* *(Delete if inapplicable)* hold the Downpayment in an interest-bearing account for the benefit of the parties. If interest is held for the benefit of the parties, it shall be paid to the party entitled to the Down-payment and the party receiving the interest shall pay any income taxes thereon. If interest is not held for the benefit of the parties, the Down-payment shall be placed in an IOLA account or as otherwise permitted or required by law. The Social Security or Federal Identification numbers of the parties shall be furnished to Escrowee upon request. At closing, the Downpayment shall be paid by Escrowee to Seller. If for any reason Closing does not occur and either party gives Notice (as defined in paragraph 14) to Escrowee demanding payment of the Downpayment, Escrowee shall give prompt Notice to the other party of such demand. If Escrowee does not receive Notice of objection from such other party to the proposed payment within 10 business days after the giving of such Notice, Escrowee is hereby authorized and directed to make such payment. If Escrowee does receive such Notice of objection within such 10 day period or if for any other reason Escrowee in good faith shall elect not to make such payment, Escrowee shall continue to hold such amount until otherwise directed by Notice from the parties to this Contract or a final, nonappealable judgment, order or decree of a court. However, Escrowee shall have the right at any time to deposit the Downpayment with the clerk of a court in the county in which the Unit is located and shall give Notice of such deposit to Seller and Purchaser. Upon such deposit or other disbursement in accordance with the terms of this para. 16, Escrowee shall be relieved and discharged of all further obligations and responsibilities hereunder.

(b) The parties acknowledge that, although Escrowee is holding the Downpayment for Seller's account, for all other purposes Escrowee is

Exhibit 6.1: *(Continued)*

22. Broker: Seller and Purchaser represent and warrant to each other that the only real estate broker with whom they have dealt in connection with this Contract and the transaction set forth herein is

and that they know of no other real estate broker who has claimed or may have the right to claim a commission in connection with this transaction. The commission of such real estate broker shall be paid by Seller pursuant to separate agreement. If no real estate broker is specified above, the parties acknowledge that this Contract was brought about by direct negotiation between Seller and Purchaser and each represents to the other that it knows of no real estate broker entitled to a commission in connection with this transaction. Seller and Purchaser shall indemnify and defend each other against any costs, claims or expenses (including reasonable attorneys' fees) arising out of the breach on their respective parts of any representation, warranty or agreement contained in this para. 22. The provisions of this para. 22 shall survive the Closing or, if the Closing does not occur, the termination of this Contract.

23. Mortgage Contingency: *(Delete if inapplicable)* (a) The obligations of Purchaser hereunder are conditioned upon issuance on or before (the "Commitment Date") of a written commitment from any Institutional Lender pursuant to which such Institutional Lender agrees to make a loan, other than a VA, FHA or other governmentally insured loan to Purchaser, at Purchaser's sole cost and expense, of $

or such lesser sum as Purchaser shall be willing to accept, at the prevailing fixed rate of interest not to exceed or initial adjustment rate of interest not to exceed for a term of at least years and on other customary commitment terms, whether or not conditioned upon any factors other than an appraisal satisfactory to the Institutional Lender, secured by a first mortgage on the Unit together with its undivided interest in the Common Elements. Purchaser shall (i) make prompt application to an Institutional Lender for such mortgage loan, (ii) furnish accurate and complete information on Purchaser and members of Purchaser's family, as required, (iii) pay all fees, points and charges required in connection with such application and loan, (iv) pursue such application with diligence, (v) cooperate in good faith with such Institutional Lender to the end of securing such first mortgage loan and (vi) promptly give Notice to Seller of the name and address of each Institutional Lender to which Purchaser has made such application. Purchaser shall comply with all requirements of such commitment (or of any commitment accepted by Purchaser) and shall furnish Seller with a copy thereof promptly after receipt thereof. If such commitment is not issued on or before the Commitment Date, then, unless Purchaser has accepted a commitment that does not comply with the requirements set forth above, Purchaser may cancel this Contract by giving Notice to Seller within 5 business days after the Commitment Date, in which case this Contract shall be deemed cancelled and thereafter neither party shall have any further rights against, or obligations or liabilities to, the other by reason of this Contract except that the Downpayment shall be promptly refunded to Purchaser and except as set forth in para. 22. If Purchaser fails to give Notice of cancellation or if Purchaser shall accept a commitment that does not comply with the terms set forth above, then Purchaser shall be deemed to have waived Purchaser's right to cancel this Contract and to

receive a refund of the Downpayment by reason of the contingency contained in this para. 23.

(b) For purposes of this Contract, an "Institutional Lender" is any bank, savings bank, private banker, trust company, savings and loan association and credit union or similar banking institution whether organized under the laws of this state, the United States or any other state; foreign banking corporation licensed by the Superintendent of Banks of New York or the Comptroller of the Currency to transact business in New York State; insurance company duly organized or licensed to do business in New York State; mortgage banker licensed pursuant to Article 12-D of the Banking Law; and any instrumentality created by the United States or any state with the power to make mortgage loans.

(Delete if inapplicable) (c) Purchaser and Seller agree that the submission of an application to a mortgage broker registered pursuant to Article 12-D of the New York Banking Law ("Mortgage Broker") shall constitute full compliance with the terms and conditions set forth in para. 23(a)(i) of this Contract, and that Purchaser's cooperation in good faith with such Mortgage Broker to obtain a commitment from an Institutional Lender (together with Purchaser's cooperation in good faith with any Institutional Lender to which Purchaser's application has been submitted by such Mortgage Broker), and the prompt giving of Notice by Purchaser to Seller of the name and address of each Mortgage Broker to which Purchaser has submitted such an application shall constitute full compliance with the terms and conditions set forth in para. 23(a)(v) and (vi) of this Contract.

24. Gender, Etc.: As used in this Contract, the neuter includes the masculine and feminine, the singular includes the plural and the plural includes the singular, as the context may require.

25. Entire Contract: All prior understandings and agreements between Seller and Purchaser are merged in this Contract and this Contract supersedes any and all understandings and agreements between the parties and constitutes the entire agreement between them with respect to the subject matter hereof.

26. Captions: The captions in this Contract are for convenience and reference only and in no way define, limit or describe the scope of this Contract and shall not be considered in the interpretation of this Contract or any provision hereof.

27. No Assignment by Purchaser: Purchaser may not assign this Contract or any of Purchaser's rights hereunder.

28. Successors and Assigns: Subject to the provisions of para. 27, the provisions of this Contract shall bind and inure to the benefit of both Purchaser and Seller and their respective distributees, executors, administrators, heirs, legal representatives, successors and permitted assigns.

29. No Oral Changes: This Contract cannot be changed or terminated orally. Any changes or additional provisions must be set forth in a rider attached hereto or in a separate written agreement signed by both parties to this Contract.

30. Contract Not Binding Until Signed: This Contract shall not be binding or effective until properly executed and delivered by Seller and Purchaser.·

In Witness Whereof, the parties hereto have duly executed this Contract on the day and year first above written.

Seller	(Soc. Sec. No.)	Purchaser	(Soc. Sec. No.)

Seller	(Soc. Sec. No.)	Purchaser	(Soc. Sec. No.)

Agreed to as to para. 16: _____
Escrowee

Escrow Depository: _____

SCHEDULE A - Permitted Exceptions

1. Zoning laws and regulations and landmark, historic or wetlands designation which are not violated by the Unit and which are not violated by the Common Elements to the extent that access to or use of the Unit would be materially and adversely affected.

2. Consents for the erection of any structure or structures on, under or above any street or streets on which the Building may abut.

3. The terms, burdens, covenants, restrictions, conditions, easements and rules and regulations set forth in the Declaration, By-Laws and rules and regulations of the Condominium, the Power of Attorney from Purchaser to the board of managers of the Condominium and the floor plans of the Condominium, all as may be amended from time to time.

4. Rights of utility companies to lay, maintain, install and repair pipes, lines, poles, conduits, cable boxes and related equipment on, over and under the Building and Common Elements, provided that none of such rights imposes any monetary obligation on the owner of the Unit or materially interferes with the use of or access to the Unit.

5. Encroachments of stoops, areas, cellar steps, trim, cornices, lintels, window sills, awnings, canopies, ledges, fences, hedges, coping and retaining walls projecting from the Building over any street or highway or over any adjoining property and encroachments of similar elements projecting from adjoining property over the Common Elements.

6. Any state of facts which an accurate survey or personal inspection of the Building, Common Elements or Unit would disclose, provided that

The survey referred to in No. 6 above was prepared by
dated   and last revised

such facts do not prevent the use of the Unit for dwelling purposes. For the purposes of this Contract, none of the facts shown on the survey, if any, identified below, shall be deemed to prevent the use of the Unit for dwelling purposes, and Purchaser shall accept title subject thereto.

7. The lien of any unpaid common charge, real estate tax, water charge, sewer rent or vault charge, provided the same are paid or apportioned at the Closing as herein provided.

8. The lien of any unpaid assessments to the extent of installments thereof payable after the Closing.

9. Liens, encumbrances and title conditions affecting the Common Elements which do not materially and adversely affect the right of the Unit owner to use and enjoy the Common Elements,

10. Notes or notices of violations of law or governmental orders, ordinances or requirements (a) affecting the Unit and noted or issued subsequent to the date of this Contract by any governmental department, agency or bureau having jurisdiction and (b) any such notes or notices affecting only the Common Elements which were noted or issued prior to or on the date of this Contract or at any time hereafter.

11. Any other matters or encumbrances subject to which Purchaser is required to accept title to the Unit pursuant to this Contract.

Exhibit 6.1: *(Continued)*

acting solely as a stakeholder at their request and for their convenience and that Escrowee shall not be liable to either party for any act or omission on its part unless taken or suffered in bad faith or in willful disregard of this Contract or involving gross negligence on the part of Escrowee. Seller and Purchaser jointly and severally agree to defend, indemnify and hold Escrowee harmless from and against all costs, claims and expenses (including reasonable attorneys' fees) incurred in connection with the performance of Escrowee's duties hereunder, except with respect to actions or omissions taken or suffered by Escrowee in bad faith or in willful disregard of this Contract or involving gross negligence on the part of Escrowee.

(c) Escrowee may act or refrain from acting in respect of any matter referred to herein in full reliance upon and with the advice of counsel which may be selected by it (including any member of its firm) and shall be fully protected in so acting or refraining from action upon the advice of such counsel.

(d) Escrowee acknowledges receipt of the Downpayment by check subject to collection and Escrowee's agreement to the provisions of this para. 16 by signing in the place indicated in this Contract.

(e) Escrowee or any member of its firm shall be permitted to act as counsel for Seller in any dispute as to the disbursement of the Downpayment or any other dispute between the parties whether or not Escrowee is in possession of the Downpayment and continues to act as Escrowee.

17. New York State Gains Tax: (a) Seller and Purchaser agree to comply in a timely manner with the requirements of article 31-B of the Tax Law and the regulations applicable thereto, as the same from time to time may be amended (collectively, the "Gains Tax Law"). Purchaser agrees to deliver to Seller a duly executed and acknowledged Transferee Questionnaire simultaneously with the execution of this Contract or within 5 business days after subsequent written request from Seller or Seller's attorney. At the Closing, Seller shall deliver (i) an Official Statement of No Tax Due or (ii) an Official Tentative Assessment and Return accompanied by a certified or official bank check drawn on any banking institution described in subpara. 3(b), payable to the order of the State Tax Commission, in the amount of the tax shown to be due thereon, or (iii) if applicable, a duly executed and acknowledged affidavit in form permitted under the Gains Tax Law claiming exemption therefrom.

(b) Seller agrees (i) to pay promptly any tax due under the Gains Tax Law and any interest and penalties thereon which may be assessed or due after the Closing, (ii) to indemnify and save Purchaser harmless from and against any of the foregoing and any cost, claim and expense (including reasonable attorneys' fees) incurred by Purchaser by reason of the non-payment thereof, and (iii) to make any other payments and execute, acknowledge and deliver such further documents as may be necessary to comply with the Gains Tax Law.

(c) The obligations under this para. 17 shall survive the Closing.

18. FIRPTA: Seller represents and warrants to Purchaser that Seller is not a "foreign person" as defined in IRC § 1445, as amended, and the regulations issued thereunder ("Code Withholding Section"). At the Closing Seller shall deliver to Purchaser a certification stating that Seller is not a foreign person in the form then required by the Code Withholding Section. In the event Seller fails to deliver the aforesaid certification or in the event that Purchaser is not entitled under the Code Withholding Section to rely on such certification, Purchaser shall deduct and withhold from the Purchase Price a sum equal to 10% thereof and shall at Closing remit the withheld amount with the required forms to the Internal Revenue Service.

19. Title Report; Acceptable Title: (a) Purchaser shall,promptly after the date hereof, or after receipt of the mortgage commitment letter, if applicable, order a title insurance report from the Title Company. Promptly after receipt of the title report and thereafter of any continuations thereof and supplements thereto, Purchaser shall forward a copy of each such report, continuation or supplement to the attorney for Seller. Purchaser shall further notify Seller's attorney of any other objections to title not reflected in such title report of which Purchaser becomes aware following the delivery of such report, reasonably promptly after becoming aware of such objections.

(b) Any unpaid taxes, assessments, water charges and sewer rents, together with the interest and penalties thereon to a date not less than two days following the date of Closing, and any other liens and encumbrances which Seller is obligated to pay and discharge or which are against corporations, estates or other persons in the chain of title, together with the cost of recording or filing any instruments necessary to discharge such liens and encumbrances of record, may be paid out of the proceeds of the monies payable at the Closing if Seller delivers to Purchaser at the Closing official bills for such taxes, assessments, water charges, sewer rents, interest and penalties and instruments in recordable form sufficient to discharge any other liens and encumbrances of record. Upon request made not less than 3 business days before the Closing, Purchaser shall provide at the Closing separate checks for the foregoing payable to the order of the holder of any such lien, charge or encumbrance and otherwise complying with subpara. 3(b). If the Title Company is willing to insure Purchaser that such charges, liens and encumbrances will not be collected out of or enforced against the Unit and is willing to insure the lien of Purchaser's Institutional Lender (as hereinafter defined) free and clear of any such charges, liens and encumbrances, then Seller shall have the right in lieu of payment and discharge to deposit with the Title Company such funds or to give such assurances or to pay such special or additional premiums as the Title Company may require in order to so insure. In such case the charges, liens and encumbrances with respect to which the Title Company has agreed so to insure shall not be considered objections to title.

(c) Seller shall convey and Purchaser shall accept fee simple title to the Unit in accordance with the terms of this Contract, subject only to: (a) the Permitted Exceptions and (b) such other matters as (i) the Title Company or any other title insurer licensed to do business by the State of New York shall be willing, without special or additional premium, to omit as exceptions to coverage or to except with insurance against collection out of or

enforcement against the Unit and (ii) shall be accepted by any lender which has committed in writing to provide mortgage financing to Purchaser for the purchase of the Unit ("Purchaser's Institutional Lender"), except that if such acceptance by Purchaser's Institutional Lender is unreasonably withheld or delayed, such acceptance shall be deemed to have been given.

(d) Notwithstanding any contrary provisions in this Contract, express or implied, or any contrary rule of law or custom, if Seller shall be unable to convey the Unit in accordance with this Contract (provided that Seller shall release, discharge or otherwise cure at or prior to Closing any matter created by Seller after the date hereof and any existing mortgage, unless this sale is subject to it) and if Purchaser elects not to complete this transaction without abatement of the Purchase Price, the sole obligation and liability of Seller shall be to refund the Downpayment to Purchaser, together with the reasonable cost of the examination of title to, and departmental violation searches in respect of, the Unit, and upon the making of such refund and payment, this Contract shall be deemed cancelled and of no further force or effect and neither party shall have any further rights against, or obligations or liabilities to, the other by reason of this Contract. However, nothing contained in this subpara. 19(d) shall be construed to relieve Seller from liability due to a willful default.

20. Risk of Loss; Casualty: (a) The risk of loss or damage to the Unit or the personal property included in this sale, by fire or other casualty, until the earlier of the Closing or possession of the Unit by Purchaser, is assumed by Seller, but without any obligation of Seller to repair or replace any such loss or damage unless Seller elects to do so as hereinafter provided. Seller shall notify Purchaser of the occurrence of any such loss or damage to the Unit or the personal property included in this sale within 10 days after such occurrence or by the date of Closing, whichever first occurs, and by such notice shall state whether or not Seller elects to repair or restore the Unit and/or the personal property, as the case may be. If Seller elects to make such repairs and restorations, Seller's notice shall set forth an adjourned date for the Closing, which shall be not more than 60 days after the date of the giving of Seller's notice. If Seller either does not elect to do so or, having elected to make such repairs and restorations, fails to complete the same on or before said adjourned date for the Closing, Purchaser shall have the following options:

(i) To declare this Contract cancelled and of no further force or effect and receive a refund of the Downpayment in which event neither party shall thereafter have any further rights against, or obligations or liabilities to, the other by reason of this Contract; or

(ii) To complete the purchase in accordance with this Contract without reduction in the Purchase Price, except as provided in the next sentence. If Seller carries hazard insurance covering such loss or damage, Seller shall turn over to Purchaser at the Closing the net proceeds actually collected by Seller under the provisions of such hazard insurance policies to the extent that they are attributable to loss of or damage to any property included in this sale, less any sums theretofore expended by Seller in repairing or replacing such loss or damage or in collecting such proceeds; and Seller shall assign (without recourse to Seller) Seller's right to receive any additional insurance proceeds which are attributable to the loss of or damage to any property included in this sale.

(b) If Seller does not elect to make such repairs and restorations, Purchaser may exercise the resulting option under (i) or (ii) of (a) above only by notice given to Seller within 10 days after receipt of Seller's notice. If Seller elects to make such repairs and restorations and fails to complete the same on or before the adjourned closing date, Purchaser may exercise either of the resulting options within 10 days after the adjourned closing date.

(c) In the event of any loss of or damage to the Common Elements which materially and adversely affects access to or use of the Unit, arising after the date of this Contract but prior to the Closing, Seller shall notify Purchaser of the occurrence thereof within 10 days after such occurrence or by the date of Closing, whichever occurs first, in which event Purchaser shall have the following options:

(i) To complete the purchase in accordance with this Contract without reduction in the Purchase Price; or

(ii) To adjourn the Closing until the first to occur of (1) completion of the repair and restoration of the loss or damage to the point that there is no longer a materially adverse effect on the access to or use of the Unit or (2) the 60th day after the date of the giving of Seller's aforesaid notice. In the event Purchaser elects to adjourn the Closing as aforesaid and such loss or damage is not so repaired and restored within 60 days after the date of the giving of Seller's aforesaid notice, then Purchaser shall have the right either to (x) complete the purchase in accordance with this Contract without reduction in the Purchase Price or (y) declare this Contract cancelled and of no further force or effect and receive a refund of the Downpayment, in which latter event neither party shall thereafter have any further rights against, or obligations or liabilities to, the other by reason of this Contract.

(d) In the event of any loss of or damage to the Common Elements which does not materially and adversely affect access to or use of the Unit, Purchaser shall accept title to the Unit in accordance with this Contract without abatement of the Purchase Price.

21. Internal Revenue Service Reporting Requirement: Each party shall execute, acknowledge and deliver to the other party such instruments, and take such other actions, as such other party may reasonably request in order to comply with IRC § 6045(e), as amended, or any successor provision or any regulations promulgated pursuant thereto, insofar as the same requires reporting of information in respect of real estate transactions. The provisions of this para. 21 shall survive the Closing. The parties designate

as the attorney responsible for reporting this information as required by law.

Exhibit 6.2: Sales Contract for a Cooperative

Blumbergs Law Products   **123**-Contract of sale cooperative apartment, 7-01

Prepared by The Committee on Condominiums and Cooperatives of the Real Property Section of the New York State Bar Association

BlumbergExcelsior Inc., Publisher NYC 10013
www.blumberg.com

CONSULT YOUR LAWYER BEFORE SIGNING THIS AGREEMENT

Contract of Sale – Cooperative Apartment

This Contract is made as of   between the **"Seller"** and the **"Purchaser"** identified below.

1 Certain Definitions and Information
1.1 The "Parties" are:
1.1.1 "Seller":

Prior names used by Seller:
Address:

S.S. No.:
1.1.2 "Purchaser":

Address:

S.S. No.:
1.2 The "Attorneys" are *(name, address and telephone, fax):*
    1.2.1 "Seller's Attorney"

    1.2.2 "Purchaser's Attorney"

1.3 The "Escrowee" is the [*Seller's*] [*Purchaser's*] Attorney.

1.4 The Managing Agent is *(name, address and telephone, fax):*

1.5 The real estate "Broker(s)" (see ¶12) is/are:

Company Name:

1.6 The name of the cooperative housing corporation ("Corporation") is:

1.7 The "Unit" number is:

1.8 The Unit is located in "Premises" known as:

1.9 The "Shares" are the   shares of the Corporation allocated to the Unit.

1.10 The "Lease" is the Corporation's proprietary lease or occupancy agreement for the Unit, given by the Corporation which expires on   .

1.11 "Personalty" is the following personal property, to the extent existing in the Unit on the date hereof: the refrigerators, freezers, ranges, ovens, built-in microwave ovens, dishwashers, garbage disposal units, cabinets and counters, lighting fixtures, chandeliers, wall-to-wall carpeting, plumbing and heating fixtures, central air-conditioning and/or window or sleeve units, washing machines, dryers, screens and storm windows, window treatments, switch plates, door hardware, mirrors, built-ins not excluded in ¶ 1.12 and

1.12 Specifically excluded from this sale is all personal property not included in ¶ 1.11 and:

1.13 The sale [*does*] [*does not*] include Seller's interest in [*Storage*]/[*Servant's Rm*]/[*Parking Space*] ("Included Interests")
1.14 The "Closing" is the transfer of ownership of the Shares and Lease.
1.15 The date scheduled for Closing is
("Scheduled Closing Date") at   .M (See ¶¶ 9 and 10)
1.16 The "Purchase Price" is: $
    1.16.1 The "Contract Deposit" is: $
    1.16.2 The "Balance" of the Purchase Price due at Closing is:
$ (See ¶ 2.2.2)
1.17 The monthly "Maintenance" charge is
$ (See ¶ 4)
1.18 The "Assessment", if any, payable to the Corporation, at the date of this Contract is $, payable as follows:

1.19 [*Seller*] [*Purchaser*] shall pay the Corporation's flip tax, transfer fee (apart from the transfer agent fee) and/or waiver of option fee ("Flip Tax"), if any.
1.20 Financing Options *(Delete **two** of the following ¶¶ 1.20.1, 1.20.2 or 1.20.3)*

1.20.1 Purchaser may apply for financing in connection with this sale and Purchaser's obligation to purchase under this Contract is contingent upon issuance of a Loan Commitment Letter by the Loan Commitment Date (¶ 18.1.2).

1.20.2 Purchaser may apply for financing in connection with this sale but Purchaser's obligation to purchase under this Contract is not contingent upon issuance of a Loan Commitment Letter.

1.20.3 Purchaser shall not apply for financing in connection with this sale.
1.21 If ¶ 1.20.1 or 1.20.2 applies, the "Financing Terms" for ¶ 18 are:
a loan of $ for a term of   years or
such lesser amount or shorter term as applied for or acceptable to

Exhibit 6.2: *(Continued)*

Purchaser; and the "Loan Commitment Date" for ¶ 18 is   calendar days after the Delivery Date.

1.22 The "Delivery Date" of this Contract is the date on which a fully
executed counterpart of this Contract is deemed given to and
received by Purchaser or Purchaser's Attorney as provided in ¶ 17.3.

1.23 All "Proposed Occupants" of the Unit are:

1.23.1 persons and relationship to Purchaser:

1.23.2 pets:

1.24 The Contract Deposit shall be held in [*a non-*] [*an*] IOLA
escrow account. If the account is a non-IOLA account then interest
shall be paid to the Party entitled to the Contract Deposit. The Party
receiving the interest shall pay any income taxes thereon. The
escrow account shall be a segregated bank account at

Depository:

Address:

(See ¶ 27)

1.25 This Contract is [*not*] continued on attached rider(s).

2 Agreement to Sell and Purchase; Purchase Price; Escrow

2.1 Seller agrees to sell to Purchaser, and Purchaser agrees to pur-
chase from Seller, the Seller's Shares, Lease, Personalty and any
Included Interests and all other items included in this sale, for the
Purchase Price and upon the terms and conditions set forth in this
Contract.

2.2   The Purchase Price is payable to Seller by Purchaser as follows:

2.2.1 the Contract Deposit at the time of signing this Contract,
by Purchaser's good check to the order of Escrowee; and

2.2.2 the Balance at Closing, only by cashier's or official bank check
or certified check of Purchaser payable to the direct order of Seller.
The check(s) shall be drawn on and payable by a branch of a
commercial or savings bank, savings and loan association or trust
company located in the same City or County as the Unit. Seller may
direct, on reasonable Notice (defined in ¶ 17) prior to Closing, that
all or a portion of the Balance shall be made payable to persons other
than Seller (see ¶ 17.7).

3 Personalty

3.1 Subject to any rights of the Corporation or any holder of a mortgage to which the Lease is subordinate, this sale includes all of the
Seller's interest, if any, in the Personalty and the Included Interests.

3.2 No consideration is being paid for the Personalty or for the
Included Interests; nothing shall be sold to Purchaser if the Closing
does not occur.

3.3 Prior to Closing, Seller will remove from the Unit all the furniture, furnishings and other property not included in this sale, and
repair any damage caused by such removal.

4 Representations and Covenants

4.1 Subject to any matter affecting title to the Premises (as to which
Seller makes no representations or covenants), Seller represents and
covenants that:

4.1.1 Seller is, and shall at Closing be, the sole owner of the
Shares, Lease, Personalty and Included Interests, with the full right,
power and authority to sell and assign them. Seller shall make timely provision to satisfy existing security interest(s) in the Shares and
Lease and have the same delivered at Closing (See ¶ 10.1);

4.1.2 the Shares were duly issued, fully paid for and are non-assessable;

4.1.3 the Lease is, and will at Closing be, in full force and effect
and no notice of default under the Lease is now or will at Closing be
in effect;

4.1.4 the Maintenance and Assessments payable as of the date
hereof are as specified in ¶ 1.17 and 1.18;

4.1.5 as of this date, Seller neither has actual knowledge nor has
received any written notice of any increase in Maintenance or any
Assessment which has been adopted by the Board of Directors of
the Corporation and is not reflected in the amounts set forth in
¶¶ 1.17 and 1.18;

4.1.6 Seller has not made any material alterations or additions to
the Unit without any required consent of the Corporation or, to
Seller's actual knowledge, without compliance with all applicable

law. This provision shall not survive Closing.

4.1.7 Seller has not entered into, shall not enter into, and has no
actual knowledge of any agreement (other than the Lease) affecting
title to the Unit or its use and/or occupancy after Closing, or which
would be binding on or adversely affect Purchaser after Closing (e.g.
a sublease or alteration agreement);

4.1.8 Seller has been known by no other name for the past
10 years except as set forth in ¶ 1.1.1.

4.1.9 at Closing in accordance with ¶ 15.2:

4.1.9.1 there shall be no judgments outstanding against
Seller which have not been bonded against collection out of the Unit
("Judgments");

4.1.9.2 the Shares, Lease, Personalty and any Included Interests
shall be free and clear of liens (other than the Corporation's general
lien on the Shares for which no monies shall be owed), encumbrances and adverse interests ("Liens");

4.1.9.3 all sums due to the Corporation shall be fully paid
by Seller to the end of the payment period immediately preceding the
date of Closing;

4.1.9.4 Seller shall not be indebted for labor or material
which might give rise to the filing of a notice of mechanic's lien
against the Unit or the Premises; and

4.1.9.5 no violations shall be of record which the owner of
the Shares and Lease would be obligated to remedy under the Lease.

4.2 Purchaser represents and covenants that:

4.2.1 Purchaser is acquiring the Shares and Lease for
residential occupancy of the Unit solely by the Proposed Occupants
identified in ¶ 1.23

4.2.2 Purchaser is not, and within the past 7 years has not been,
the subject of a bankruptcy proceeding;

4.2.3 if ¶ 1.20.3 applies, Purchaser shall not apply for financing
in connection with this purchase.

4.2.4 Each individual comprising Purchaser is over the age of
18 and is purchasing for Purchaser's own account (beneficial and of
record);

4.2.5 Purchaser shall not make any representations to the
Corporation contrary to the foregoing and shall provide all documents in support thereof required by the Corporation in connection
with Purchaser's application for approval of this transaction; and

4.2.6 there are not now and shall not be at Closing any unpaid
tax liens or monetary judgments against Purchaser.

4.3 Each Party covenants that its representations and covenants
contained in ¶ 4 shall be true and complete at Closing and, except
for ¶ 4.1.6, shall survive Closing but any action based thereon must
be instituted within one year after Closing.

5 Corporate Documents

Purchaser has examined and is satisfied with, or (except as to any
matter represented in this Contract by Seller) accepts and assumes
the risk of not having examined, the Lease, the Corporation's
Certificate of Incorporation, By-laws, House Rules, minutes of
shareholders' and directors' meetings, most recent audited financial
statement and most recent statement of tax deductions available to
the Corporation's shareholders under Internal Revenue Code ("IRC")
§216 (or any successor statute).

6 Required Approval and References

6.1 This sale is subject to the unconditional consent of the
Corporation.

6.2 Purchaser shall in good faith:

6.2.1 submit to the Corporation or the Managing Agent an
application with respect to this sale on the form required by the
Corporation, containing such data and together with such documents
as the Corporation requires, and pay the applicable fees and charges
that the Corporation imposes upon Purchaser. All of the foregoing
shall be submitted within 10 business days after the Delivery Date,
or, if ¶ 1.20.1 or 1.20.2 applies and the Loan Commitment Letter is
required by the Corporation, within 3 business days after the earlier
of (i) the Loan Commitment Date (defined in ¶ 1.21) or (ii) the date
of receipt of the Loan Commitment Letter (defined in ¶ 18.1.2);

6.2.2 attend (and cause any Proposed Occupant to attend) one
or more personal interviews, as requested by the Corporation; and

6.2.3 promptly submit to the Corporation such further
references, data and documents reasonably requested by the
Corporation.

Exhibit 6.2: *(Continued)*

6.3 Either Party, after learning of the Corporation's decision, shall promptly advise the other Party thereof. If the Corporation has not made a decision on or before the Scheduled Closing Date, the Closing shall be adjourned for 30 business days for the purpose of obtaining such consent. If such consent is not given by such adjourned date, either Party may cancel this Contract by Notice, provided that the Corporation's consent is not issued before such Notice of cancellation is given. If such consent is refused at any time, either Party may cancel this Contract by Notice. In the event of cancellation pursuant to this ¶ 6.3, the Escrowee shall refund the Contract Deposit to Purchaser.

6.4 If such consent is refused, or not given, due to Purchaser's bad faith conduct, Purchaser shall be in default and ¶ 13.1 shall govern.

7 Condition of Unit and Personalty; Possession

7.1 Seller makes no representation as to the physical condition or state of repair of the Unit, the Personalty, the Included Interests or the Premises. Purchaser has inspected or waived inspection of the Unit, the Personalty and the Included Interests and shall take the same "as is", as of the date of this Contract, except for reasonable wear and tear. However, at the time of Closing, the appliances shall be in working order and required smoke detector(s) shall be installed and operable.

7.2 At Closing, Seller shall deliver possession of the Unit, Personalty and Included Interests in the condition required by ¶ 7.1, broom-clean, vacant and free of all occupants and rights of possession.

8 Risk of Loss

8.1 The provisions of General Obligations Law Section 5-1311, as modified herein, shall apply to this transaction as if it were a sale of realty. For purposes of this paragraph, the term "Unit" includes built-in Personalty.

8.2 Destruction shall be deemed "material" under GOL 5-1311, if the reasonably estimated cost to restore the Unit shall exceed 5% of the Purchase Price.

8.3 In the event of any destruction of the Unit or the Premises, when neither legal title nor the possession of the Unit has been transferred to Purchaser, Seller shall give Notice of the loss to Purchaser ("Loss Notice") by the earlier of the date of Closing or 7 business days after the date of the loss.

8.4 If there is material destruction of the Unit without fault of Purchaser, this Contract shall be deemed canceled in accordance with ¶ 16.3, unless Purchaser elects by Notice to Seller to complete the purchase with an abatement of the Purchase Price; or

8.5 Whether or not there is any destruction of the Unit, if, without fault of Purchaser, more than 10% of the units in the Premises are rendered uninhabitable, or reasonable access to the Unit is not available, then Purchaser shall have the right to cancel this Contract in accordance with ¶ 16.3 for any destruction.

8.6 Purchaser's Notice pursuant to ¶ 8.4 or ¶ 8.5 shall be given within 7 business days following the giving of the Loss Notice except that if Seller does not give a Loss Notice, Purchaser's Notice may be given at any time at or prior to Closing

8.7 In the event of any destruction of the Unit, Purchaser shall not be entitled to an abatement of the Purchase Price (i) that exceeds the reasonably estimated cost of repair and restoration or (ii) for any loss that the Corporation is obliged to repair or restore; but Seller shall assign to Purchaser, without recourse, Seller's claim, if any, against the Corporation with respect to such loss.

9 Closing Location

The Closing shall be held at the location designated by the Corporation or, if no such designation is made, at the office of Seller's Attorney.

10 Closing

10.1 At Closing, Seller shall deliver or cause to be delivered:

10.1.1 Seller's certificate for the Shares duly endorsed for transfer to Purchaser or accompanied by a separate duly executed stock power to Purchaser, and in either case, with any guarantee of Seller's signature required by the Corporation;

10.1.2 Seller's counterpart original of the Lease, all assignments and assumptions in the chain of title and a duly executed assignment thereof to Purchaser in the form required by the Corporation;

10.1.3 FIRPTA documents required by ¶ 25;

10.1.4 keys to the Unit, building entrance(s) and, if applicable, garage, mailbox, storage unit and any locks in the Unit;

10.1.5 if requested, an assignment to Purchaser of Seller's interest in the Personalty and Included Interests;

10.1.6 any documents and payments to comply with ¶ 15.2

10.1.7 If Seller is unable to deliver the documents required in ¶ 10.1.1 or 10.1.2 then Seller shall deliver or cause to be delivered all documents and payments required by the Corporation for the issuance of a new certificate for the Shares or a new Lease.

10.2 At Closing, Purchaser shall:

10.2.1 pay the Balance in accordance with ¶ 2.2.2;

10.2.2 execute and deliver to Seller and the Corporation an agreement assuming the Lease, in the form required by the Corporation; and

10.2.3 if requested by the Corporation, execute and deliver counterparts of a new lease substantially the same as the Lease, for the balance of the Lease term, in which case the Lease shall be canceled and surrendered to the Corporation together with Seller's assignment thereof to Purchaser.

10.3 At Closing, the Parties shall complete and execute all documents necessary:

10.3.1 for Internal Revenue Service ("IRS") form 1099-S or other similar requirements;

10.3.2 to comply with smoke detector requirements and any applicable transfer tax filings; and

10.3.3 to transfer Seller's interest, if any, in and to the Personalty and Included Interests.

10.4 Purchaser shall not be obligated to close unless, at Closing, the Corporation delivers:

10.4.1 to Purchaser a new certificate for the Shares in the name, of Purchaser; and

10.4.2 a written statement by an officer or authorized agent of the Corporation consenting to the transfer of the Shares and Lease to Purchaser and setting forth the amounts of and payment status of all sums owed by Seller to the Corporation, including Maintenance and any Assessments, and the dates to which each has been paid.

11 Closing Fees, Taxes and Apportionments

11.1 At or prior to Closing,

11.1.1 Seller shall pay, if applicable:

11.1.1.1 the cost of stock transfer stamps; and

11.1.1.2 transfer taxes, except as set forth in ¶ 11.1.2.2

11.1.2 Purchaser shall pay, if applicable:

11.1.2.1 any fee imposed by the Corporation relating to Purchaser's financing; and

11.1.2.2 transfer taxes imposed by statute primarily on Purchaser (e.g., the "mansion tax").

11.2 The Flip Tax, if any, shall be paid by the Party specified in ¶ 1.19.

11.3 Any fee imposed by the Corporation and not specified in this Contract shall be paid by the Party upon whom such fee is expressly imposed by the Corporation, and if no Party is specified by the Corporation, then such fee shall be paid by Seller.

11.4 The Parties shall apportion as of 11:59 P.M. of the day preceding the Closing, the Maintenance, and any other periodic charges due the Corporation (other than Assessments) and STAR Tax Exemption (if the Unit is the beneficiary of same), based on the number of the days in the month of Closing.

11.5 Assessments, whether payable in a lump sum or installments, shall not be apportioned, but shall be paid by the Party who is the owner of the Shares on the date specified by the Corporation for payment. Purchaser shall pay any installments payable after Closing provided Seller had the right and elected to pay the Assessment in installments.

11.6 Each Party shall timely pay any transfer taxes for which it is primarily liable pursuant to law by cashier's, official bank, certified, or attorney's escrow check. This ¶ 11.6 shall survive Closing.

11.7 Any computational errors or omissions shall be corrected within 6 months after Closing. This ¶ 11.7 shall survive Closing.

12 Broker

12.1 Each Party represents that such Party has not dealt with any person acting as a broker, whether licensed or unlicensed, in connection with this transaction other than the Broker(s) named in ¶ 1.5.

12.2 Seller shall pay the Broker's commission pursuant to a separate

Exhibit 6.2: *(Continued)*

agreement. The Broker(s) shall not be deemed to be a third-party beneficiary of this Contract.

12.3 This ¶ 12 shall survive Closing, cancellation or termination of this Contract.

13 Defaults, Remedies and Indemnities

13.1 In the event of a default or misrepresentation by Purchaser, Seller's sole and exclusive remedies shall be to cancel this Contract, retain the Contract Deposit as liquidated damages and, if applicable, Seller may enforce the indemnity in ¶ 13.3 as to brokerage commission or sue under ¶ 13.4. Purchaser prefers to limit Purchaser's exposure for actual damages to the amount of the Contract Deposit, which Purchaser agrees constitutes a fair and reasonable amount of compensation for Seller's damages under the circumstances and is not a penalty. The principles of real property law shall apply to this liquidated damages provision.

13.2 In the event of a default or misrepresentation by Seller, Purchaser shall have such remedies as Purchaser is entitled to at law or in equity, including specific performance, because the Unit and possession thereof cannot be duplicated.

13.3 Subject to the provisions of ¶ 4.3, each Party indemnifies and holds harmless the other against and from any claim, judgment, loss, liability, cost or expense resulting from the indemnitor's breach of any of its representations or covenants stated to survive Closing, cancellation or termination of this Contract. Purchaser indemnifies and holds harmless Seller against and from any claim, judgment, loss, liability, cost or expense resulting from the Lease obligations accruing from and after the Closing. Each indemnity includes, without limitation, reasonable attorneys' fees and disbursements, court costs and litigation expenses arising from the defense of any claim and enforcement or collection of a judgment under this indemnity, provided the indemnitee is given Notice and opportunity to defend the claim. This ¶ 13.3 shall survive Closing, cancellation or termination of this Contract.

13.4 In the event any instrument for the payment of the Contract Deposit fails of collection, Seller shall have the right to sue on the uncollected instrument. In addition, such failure of collection shall be a default under this Contract, provided Seller gives Purchaser Notice of such failure of collection and, within 3 business days after Notice is given, Escrowee does not receive from Purchaser an unendorsed good certified check, bank check or immediately available funds in the amount of the uncollected funds. Failure to cure such default shall entitle Seller to the remedies set forth in ¶ 13.1 and to retain all sums as may be collected and/or recovered.

14 Entire Agreement; Modification

14.1 All prior oral or written representations, understandings and agreements had between the Parties with respect to the subject matter of this Contract, and with the Escrowee as to ¶ 27, are merged in this Contract, which alone fully and completely expresses the Parties' and Escrowee's agreement.

14.2 The Attorneys may extend in writing any of the time limitations stated in this Contract. Any other provision of this Contract may be changed or waived only in writing signed by the Party or Escrowee to be charged.

15 Removal of Liens and Judgments

15.1 Purchaser shall deliver or cause to be delivered to Seller or Seller's Attorney, not less than 10 calendar days prior to the Scheduled Closing Date a Lien and Judgment search, except that Liens or Judgments first disclosed in a continuation search shall be reported to Seller within 2 business days after receipt thereof, but not later than the Closing. Seller shall have the right to adjourn the Closing pursuant to ¶ 16 to remove any such Liens and Judgments. Failure by Purchaser to timely deliver such search or continuation search shall not constitute a waiver of Seller's covenants in ¶ 4 as to Liens and Judgments. However, if the Closing is adjourned solely by reason of untimely delivery of the Lien and Judgment search, the apportionments under ¶ 11.3 shall be made as of 11:59 P.M. of the day preceding the Scheduled Closing Date in ¶ 1.15.

15.2 Seller, at Seller's expense, shall obtain and deliver to the Purchaser the documents and payments necessary to secure the release, satisfaction, termination and discharge or removal of record of any Liens and Judgments. Seller may use any portion of the Purchase Price for such purposes.

15.3 This ¶ 15 shall survive Closing.

16 Seller's Inability

16.1 If Seller shall be unable to transfer the items set forth in ¶ 2.1 in accordance with this Contract for any reason other than Seller's failure to make a required payment or other willful act or omission, then Seller shall have the right to adjourn the Closing for periods not exceeding 60 calendar days in the aggregate, but not extending beyond the expiration of Purchaser's Loan Commitment Letter, if ¶ 1.20.1 or 1.20.2 applies.

16.2 If Seller does not elect to adjourn the Closing or (if adjourned) on the adjourned date of Closing Seller is still unable to perform, then unless Purchaser elects to proceed with the Closing without abatement of the Purchase Price, either Party may cancel this Contract on Notice to the other Party given at any time thereafter.

16.3 In the event of such cancellation, the sole liability of Seller shall be to cause the Contract Deposit to be refunded to Purchaser and to reimburse Purchaser for the actual costs incurred for Purchase's lien and title search, if any.

17 Notices and Contract Delivery

17.1 Any notice or demand ("Notice") shall be in writing and delivered either by hand, overnight delivery or certified or registered mail, return receipt requested, to the Party and simultaneously, in like manner, to such Party's Attorney, if any, and to Escrowee at their respective addresses or to such other address as shall hereafter be designated by Notice given pursuant to this ¶ 17.

17.2 The Contract may be delivered as provided in ¶ 17.1 or by ordinary mail.

17.3 The Contract or each Notice shall be deemed given and received:

17.3.1 on the day delivered by hand;

17.3.2 on the business day following the date sent by overnight delivery;

17.3.3 on the 5th business day following the date sent by certified or registered mail; or

17.3.4 as to the Contract only, 3 business days following the date of ordinary mailing.

17.4 A Notice to Escrowee shall be deemed given only upon actual receipt by Escrowee.

17.5 The Attorneys are authorized to give and receive any Notice on behalf of their respective clients.

17.6 Failure or refusal to accept a Notice shall not invalidate the Notice.

17.7 Notice pursuant to ¶¶ 2.2.2 and 13.4 may be delivered by confirmed facsimile to the Party's Attorney and shall be deemed given when transmission is confirmed by sender's facsimile machine.

18 Financing Provisions

18.1 The provisions of ¶¶ 18.1 and 18.2 are applicable only if ¶ 1.20.1 or 1.20.2 applies.

18.1.1 An "Institutional Lender" is any of the following that is authorized under Federal or New York State law to issue a loan secured by the Shares and Lease and is currently extending similarly secured loan commitments in the county in which the Unit is located: a bank, savings bank, savings and loan association, trust company, credit union of which Purchaser is a member, mortgage banker, insurance company or governmental entity.

18.1.2 A "Loan Commitment Letter" is a written offer from an Institutional Lender to make a loan on the Financing Terms (see ¶ 1.21) at prevailing fixed or adjustable interest rates and on other customary terms generally being offered by Institutional Lenders making cooperative share loans. An offer to make a loan conditional upon obtaining an appraisal satisfactory to the Institutional Lender shall not become a Loan Commitment Letter unless and until such condition is met. An offer conditional upon any factor concerning Purchaser (e.g. sale of current home, payment of outstanding debt, no material adverse change in Purchaser's financial condition, etc.) is a Loan Commitment Letter whether or not such condition is met. Purchaser accepts the risk that, and cannot cancel this Contract if, any condition concerning Purchaser is not met.

18.2 Purchaser, directly or through a mortgage broker registered pursuant to Article 12-D of the Banking Law, shall diligently and in good faith:

18.2.1 apply only to an Institutional Lender for a loan on

Exhibit 6.2: *(Continued)*

the Financing Terms (see ¶ 1.21) on the form required by the Institutional Lender containing truthful and complete information, and submit such application together with such documents as the Institutional Lender requires, and pay the applicable fees and charges of the Institutional Lender, all of which shall be performed within 5 business days after the Delivery Date;

18.2.2 promptly submit to the Institutional Lender such further references, data and documents requested by the Institutional Lender; and

18.2.3 accept a Loan Commitment Letter meeting the Financing Terms and comply with all requirements of such Loan Commitment Letter (or any other loan commitment letter accepted by Purchaser) and of the Institutional Lender in order to close the loan; and

18.2.4 furnish Seller with a copy of the Loan Commitment Letter promptly after Purchaser's receipt thereof.

18.2.5 Purchaser is not required to apply to more than one Institutional Lender.

18.3 If ¶ 1.20.1 applies, then

18.3.1 provided Purchaser has complied with all applicable provisions of ¶ 18.2 and this ¶ 18.3, Purchaser may cancel this Contract as set forth below, if:

18.3.1.1 any Institutional Lender denies Purchaser's application in writing prior to the Loan Commitment Date (see ¶ 1.21); or

18.3.1.2 a Loan Commitment Letter is not issued by the Institutional Lender on or before the Loan Commitment Date; or

18.3.1.3 any requirement of the Loan Commitment Letter other than one concerning Purchaser is not met (e.g. failure of the Corporation to execute and deliver the Institutional Lender's recognition agreement or other document, financial condition of the Corporation, owner occupancy quota, etc.); or

18.3.1.4 (i) the Closing is adjourned by Seller or the Corporation for more than 30 business days from the Scheduled Closing Date and (ii) the Loan Commitment Letter expires on a date more than 30 business days after the Scheduled Closing Date and before the new date set for Closing pursuant to this paragraph and (iii) Purchaser is unable in good faith to obtain from the Institutional Lender an extension of the Loan Commitment Letter or a new Loan Commitment Letter on the Financing Terms without paying additional fees to the Institutional Lender, unless Seller agrees, by Notice to Purchaser within 5 business days after receipt of Purchaser's Notice of cancellation on such ground, that Seller will pay such additional fees and Seller pays such fees when due. Purchaser may not object to an adjournment by Seller for up to 30 business days solely because the Loan Commitment Letter would expire before such adjourned Closing date.

18.3.2 Purchaser shall deliver Notice of cancellation to Seller within 5 business days after the Loan Commitment Date if cancellation is pursuant to ¶ 18.3.1.1 or 18.3.1.2 and on or prior to the Scheduled Closing Date if cancellation is pursuant to ¶ 18.3.1.3 or 18.3.1.4.

18.3.3 If cancellation is pursuant to ¶ 18.3.1.1, then Purchaser shall deliver to Seller, together with Purchaser's Notice, a copy of the Institutional Lender's written denial of Purchaser's loan application. If cancellation is pursuant to ¶ 18.3.1.3, then Purchaser shall deliver to Seller together with Purchaser's Notice evidence that a requirement of the Institutional Lender was not met.

18.3.4 Seller may cancel this Contract by Notice to Purchaser, sent within 5 days after the Loan Commitment Date, if Purchaser shall not have sent by then either (i) Purchaser's Notice of cancellation or (ii) a copy of the Loan Commitment Letter to Seller, which cancellation shall become effective if Purchaser does not deliver a copy of such Loan Commitment Letter to Seller within 10 business days after the Loan Commitment Date.

18.3.5 Failure by either Purchaser or Seller to deliver Notice of cancellation as required by this ¶ 18.3 shall constitute a waiver of the right to cancel under this ¶ 18.3.

18.3.6 If this Contract is canceled by Purchaser pursuant to this ¶ 18.3, then thereafter neither Party shall have any further rights against, or obligations or liabilities to, the other by reason of this Contract, except that the Contract Deposit shall be promptly refunded to Purchaser and except as set forth in ¶ 12. If this Contract is canceled by Purchaser pursuant to ¶ 18.3.1.4, then Seller shall reim-

burse Purchaser for any non-refundable financing and inspection expenses and other sums reimbursable pursuant to ¶ 16.

18.3.7 Purchaser cannot cancel this Contract pursuant to ¶ 18.3.1.4 and cannot obtain a refund of the Contract Deposit if the Institutional Lender fails to fund the loan:

18.3.7.1 because a requirement of the Loan Commitment Letter concerning Purchaser is not met (e.g., Purchaser's financial condition or employment status suffers an adverse change; Purchaser fails to satisfy a condition relating to the sale of an existing residence, etc.) or

18.3.7.2 due to the expiration of a Loan Commitment Letter issued with an expiration date that is not more than 30 business days after the Scheduled Closing Date.

19 Singular/Plural and Joint/Several
The use of the singular shall be deemed to include the plural and vice versa, whenever the context so requires. If more than one person constitutes Seller or Purchaser, their obligations as such Party shall be joint and several.

20 No Survival
No representation and/or covenant contained herein shall survive Closing except as expressly provided. Payment of the Balance shall constitute a discharge and release by Purchaser of all of Seller's obligations hereunder except those expressly stated to survive Closing.

21 Inspections
Purchaser and Purchaser's representatives shall have the right to inspect the Unit within 48 hours prior to Closing, and at other reasonable times upon reasonable request to Seller.

22 Governing Law and Venue
This Contract shall be governed by the laws of the State of New York without regard to principles of conflict of laws. Any action or proceeding arising out of this Contract shall be brought in the county or Federal district where the Unit is located and the Parties hereby consent to said venue.

23 No Assignment by Purchaser; Death of Purchaser
23.1 Purchaser may not assign this Contract or any of Purchaser's rights hereunder. Any such purported assignment shall be null and void.

23.2 This Contract shall terminate upon the death of all persons comprising Purchaser and the Contract Deposit shall be refunded to the Purchaser. Upon making such refund and reimbursement, neither Party shall have any further liability or claim against the other hereunder, except as set forth in Par. 12.

24 Cooperation of Parties
24.1 The Parties shall each cooperate with the other, the Corporation and Purchaser's Institutional Lender and title company, if any, and obtain, execute and deliver such documents as are reasonably necessary to consummate this sale.

24.2 The Parties shall timely file all required documents in connection with all governmental filings that are required by law. Each Party represents to the other that its statements in such filings shall be true and complete. This ¶ 24.2 shall survive Closing.

25 FIRPTA
The parties shall comply with IRC §§ 897, 1445 and the regulations thereunder as same may be amended ("FIRPTA"). If applicable, Seller shall execute and deliver to purchaser at Closing a Certification of Non-Foreign Status ("CNS") or deliver a Withholding Certificate from the IRS. If Seller fails to deliver a CNS or a Withholding Certificate, Purchaser shall withhold from the Balance, and remit to the IRS, such sum as may be required by law. Seller hereby waives any right of action against Purchaser on account of such withholding and remittance. This ¶ 25 shall survive Closing.

26 Additional Requirements
26.1 Purchaser shall not be obligated to close unless all of the following requirements are satisfied at the time of the Closing:

26.1.1 the Corporation is in good standing;

26.1.2 the Corporation has fee or leasehold title to the Premises, whether or not marketable or insurable; and

26.1.3 there is no pending *in rem* action, tax certificate/lien sale or foreclosure action of any underlying mortgage affecting the Premises.

26.2 If any requirement in ¶ 26.1 is not satisfied at the time of the Closing, Purchaser shall give Seller Notice and if the same is not satisfied within a reasonable period of time thereafter, then either Party may cancel this Contract (pursuant to ¶ 16.3) by Notice.

Exhibit 6.2: *(Continued)*

27 Escrow Terms
27.1 The Contract Deposit shall be deposited by Escrowee in an escrow account as set forth in ¶ 1.24 and the proceeds held and disbursed in accordance with the terms of this Contract. At Closing, the Contract Deposit shall be paid by Escrowee to Seller. If the Closing does not occur and either Party gives Notice to Escrowee demanding payment of the Contract Deposit, Escrowee shall give prompt Notice to the other Party of such demand. If Escrowee does not receive a Notice of objection to the proposed payment from such other Party within 10 business days after the giving of Escrowee's Notice, Escrowee is hereby authorized and directed to make such payment to the demanding party. If Escrowee does receive such a Notice of objection within said period, or if for any reason Escrowee in good faith elects not to make such payment, Escrowee may continue to hold the Contract Deposit until otherwise directed by a joint Notice by the Parties or a final, non-appealable judgment, order or decree of a court of competent jurisdiction. However, Escrowee shall have the right at any time to deposit the Contract Deposit and the interest thereon, if any, with the clerk of a court in the county as set forth in ¶ 22 and shall give Notice of such deposit to each Party. Upon disposition of the Contract Deposit and interest thereon, if any, in accordance with this ¶ 27, Escrowee shall be released and discharged of all escrow obligations and liabilities.

27.2 The Party whose Attorney is Escrowee shall be liable for loss of the Contract Deposit. If the Escrowee is Seller's attorney, then Purchaser shall be credited with the amount of the contract Deposit at Closing.

27.3 Escrowee will serve without compensation. Escrowee is acting solely as a stakeholder at the Parties' request and for their convenience. Escrowee shall not be liable to either Party for any act or omission unless it involves bad faith, willful disregard of this Contract or gross negligence. In the event of any dispute, Seller and

Purchaser shall jointly and severally (with right of contribution) defend (by attorneys selected by Escrowee), indemnify and hold harmless Escrowee from and against any claim, judgment, loss, liability, cost and expenses incurred in connection with the performance of Escrowee's acts or omissions not involving bad faith, willful disregard of this Contract or gross negligence. This indemnity includes, without limitation, reasonable attorneys' fees either paid to retain attorneys or representing the fair value of legal services rendered by Escrowee to itself and disbursements, court costs and litigation expenses.

27.4 Escrowee acknowledges receipt of the Contract Deposit, by check subject to collection.

27.5 Escrowee agrees to the provisions of this ¶ 27.

27.6 If Escrowee is the Attorney for a Party, Escrowee shall be permitted to represent such Party in any dispute or lawsuit.

27.7 This ¶ 27 shall survive Closing, cancellation or termination of this Contract.

28 Margin Headings
The margin headings do not constitute part of the text of this Contract.

29 Miscellaneous
This Contract shall not be binding unless and until Seller delivers a fully executed counterpart of this Contract to Purchaser (or Purchaser's Attorney) pursuant to ¶17.2 and 17.3. This Contract shall bind and inure to the benefit of the Parties hereto and their respective heirs, personal and legal representatives and successors in interest.

30 Lead Paint
If applicable, the complete and fully executed Disclosure of Information on Lead Based Paint and or Lead-Based Paint Hazards is attached hereto and made a part hereof.

In Witness Whereof, the Parties hereto have duly executed this Contract as of the date first above written.

ESCROW TERMS AGREED TO: SELLER: PURCHASER:

_____   _____   _____

ESCROWEE

                                 _____   _____

Rider to, and Part of, Contract of Sale Between   **as Seller**
and   **as Purchaser for Unit**   **at**

Suggested Purchaser's representations for use when applicable.

31 Purchaser's Additional Representations and Covenants
31.1 Supplementing ¶ 4.2 of the Contract. Purchaser also represents and covenants that:

 31.1.1 Purchaser has, and will at Closing have, available unencumbered cash and cash equivalents (including publicly traded securities) in a sum at least equal to (and having a then current value of) the Balance; and

 31.1.2 Purchaser has, and will at and immediately following the Closing have, a positive net worth.

31.2 the Maintenance and the monthly amount of the Assessment (if any) do not aggregate more than 25% of the current total gross monthly income of the individuals comprising the Purchaser;

31.3 (if ¶ 1.20.1 or ¶ 1.20.2 applies) the monthly debt service (interest and amortization of principal, if any) of the proposed financing, together with the Maintenance and the monthly Assessment amount (if any), do not aggregate more than 35% of said current total gross monthly income.

32 Supplementing paragraph 4.1. Seller has no actual knowledge of a material default or condition which the Lessee is required to cure under the Lease and which remains uncured. If, prior to Closing, Seller acquires knowledge of a such default or condition which the Lessee would be required to cure, then Seller shall cure same at or prior to Closing. This provision shall not survive closing.

The Parties have duly executed this Rider as of the same date as the Contract.

                SELLER: PURCHASER:

                _____   _____

                _____   _____

Exhibit 6.3: Land Description of a Commercial Property

VINTAGE ALLEY 20'

S 9°38'30"W

BRICK GARAGE

PROPOSED 6' SOLID FENCE w/gates

2 STORY BRICK DWELLING

2 STORY BRICK DWELLING NO. 472

2 STORY BRICK DWELLING

40.00'
N 9°38'30"E

SOUTH GRAHAM STREET 50'
(FORMERLY GRAHAM STREET)

PLAN OF SURVEY
SITUATE IN
8TH WARD, CITY OF PITTSBURGH, ALLEG. CO., PA.

SURVEYED FOR
JOHN P.

JAN. 23, 1995   SCALE: 1" = 20'

JOSEPH M. PUSKAR PROFESSIONAL LAND SURVEYOR
PITTSBURGH, PENNSYLVANIA

7

Landlord-Tenant Law

CHAPTER OVERVIEW

As explained in Chapter 1, property is divided into two broad categories: freeholds and leaseholds. The preceding chapters concentrated on various aspects of freehold estates; this chapter focuses on the second group of estates — the leasehold.

A **leasehold** is a possessory interest in property, either real or personal, that is created and governed by the terms of a lease. A **lease** is the contract that establishes the possessory rights and obligations and, for the most part, is governed by general contract law. Various aspects of contract law have been discussed in earlier chapters and a detailed examination of the law of contracts is beyond the scope of this text. However, the legal professional must always be cognizant of the fact that the rights and obligations of the lessor and the lessee are determined by the provisions of the lease.

This chapter highlights the various types of leasehold arrangements that may exist, as well as the rights (and responsibilities) of both the landlord and the tenant. Note that personal property as well as real property can be subject to lease arrangements.

The Lease

A *lease* is a contract that establishes the relationship between the lessor and the lessee. The **lessor** is the person who has rights in the subject property sufficient to permit him or her to transfer a right of possession. The **lessee** is the person who contracts for the right of possession of the leased property. It must be borne in mind that the lessee, as such, only acquires a possessory right in the property.

EXAMPLE:

A widow decides to take a one-year trip around the world and to let her house for that period. The widow owns the house as a tenant in severalty, which gives her the right to transfer any estate up to the one she has to another person. She rents her house for the one-year period to a middle-aged couple who, pursuant to the terms of the lease, have the right to use and enjoy the house for the year, but they do not "own" the house, and the lease has prohibitions against the couple transferring their interests (see below).

If the property that is subject to the lease is realty, it is referred to as a *leasehold*; leases of personalty are referred to simply as leases.

Generally, there are four types of leaseholds that may be created:

1. **Tenancy for years:** These tenancies are created for a fixed period of time. If the leasehold period is intended to exist for more than one year, the Statute of Frauds requires that the lease be in writing to be enforceable, and the lease automatically terminates at the date specified in the lease. Furthermore, most jurisdictions permit the landlord to retain a **right of entry** to gain access to the premises in the event the tenant breaches any of the lease covenants. **Landlord** is the term generally employed to refer to the lessor of realty.

EXAMPLE:

A student has enrolled in a law school in a city several hundred miles from her home. She enters into a lease for an apartment near the school for a term of three years. At the end of three years the lease will automatically terminate.

A tenancy for years may be terminated by the landlord earlier than the termination date if the tenant fails to pay the specified rent (see below), or the tenant may surrender the property to the landlord prior to the expiration of the lease, which will excuse further obligations *if* the landlord accepts such early termination. The rights of early termination depend on the specific jurisdiction in which the property is located.

2. **Periodic tenancy:** This type of lease continues for successive periods specified in the lease until terminated by notice of either party. Periodic tenancies may be created by:
   (a) an express agreement; "AN *EASEMENT*"
   (b) implication, if the lease specifies a monthly or weekly rental and no specific termination; and

(c) operation of law if a tenant remains in possession after the termination of a tenancy for years.

Periodic tenancies typically remain in effect until one party informs the other of its termination.

EXAMPLE:

A student rents an apartment for a one-year lease for a yearly rental of $6000, payable in monthly installments of $500. At the termination of the lease the student does not leave, and the landlord continues to accept the student's rent check of $500 for each of the next three months. After the third month the landlord sends the student a notice of termination to be effective at the end of the current month. The tenancy for years turned into a periodic tenancy but was terminated by the landlord's notice.

3. **Tenancy at will:** This tenancy is created by the will and intent of either the lessor or the lessee, and must be created by an express agreement (not necessarily a writing). This type of tenancy may be terminated at any time without notice, or automatically by operation of law if one of the parties dies or the tenant acquires title to the property.

EXAMPLE:

A writer who lives in the city wants to go into seclusion to complete his novel. His friend has a mountain cabin that he uses infrequently, and the friend agrees to let the writer live in the cabin to finish the novel. In consideration of this use, the writer agrees to pay all utilities and taxes due on the property while he is in possession. After six months the novel is complete and the writer quits the cabin. The writer is obligated for utilities and taxes attributable to these six months, and the tenancy is terminated.

4. **Tenancy at sufferance:** A tenancy at sufferance is created when a tenant unlawfully remains in possession of the property after the termination of a lawful tenancy. This tenancy only remains in effect until the lessor takes steps to evict the tenant, and no notice of the termination is required.

EXAMPLE:

A tenancy for years has ended, but the tenant refuses to leave. The landlord commences eviction proceedings. Until the tenant is evicted, the tenant is a tenant at sufferance.

If a tenant remains in possession after the termination of the lease, the lessor has two options:

(a) the lessor may commence proceedings in a court of competent jurisdiction to **evict** the tenant, meaning that the court will order the tenant to quit the premises and have the order enforced by a marshal; or

(b) the lessor may bind the lessee to a new periodic tenancy, under the terms of the expired lease or at an increased rent *if* the lessor has notified the lessee of an increased rental prior to the expiration of the valid lease.

Be alert to the fact that this right, known as the **holdover doctrine**, does not apply if the lessee only remains in possession for a few hours after the lease expired or is delayed in quitting because of reasons not the tenant's fault, such as a severe illness.

The typical lease for realty will include the names of the parties; a description of the property to be rented, referred to as the **premises**; the use to which the property may be put; and the termination of the lease. Because the lease is a contract, the tenant's right of possession or use is granted in consideration of the tenant's obligation to compensate the landlord. The most common form of such obligation is the payment of money, referred to as **rent.**

Rent clauses fall into one of two categories: gross lease or a net rent lease. A **gross lease** requires the tenant to pay rent, and all operating costs on the premises — taxes, water, utilities, and so forth — are the obligation of the landlord. In a **net rent lease** the tenant pays the rent to the landlord and further is responsible for the operating costs, which the tenant pays directly to the provider of such services.

In many instances, residential rent may be regulated by the government, in which case rent renewals of the lease may be guaranteed to the tenant, and rent increases for the new lease are established under the provisions of the particular statute. In other locations and with commercial leases, the lessor may indicate a **rent escalation clause** in which the parties agree to periodic rent increases based on either costs or inflation.

Many commercial leases contain a **percentage rent** that requires the tenant to pay the landlord a set percentage of the tenant's gross sales. With this type of lease rent is usually due on a quarterly or annual basis to correspond to the tenant's payment of taxes. A variation on this type of lease is a **percentage breakpoint** clause in which a set rent is established, but if the tenant's gross receipts exceed a stated dollar amount, called the breakpoint, the landlord is entitled to additional rent based on a percentage of the gross sales above the breakpoint amount. In certain instances, this type of lease may also contain a **radius clause** that prohibits the tenant from operating a similar enterprise within a specific geographic distance from the rented premises, which could limit the tenant's gross sales at the leased location.

EXAMPLE:

A man rents an apartment under a net rent lease. According to the lease, he must pay the landlord a monthly rental of $750 and is responsible for his own utilities — gas, electricity, and water. The landlord remains responsible for taxes and insurance.

EXAMPLE:

A man rents a location to open a bookstore. Under the terms of the lease, the tenant must pay the landlord a monthly net rent based on a yearly rental of $200 per square foot of leased space. Furthermore, if the bookstore's gross sales exceed $500,000, the tenant must pay the landlord an additional 1% of all sales in excess of $500,000. This lease also restricts the tenant from opening another bookstore within ten blocks of this location. This is an example of a percentage breakpoint lease with a radius clause.

In addition, a lease will usually indicate which party is responsible for the maintenance and repair of the premises and, for commercial leases, may specify that one of the parties must maintain minimum insurance on the property. See Exhibit 7.1 at the end of this chapter for a sample lease.

Tenants' Duties

Under a typical lease agreement, the tenant warrants to maintain the property in good repair. In this context the tenant is precluded from committing waste on the property (see Chapter 2). If the tenant, under the lease contract, has specifically covenanted to make repairs, the tenant's duty will be higher than that imposed under the law of contract, and she may even be obligated to reconstruct the property if the property is destroyed, even if the property is destroyed without the fault of the tenant or the landlord. Furthermore, even absent such a contract, if the premises are destroyed without fault, in most jurisdictions the tenant, absent an agreement to the contrary, is still obligated to continue paying rent for the duration of the lease.

EXAMPLE:

A man enters into a lease to rent a house for a two-year period. Three months later the house is destroyed by a tornado. In most jurisdictions the tenant may still be liable to pay rent on the now nonexistent house for the next 21 months. If the tenant had specifically contracted to make repairs, he might be obligated to rebuild the house. In this type of contract the tenant is usually further obligated to maintain insurance on the property, for obvious reasons.

A tenant is precluded from using the leased premises for an unlawful purpose. Such unlawful use gives the landlord the right to terminate the lease, sue for damages, and/or seek injunctive relief.

 EXAMPLE:

A woman rents a large apartment. She then uses that apartment as a brothel. When the landlord finds out he may either terminate the lease and evict the tenant or seek an injunction, a court order requiring the woman to stop using the premises for an unlawful purpose.

The primary obligation of a tenant is to pay the agreed-upon rent at the time and manner specified in the lease. A landlord may also require the tenant to give a **security deposit** to cover a portion of the rent in the case of a default. At the termination of the lease the tenant's rent obligation terminates and the tenant is entitled to the return of the security deposit, less any amount deducted for damage to the premises caused by the tenant. Also, the tenant is entitled to receive interest accruing on the security deposit during the tenancy.

If the tenant fails to pay the rent when due, the landlord, in most states, is entitled to one of two options:

1. the landlord may sue the tenant for money damages for the amount of rent that was due and unpaid; or
2. the landlord may sue to have the tenant evicted.

If the tenant abandons the premises without justification, most states require the landlord to attempt to re-rent the property to lessen the amount of rent the tenant owes under the lease. This obligation is known as the duty of **mitigation of damages.** If the new tenant pays less rent than the abandoning tenant, the abandoning tenant is obligated to the landlord for the difference. Conversely, if the new tenant pays a higher rent, the abandoning tenant is discharged. Note, though, that if the landlord accepts the surrender of the premises the tenant will not be obligated for rent under the lease.

 EXAMPLE:

The owner of a two-family house rents one of the units to a family. However, the man and the family have constant arguments over matters not concerned with the property. The family decides to move with nine months left on the lease. If the man accepts their departure, they are not obligated under the lease. If the man does not accept their departure, he must attempt to re-rent the property, and the family will only be obligated for the difference between the their rent and the new rent if it is less. If the man refuses to attempt to find a new tenant for the property he may be denied relief from the court for failure to mitigate damages.

mitigate - to make damages less severe.

Landlord's Duties

Absent a statutory or contractual obligation, under the general law a landlord is under no duty to repair or maintain leased premises. Basically, a landlord's obligations fall into three categories:

1. The landlord has a duty to deliver actual possession to the tenant on the date agreed upon. If there are holdover tenants or squatters on the premises, it is the landlord's duty to see that they are evicted so that the tenant may take possession.
2. The landlord, under all lease agreements, has imposed a covenant of quiet enjoyment (see Chapter 5), meaning that the landlord guarantees that no one, including the landlord, will interfere with the tenant's use and possession of the property. This covenant may be breached in one of the following ways:
   (a) actual eviction, which occurs when the tenant is evicted from the entire property, at which time the tenant's rent obligation is considered terminated;
   (b) **partial eviction,** which occurs when the tenant is precluded from possession of a portion of the property. If the partial eviction is caused by the landlord, as opposed to a third person, the tenant's obligation to pay rent on the entire property is terminated.

EXAMPLE:

A man rents a house with a garage. There is a mechanic's lien on the garage and the contractor who holds the lien attaches the garage. This is an example of a partial eviction. Because the partial eviction was caused by the landlord's failure to pay the contractor, the tenant is relieved from paying rent on the property.

   (c) **constructive eviction,** which occurs if the landlord does anything that renders the property uninhabitable, such as failing to provide essential services. The tenant may terminate the lease and seek damages from the landlord. However, to terminate the lease and seek damages, the tenant must vacate the property and the condition that caused the problem must be the fault of the landlord, not a third party.

EXAMPLE:

A man rents a house under a gross rent lease. The landlord refuses to pay any utility bills although it is his obligation, and all utilities are turned off in the house, rendering it uninhabitable. The tenant may terminate the lease by vacating the house and then suing the landlord for damages, or he may pay the utilities himself and sue the landlord for reimbursement.

3. Most jurisdictions impose an implied **warranty of habitability** on residential leases, which is deemed to be non-waivable (exclusively) by the tenant. What is considered "habitable" is determined by local housing codes. If this warranty is breached, the tenant may:
   (a) terminate the lease;
   (b) make the necessary repairs and offset the cost against the rent;
   (c) seek an **abatement** whereby the rent is proportionately reduced for the lack of use; or
   (d) remain in possession but sue for damages.

If a tenant attempts to assert his or her legal rights, the landlord is prohibited, in most states, from terminating the lease or otherwise penalizing the tenant in retribution. Any attempt to do so is considered **retaliatory eviction**, which, depending on the jurisdiction, may entitle the tenant to certain legal remedies against the landlord. Each state's statutes must be individually analyzed.

If the entire property is condemned by the government, or taken over under a right of eminent domain (see Chapter 3), the lease is deemed terminated. However, a partial or temporary taking does not relieve the tenant of his or her obligation under the lease.

Assignments and Subleases

Unless the parties have agreed to the contrary, tenants are typically permitted to assign or sublease their rights. An **assignment** is a transfer of all rights the tenant has under the lease. A **sublease** is a transfer of a portion of the tenant's rights under the lease. If the tenant retains the right to return to the property any time prior to the termination of the lease, including the right to renew the lease, the transfer is deemed to be a sublease.

EXAMPLE:

> Three young women share an apartment, but do not get along. One of them finds a fourth young woman to take over her portion of the lease. When the dissatisfied tenant transfers all of her rights to the fourth woman, she has effectuated an assignment; however, if she retained the right to renew the lease in her own name this is considered a sublease.

The effect of an assignment is to make the **assignee** (the transferee) primarily obligated to the landlord for the rent. The **assignor** (the transferor) remains secondarily liable, meaning that if the assignee defaults the assignor will be liable for the rent to the landlord.

With a sublease, the original tenant remains obligated to the landlord, and he or she is the only one who can enforce the lease's covenants against the landlord. The tenant and the sublessee are contractually obligated to each other, and the sublessee's only remedies are against the tenant/sublessor.

A lease may contain a provision prohibiting assignments and subleases, but such provisions are generally construed against the landlord. In jurisdictions that provide for regulated residential leases, such provisions may be prohibited, but each state's statutes must be independently analyzed. If a transfer is made in violation of the lease, and the landlord knows about it but does not object, the lease provision prohibiting the transfer is deemed waived. If the landlord does object, the landlord may be able to terminate the lease.

EXAMPLE:

> A lease contains a non-assignment provision. Six months after the lease starts the tenant must move to a new city, and assigns her lease to a friend. The landlord accepts the friend's rent check. Under these circumstances, the law will assume that the landlord has waived his right to object to the assignment.

The landlord may assign any and all of his or her rights without the tenant's consent. The tenant's obligation will be to the landlord's assignee, and the tenant must be given a notice to attorn (see Chapter 5).

Practical Tips

- Leases for rentals exceeding one year must be in writing, and long-term leases may be recorded to protect the parties.
- If a lease is going to be recorded, only record a memorandum of the lease provisions. It is not necessary to record all the terms of the lease itself.

- review all leases in the same manner in which a contract would be reviewed — it must meet all the requirements of a valid contract to be enforceable.
- Only use a form lease as a guide; make sure to personalize each lease to protect the client.

Chapter Review

Landlord-tenant law is a subset of general real property law that is governed by contract. This contract, known as a lease, determines the rights and obligations of the parties.

There are four types of lease agreements generally in effect: a tenancy for years, in which property is leased for a fixed period of time; a periodic tenancy, created for successive periods; a tenancy at will, which is formed by agreement and which may be terminated at any time without notice; and a tenancy at sufferance, which comes about when a tenant remains in unlawful possession of a formerly leased premise.

The consideration given to the landlord to support the contract is known as rent, and the tenant may be obligated for utilities, or they may be the landlord's responsibility. For commercial tenants, the landlord may also contract for a portion of the tenant's gross sales or profit.

The tenant is required to maintain the premises in good repair, absent an agreement or statute to the contrary, and may even have to rebuild a premise that is destroyed.

Leases, as a general rule, are freely assignable, which means all the tenant's rights are transferred, and capable of being sublet, which means the tenant retains some interest in the lease, even if just the ability to renew the contract.

Ethical Concern

Leases are fairly common legal documents, and most law offices maintain a form lease on file. It is unethical to charge every client the cost of creating the same lease. This is known as double billing. However, it is permissible to charge each client for the particular work that was performed to personalize that form lease for the client.

Key Terms

Abatement	Assignor
Assignee	Constructive eviction
Assignment	Evict

Gross lease	Premises
Holdover doctrine	Radius clause
Landlord	Rent
Lease	Rent escalation clause
Leasehold	Retaliatory eviction
Lessee	Right of entry
Lessor	Security deposit
Mitigation of damages	Sublease
Net rent lease	Tenancy at sufferance
Partial eviction	Tenancy at will
Percentage breakpoint	Tenancy for years
Percentage rent	Warranty of habitability
Periodic tenancy	

Exercises

1. Using the library or the Internet, determine whether your locality provides for residential rent regulation. If so, analyze its provisions.
2. Obtain a form lease for your jurisdiction and analyze its provisions.
3. Determine what constitutes "habitability" in your locality.
4. Many states have a landlord-tenant court for housing disputes. Find out whether such a court exists for your county, and if so, list its jurisdictional requirements.
5. Briefly discuss how the parties could determine "gross sales" under a percentage lease.

Situational Analysis

A tenant leases a two-bedroom apartment in a major city. She is the only tenant on the lease. To meet expenses, she lets one of the bedrooms to another woman by an oral agreement. The other woman is not listed on the lease. Each woman pays one-half the rent by check, and the landlord accepts these checks. After one year they begin to have problems living with each other, and the woman named on the lease asks the other woman to leave, but she refuses. What are the rights of the parties? How would you advise each woman?

Edited Cases

Ballesteros v. Rosello is a New York case dealing with a holdover tenant, and the *Bourgeois* decision concerns the breach of a sublease.

Ballesteros v. Rosello
183 Misc. 2d 448, 703 N.Y.S.2d 686 (1999)

Petitioner commenced these two summary holdover proceedings, L&
T index No. 91705/99, against respondent Calexi Rosello, and L&T index
No. 91706/99 against respondent Rose Cardona, to recover possession of
the subject premises, 199 Jackson Street, apartment No. 1 and apartment
No. 2, respectively, in Brooklyn, New York. Both proceedings were initi-
ated by service of separate 30-day notices of termination, dated July 15,
1999, on the identical basis that respondents had no current lease, were
neither rent stabilized nor rent controlled, and were month-to-month tenants whose respective tenancies would be terminated as of August 31,
1999. Petitioner subsequently served these two instant petitions alleging
each respondent was a tenant who entered into possession of their respective apartments under a rental agreement between herself and petitioner's
predecessor. The proceedings are consolidated for decision.

On October 15, 1999, the Honorable Delores Thomas consolidated
both the instant proceedings; dismissed respondents' cross motions seeking dismissal of the petitions based on the argument that there was no
existing landlord tenant relationship, and that the proceedings were not
brought under the appropriate section of the Real Property Actions and
Proceedings Law with leave to renew at trial; and granted petitioner's
motions solely to the extent of striking respondents' defenses of a lack of
personal and subject matter jurisdiction. Both matters were adjourned to
November 3, 1999 for trial.

On November 3, 1999, counsel for both parties agreed that in lieu of a
trial they would submit papers on the sole legal issue for both proceedings,
namely, whether or not respondents in this particular instance have a landlord-tenant relationship with petitioner, and are month-to-month tenants;
or have no landlord-tenant relationship with petitioner and are licensees.
It is undisputed that respondents are neither rent stabilized nor rent controlled, and have never tendered rent nor use and occupancy to, or executed a lease with, the current petitioner. It is also undisputed that respondents and the petitioner's predecessor in interest entered into rental
agreements for respondents' respective apartments, and had a landlord-
tenant relationship.

Respondents submitted a supplemental affirmation dated November
9, 1999, requesting the instant proceedings be dismissed as no landlord-
tenant relationship exists between petitioner and respondents. Respondents assert that as they have never executed a lease with, or paid any
rent or use and occupancy to petitioner, they are licensees, not month-
to-month tenants. Respondents further assert that as licensees, petitioner
should have proceeded with licensee proceedings against them by first
serving upon them 10-day notices to quit pursuant to RPAPL 713 (7),
rather than the 30-day notices to vacate they received pursuant to Real
Property Law Sec. 232-a. Respondents rely in part on an April 26, 1999
unreported Kings County Housing Part case — *Francis v. Coral* (L&T index

No. 64963/99), in which the Honorable Jose Rodriquez dismissed a hold-over petition after trial as no landlord-tenant relationship was established.

Petitioner subsequently submitted a memorandum of law dated November 15, 1999, in opposition to respondents' posttrial motion to dismiss, requesting respondents' motions be denied in their entirety and judgment entered in favor of petitioner forthwith. Petitioner asserts that as respondents enjoyed a landlord-tenant relationship with petitioner's predecessor in interest, respondents did not lose their possessory interest and therefore cannot be reduced to licensee status merely because the prior landlord sold the building. Petitioner asserts that *Francis v. Coral* (supra) has no binding stare decisis effect on this court's decision, and also distinguishes it from the facts in the instant proceedings because respondents' counsel herein has stipulated to evidence of a preexisting landlord-tenant relationship. Petitioner further asserts no other support in case law can be found. Petitioner submits that the respondents received the additional protection of 30-day notices as opposed to the 10-day notices they would have received as licensees.

The common-law principle of attornment, which is the "act or agreement of a tenant accepting one person in the place of another as his landlord," has been abolished by Real Property Law Sec. 248. (Rasch, New York Landlord and Tenant — Summary Proceedings Sec. 2:3, at 106 [3d ed].) Pursuant to Real Property Law Sec. 248, "[a]n attornment to a grantee is not requisite to the validity of a conveyance of real property occupied by a tenant, or of the rents or profits thereof, or any other interest therein."

Additionally, Real Property Law Sec. 223 states, "The grantee of leased real property, or of a reversion thereof, or of any rent, the devisee or assignee of the lessor of such a lease, or the heir or personal representative of either of them, has the same remedies, by entry, action or otherwise, for the nonperformance of any agreement contained in the assigned lease for the recovery of rent . . . or for other cause of forfeiture as his grantor or lessor had, or would have had, if the reversion had remained in him." Thus, as petitioner's predecessor in interest had a landlord-tenant relationship with respondents, and would have been entitled to institute holdover summary proceedings against them as month-to-month tenants, the petitioner has the same remedies available to it against respondents, and is correct in treating respondents as month-to-month tenants as it has in the instant matters. The petitioner, as purchaser, succeeds "to all the title and rights of the original landlord, becomes the landlord by operation of law, with all the rights and remedies of the original landlord," creating a conventional relation of landlord and tenant. (*Commonwealth Mtge. Co. v. De Waltoff*, 135 App. Div. 33, 35 [1st Dept. 1909]; see also, *Costagliola v. Home Owners' Loan Corp.*, 35 F. Supp. 930 [S.D.N.Y. 1940].) Therefore, petitioner is entitled to the same rights and obligations of the landlord-tenant relationship with respondents as they had with petitioner's predecessor in interest.

Based upon the foregoing, the court denies respondents' motions to dismiss both proceedings, and pursuant to the parties' stipulated agreement to accept the court's decision on this legal question in lieu of a trial, the petitioner is awarded a final judgment of possession against each of the respondents for their respective apartments. Issuance of the warrants of eviction against each of the respondents is forthwith, and the execution of the warrants is stayed for 10 days.

Case Questions

1. What is a holdover tenant?
2. How does the court apply the concept of attornment to this case?

Bourgeois, Dupuis, Wright & Cohen, CPAs v. Hayes et al.
457 So. 2d 231 (La. App. 1984)

This appeal arises out of a suit for the breach of a sublease.

Bourgeois, Dupuis, Wright and Cohen, sublessors, filed suit against Hayes, Durio and Richard, sublessees, seeking an acceleration of the terms of the sublease of office space, on the ground that defendants breached their obligations by failing to pay the rent due under the terms of the sublease. Defendants answered seeking a dismissal of the suit on the ground that plaintiffs had breached the terms of the sublease by refusing to allow defendants to make certain alterations in the office space as agreed upon in the sublease. Plaintiffs amended their petition by adding, as a defendant, 315 Office Ltd. (315), the original lessor, seeking judgment against 315 to cancel the original lease between plaintiffs and 315 in the event defendants were successful in asserting their defense and obtaining judgment cancelling the sublease.

From a trial court judgment dismissing their suit, plaintiffs appeal. We affirm.

Facts

On August 29, 1980, plaintiffs leased 5,754 square feet of office space from 315 located in a building owned by 315 at 315 South College Road in Lafayette, Louisiana. The primary term of the lease was for five years with an option to renew the lease for an additional five-year term. The lease contained a provision that plaintiffs could only sublease or assign the lease if the written permission of 315 was obtained. This lease was silent as to plaintiffs' right to make alterations of the premises.

In the latter part of 1981, the plaintiffs began negotiations with defendants for the subleasing of the 5,754 square feet of office space. James Dupuis, managing partner of plaintiffs, Tony Fazzio, and Stephen Durio, members of defendants' law firm, represented the respective parties in those negotiations.

It is undisputed that, in the course of the negotiations, Durio and/or Fazzio informed Dupuis that the law firm did not have need for all the space, therefore, it would be necessary that the sublease contain a provision that would allow subleasing and alterations by defendants. Durio testified that Dupuis told him that he (Dupuis) did not expect any difficulty in getting permission from 315 for him to allow defendants to sublease or for him to obtain consent for alterations.

Dupuis admitted that Durio informed him of the necessity of the clause providing for the authority of defendants to sublease and make alterations. Dupuis was agreeable to such a provision. As a result such a provision was inserted into the sublease. This instrument was prepared by the attorney for the plaintiffs. The sublease contained a povision allowing defendants to sublease and to make alterations in the premises upon giving proper notice and obtaining the written consent of plaintiffs.

Pursuant to the terms of the lease between plaintiffs and 315, Dupuis received permission from 315 to sublease the property to defendants. This letter of permission, dated November 10, 1981, made no mention of any alterations to be made by defendants.

The sublease in question was executed by plaintiffs and defendants on January 15, 1982. The defendants occupied a portion of the premises. A short time later, defendants began negotiations with Exploration of Louisiana, Inc., for the sublease of approximately 1,700 square feet of the office space. Exploration informed defendants that it would be necessary that the defendants make some alterations before they would sublease the space. These alterations consisted of the closing of one door, installing four doors, one window and a partition.

Dupuis was notified by defendants of the need for alterations and he contacted Paul Kratzer, a representative of 315, seeking the permission of 315 to allow the proposed alterations. This request by Dupuis was refused. Dupuis then informed defendants that he would not grant permission for defendants to make the alterations. The sublease to Exploration was not confected. On or about September 1, 1982, defendants vacated the premises and ceased making rental payments. This suit followed.

The trial court found that plaintiffs had breached the contract by refusing to grant permission for the alterations and dismissed the suit. The issue presented is whether the trial court was in error in its ruling.

At the outset, we feel that we should clarify the question of whether the instrument is a sublease or an assignment of the lease. The record reflects references to the instrument in some places as an assignment and in other places it is referred to as a sublease. We have examined the instrument and have determined that the instrument is a sublease and is not an assignment.

"The distinction between an assignment and a sublease is that in an assignment the original lessee transfers all of his rights in the lease, whereas in a sublease he retains some control or interest in the lease. . . ." *Bordelon v. Bordelon*, 434 So. 2d 633 (La. App. 3d Cir. 1983).

Dupuis, manager for plaintiffs, testified that defendants paid the monthly rental payments to plaintiffs and they, in turn, would pay 315. Dupuis stated that the monthly payments made by defendants were $.50 per square foot higher than the payments made to 315 by plaintiffs. Further, the primary term of the original lease to plaintiffs was five years with a five-year option, while the primary term granted to the defendants was one year with six two-month options. Since the term granted to defendants was shorter than the term of the original lease to plaintiffs, the lease interest in the premises would revert to the plaintiffs at the expiration of defendants' term. The instrument between the plaintiffs and defendants contained a provision recognizing the fact that a reversion would take place and set out the responsibility of the defendants when the expiration of the term took place.

These facts clearly show that plaintiff retained an interest in the lease[,] thus it was a sublease and was not an assignment. Having concluded that the instrument was a sublease, we now shall proceed with the disposition of the issue of the case; i.e., whether plaintiffs have breached their obligation under the sublease to defendants.

The legal principles applicable to this issue are derived from the law of lease and obligations.

When parties enter into a sublease, a new contract comes into existence which is separate and distinct from the original lease between the owner and the sublessor. The rights and obligations of the sublessor and sublessee arise out of the provisions of the sublease. There is no privity of contract between the sublessee and the original owner-lessor. When a dispute arises between the sublessee and sublessor regarding a breach of the sublease, the court looks to the terms of the sublease in order to determine the respective rights of the sublessee and sublessor. *Audubon Hotel Co. v. Braunnig*, 120 La. 1089, 46 So. 33 (La. 1908); *Ducote v. Callico*, 307 So. 2d 644 (La. App. 4th Cir. 1974), *writ den.*, 309 So. 2d 337 (La. 1974).

As we examine the sublease we find provisions wherein plaintiffs agreed that defendants could sublease the premises or any part thereof upon obtaining written consent from the plaintiffs. Plaintiffs agreed that such consent would not be unreasonably withheld. Also, plaintiffs specifically agreed to allow defendants to make any alterations, additions and/or improvements within the leased premises after obtaining the written consent of plaintiffs. The plaintiffs also agreed that such consent would not be unreasonably withheld.

James Dupuis, the managing partner for the plaintiffs, testified that, during the negotiations, he was informed that it was important and necessary that defendants have the right to sublease and/or make reasonable alterations to the premises. Dupuis knew that defendants would not have need for the entire floor space and that the defendants planned to sublease a portion of the space to other parties. Dupuis was aware of the fact that he needed to get the consent of 315 before alterations could be made by defendants.

Dupuis, before executing the sublease, obtained written permission from 315 to allow him to sublease the premises to defendants. He failed, however, to get consent from 315 that would allow him to grant the defendants the right to make alterations. Notwithstanding the lack of consent from 315 for alterations, plaintiffs agreed to the alterations clause that was inserted into the sublease. When defendants requested permission for the alterations in order to sublease, Dupuis then attempted to get the consent of 315, but to no avail. Dupuis then notified defendants that he would not give alteration consent, the reason being that he was unable to obtain the consent of 315. There is no contention that the proposed alterations were unreasonable.

The plaintiff counsel contends that the defendants, being a partnership composed of attorneys who negotiated the sublease, "was in as good a position [as was plaintiff] to have required some intervention by 315 in the said sublease agreement if for no other purpose than to guarantee that they would authorize alterations to be suggested at a later date. . . ." Plaintiffs then argue that defendants cannot complain that plaintiffs breached the sublease. We disagree.

As we have previously pointed out, the sublease between plaintiffs and defendants is a separate contract from the original lease. The defendants were under no obligation to negotiate with the original lessor, 315, in order to confect the sublease. The plaintiffs, before agreeing to the alteration clause, had a duty to ascertain whether the consent by 315 could be obtained in order that they could fulfill their obligation to consent to reasonable alterations. This consent from 315 plaintiffs neglected to get. The result was that plaintiffs agreed to an obligation that [they were] not free to perform. When the plaintiffs refused to consent to the alterations as requested, this refusal amounted to a breach of the sublease. As stated in *Fontenot v. Benoit*, 128 So. 2d 815 (La. App. 3d Cir. 1961):

> Article 2729 of our LSA-Civil Code provides that "the neglect of the lessor or lessee to fulfill his engagements, may also give cause for a dissolution of the lease . . ." Article 2692 provides that the lessor is under an obligation to maintain the lessee in peaceable possession of the leased premises. . . .

Civil Code art. 2729 gives both parties the reciprocal right to cancel or terminate the sublease if either violates the terms of the agreement. We find that plaintiffs violated the sublease by refusing to allow the defendants to make the requested alterations, thus, defendants had the right to terminate the lease. The trial court correctly dismissed plaintiffs' suit.

For these reasons, the judgment of the trial court is affirmed. Plaintiffs-appellants are to pay the costs of this appeal.

Case Questions

1. How does the court distinguish between a sublease and an assignment?

2. What does the court say are the rights of a sublessee?

Exhibit 7.1: Sample Commercial or Residential Lease

This lease made in _____ [*city*], state of _____ [*date*] between _____ of _____ as lessor, and _____ of _____ as lessee, witnesses:

Lessor, for and in consideration of the agreements of lessee mentioned below, hereby leases to lessee, and lessee hereby leases from lessor, the premises [or as the case may be] located at _____ [*city*], state of _____ described as follows: _____ excepting and reserving to lessor _____ including the right to _____.

This lease is for the terms of _____ years [or as the case may be], beginning _____ [*date*], and ending _____ [*date*], unless sooner terminated as provided below.

A. Agreements of Lessee

Lessee, in consideration of the leasing, agrees:

1. To pay as rent for premises the sum of $____ per month [or as the case may be], payable on the day of _____ each month [or as the case may be] during the term of this lease, at _____.

2. To pay all charges for light, heat, fuel, power and water furnished or supplied to or on any part of premises.

3. To pay all taxes and assessments, ordinary and extraordinary, general and specific, including the same for _____ [*year*], which may be levied or assessed on premises.

4. To pay all reasonable costs, attorneys' fees and expenses that shall be made and incurred by lessor in enforcing the agreements of this lease.

5. To use and occupy the premises for _____ purposes only, and for no other object or purpose without written consent of lessor, and to not use premises for any unlawful purpose or purpose deemed extra hazardous.

6. To keep the premises in as good repair as the same shall be at the commencement of the term, wear and tear arising from the reasonable use of the same and damages by the elements excepted.

7. To keep the buildings and improvements on the premises insured in a responsible insurance company or companies for not less than $____ payable, in case of loss, to lessor as lessor's interest may appear.

8. To permit lessor and lessor's agents to enter on the premises or any part thereof, at all reasonable hours, for purpose of examining or exhibiting same or making such repairs or alterations as may be necessary for safety or preservation thereof; also to permit lessor to place on premises notice of "For Sale" and "To Rent" and not interfere with same.

9. To deliver to lessor within _____ days from execution of this lease a surety bond in amount of $____ from a reputable bonding company, guaranteeing faithful performance by lessee of all terms and conditions of this lease.

10. Not to assign this lease nor sublet the premises or any portion thereof without written consent of _____.

11. Not to make any contract for construction, repair, or improvements on, in, of, or to premises, or any part thereof, or for any work to be done or materials to be furnished on or to premises, or any part thereof, without providing in such contract or agreement that no lien of mechanics or materialmen shall be created or shall arise against above-described land and/or the building or improvements at any time located thereon. All persons furnishing any work, labor or materials, as well as all other persons whatever, shall be bound by this provision and by the notice of it from and after date of this lease, and notice is hereby given that no mechanic's lien, materialmen's lien, or any other incumbrance made by or obtained against lessee, or lessee's interest in demised land and/or the building or improvements thereon, shall in any manner or degree affect the title or interest of lessor in land and/or the building or improvements thereon. To that end, lessee agrees not to make any contract or agreement, either oral or written, for any labor, services, fixtures, material or supplies in connection with altering, repairing or improving any building or improvement on premises without providing in such contract or agreement that contractor or contractors waive all right to a mechanic's lien, and waive all right of any subcontractor or subcontractors to mechanics' liens, by reason of furnishing any labor, services and/or material under such contract or contracts, whether written or oral, and that such contract or contracts shall, upon execution, be immediately filed in office of recorder _____ of deeds of _____ county, _____ and a copy thereof lodged with lessor.

12. Lessee has examined and knows condition of premises, and has received same in good order and repair, except as otherwise specified in this lease, and no representations as to condition or repair thereof have been made by lessor or lessor's agent, prior to, or at execution of, this lease.

13. Lessor shall have a lien on all of property of lessee used or situated on premises, to secure payment of rent (and other indebtedness owing from lessee to lessor at any time during existence of this lease) to become due under this lease, and in default of payment may take possession of and sell such of the property as may be sufficient to pay deliquent rent [or indebtedness].

14. Lessor shall have the right to sell premises, provided, however, that notice of such contemplated sale shall be given in writing to lessee at last prior to time fixed for vacation of premises by lessee, and provided, further, that during such period lessee shall have option to buy premises at price and on terms of such contemplated sale. In event of a sale of premises by lessor, after such notice and failure of lessee to exercise the option to purchase, lessee agrees to vacate and give possession of premises within days after written notice of sale, given by lessor to lessee, and after payment by lessor to lessee of $____ on or before the expiration of ____ days' notice.

15. If lessee shall abandon or vacate the premises, they may be relet by lessor for such rent and on such terms as lessor may see fit; and, if a sufficient sum shall not be thus realized, after paying all expenses of such reletting and collecting to satisfy the rent hereby reserved, lessee agrees to satisfy and pay all deficiency.

16. At expiration of this lease, to give peaceable possession of premises to lessor, in as good condition as they now are, the usual wear, inevitable accidents, and loss by fire excepted.

17. The lease may be terminated by lessor in the event of the breach of any of the agreements of lessee contained herein, in which case lessor may reenter on the premises, and this lease shall immediately terminate.

18. This lease, at option of lessor, shall terminate in case lessee shall by any court be adjudged as bankrupt or insolvent, or in case lessee shall make an assignment for benefit of creditors.

19. To observe and comply with all rules, regulations and laws now in effect or which may be enacted during the continuance of this lease by any municipal, county, state or federal authorities having jurisdiction over the premises, and to indemnify lessor for any damage caused by violation thereof.

20. In case lessor, by reason of the failure of lessee to perform any of the agreements or conditions contained herein, shall be compelled to pay or shall pay any sum of money, or shall be compelled to do or shall do any act which requires payment of money, the sum or sums so paid or required to be paid, together with all interest, costs, and damages, shall be added to instalment of rent, next becoming due or to any subsequent instalment of rent, and shall be collectable as additional rent in same manner and with same remedies as if it had been originally reserved. On failure of lessee to make repairs, as provided for herein, lessor may make necessary repairs, and add the amount of cost of such repairs to the rent due on the first month following date of repairs, and such cost of repairs shall be and constitute such rent together with the rent above provided for.

21. Failure of lessor to insist on the strict performance of the terms, agreements and conditions contained herein, or any of them, shall not constitute or be construed as a waiver or relinquishment of lessor's right to enforce any such term, agreement or condition, but the same shall continue in full force and effect.

22. Lessor shall not be liable for any damage to persons or property occurring or arising on premises from any cause whatever.

23. [add any other affirmative or negative provisions which lessor and lessee have agreed on].

B. Agreements of Lessor

Lessor, in consideration of the agreements of lessee set forth above, agrees as follows:

1. To keep leased building [or as the case may be] in good repair.

2. Lessee may make such alterations, additions, or improvements in such parts of building as lessee deems necessary, provided, however, written consent of lessor is first obtained.

3. Lessee shall have the right to assign this lease or sublet the premises or any part thereof, subject to the following limitations, viz.:

4. To extend the term of this lease for a further term of _____ years, at the same rental, payable in like manner, and subject to same agreements as are contained in this lease, provided lessee gives written notice to lessor

of a desire to renew lease, at least _____ days [or "months"] before expiration of terms of this lease, and provided lessee is not in default in performance of terms and conditions of this lease, and provided this lease is not terminated before expiration of term thereof as provided for herein.

    5. In event that at any time during the term of this lease, _____ [*state occurrence*], lessee shall have the right to terminate this lease on the giving of at least _____ days' written notice to lessor.

    6. All fixtures erected in or attached to premises by lessee may be removed by lessee at the termination of this lease, provided (a) lessee shall not then be in default in the performance of any of the agreements herein, (b) that such removal shall not permanently injure the building, and (c) that removal shall be made before the expiration of this lease or any extension thereof.

    7. Lessee shall have the right, at the end of the term of this lease, or at any time during the term thereof, to purchase property from lessor, or lessor's heirs, executors, administrators and assigns, for $_____ and, on tendering of such amount in lawful money of United States by lessee as above provided, lessor agrees immediately to deliver to lessee a sufficient warranty deed of premises.

    8. Should any more favorable condition be included in any other leases on space in this building, during the life of the instrument, pertaining to termination of lease or rate of rental per square foot, in particular or other conditions in general, these same conditions are made a part of the contract.

    9. Not to engage, during the life of this lease, in the city of _____ directly or indirectly, whether as owner, partner, stockholder, or otherwise, in the _____ [*rival*] business.

    10. Not to rent, during the term of this lease, the adjoining premises [or as the case may be], owned by lessor, for a business in competition with that of the lessee which is _____.

C. Mutual Agreements of Lessor and Lessee

    1. Lessee agrees to deposit with lessor, on signing of this lease, $_____ in cash as security for payment of rent herein received and faithful performance by lessee of all terms, conditions and agreements of lease, as well as to indemnify lessor for any costs or expense to which lessor may be put by reason of any default by lessee. Lessor agrees to pay interest to lessee on before-mentioned security deposit of $_____ at rate of $_____ per annum and to repay lessee the $_____ so deposited as security, by crediting same on account of payment of rent for last _____ months of demised term, provided that all of terms, conditions and agreements of lease shall have then been fully complied with by lessee.

    2. If during the term of this lease the premises shall be destroyed by fire, the elements, or any other cause, this lease shall cease and become null and void from date of such damage or destruction and lessee shall immediately surrender premises to lessor and shall pay rent only to time of such surrender. If premises shall be damaged by fire or other cause so as to be capable of being repaired within a reasonable time, lessor shall

have to option to repair the same and during time that repairs are being made lessor shall remit to lessee a just and fair portion of rent according to nature of damage sustained and according to extent that lessee is deprived of use of premises.

3. This lease shall be deemed renewed and extended for the further term of _____ from expiration of term hereby granted, unless either lessor or lessee, at least ____ months prior to termination thereof, shall give written notice to the other of an intention to take possession of, or to surrender, as the case may be, the premises on date fixed herein for the expiration of term. The rent during such extended term shall be at same rate as rate provided for herein, and extension shall be on the terms, conditions and agreements contained in this lease, including this clause.

4. If default be made in the payment of the rent above reserved, or any part thereof or in any of the agreements herein contained, to be kept by lessee, it shall be lawful for, and lessee hereby requests lessor without notice, to declare said term ended, and to reenter premises or any part thereof, either with or without process of law, and lessee or any other person or persons occupying the same, to expel, remove and put out, using such force as may be deemed necessary in so doing, and premises again to repossess and enjoy as in lessor's first estate; and in order to enforce a forfeiture of this lease for default in any of its conditions it shall not be necessary to make demand or to serve notice on lessee, and lessee waives all right to any demand or notice from lessor of lessor's election to declare this lease at an end or of declaring it so to be; but the fact of nonperformance of any of the agreements of this lease, shall in itself at election of lessor, without notice or demand, constitute a forfeiture of lease, and at any and all times after such default, lessee shall be deemed guilty of a forcible detainer of the premises and all notices required by any statute of the state of or otherwise are hereby waived.

5. If lessee shall hold over, after expiration of the term hereby created, with consent of lessor, if shall be deemed a renewal of this lease, and of all the conditions and agreements therein contained for term of ____ and so on from year to year until lease is terminated by either party giving to the other not less than ____ days' notice of termination prior to end of any term.

6. Notices and demands by either lessor or lessee may be given by registered mail with prepaid postage addressed to lessor at _____ or to lessee at _____ subject to the right of either the lessor or lessee to designate by notice in writing a new address to which such notices or demands must be sent. The agreements, conditions and undertakings herein contained shall extend to and be binding on the representatives, heirs, executors, administrators, successors and assigns, of respective parties hereto as if they were in all cases named.

7. Wherever the worlds "lessor" and "lessee" are used herein they shall be read as "lessors" and "lessees" in all cases where there is more than one lessor or lessee and with necessary grammatical changes as if duly made herein. In witness whereof, the parties have set their hands [and seals] the day and year first above written.

8 Personal Property

CHAPTER OVERVIEW

As stated in the first chapter, the titles that apply to real estate apply equally to personalty. However, there are certain legal rules and doctrines that are applicable only to personal property. This chapter examines the two different categories of personalty — tangible and intangible property — and then addresses the unique rules with respect to the transfer of these items. Bear in mind that the rules and procedures outlined earlier, excluding those that are exclusive to real estate transactions, apply to personalty as well.

Categories of Personal Property

Generally, all non-real property is considered to be personal property, which is divided into tangible and intangible property. **Tangible property** is anything that can be touched and moved, and its value is intrinsic to the item itself. **Intangible property** is that personal property that may have little monetary value, but is representative of something of value. This type of personal property is often referred to as a **chose in action.**

 EXAMPLE:

A man buys a gold watch from Tiffany's. The watch has intrinsic value, and therefore is tangible personal property.

EXAMPLE:

A woman opens a bank account with $5000 and receives a bankbook. The bankbook has little intrinsic value, but it represents her right to possess the $5000. The bankbook is intangible property.

General Tangibles

Most people are only superficially aware of their personal property. Because they see and use the property every day they tend not to identify it. But if a person wishes to transfer an item of personalty, the item must be identified in such a way that there will be no confusion in determining which item was meant should the transferor own similar types of property. Unlike real estate, there is no deed at a county recorder's office to provide a legally sufficient description.

EXAMPLE:

A man owns two 14K gold chains and wants to sell one. The bill of sale should make specific reference to the chain in question to identify it, such as "the 14K gold rope chain, 18 inches long, manufactured in Italy."

Intangibles

General Intangibles

General intangibles include such items as certificates of deposit, corporate stocks, corporate and government bonds, and so forth. Savings and time accounts are typical of the intangible property many people possess.

EXAMPLE:

A man inherits 1,000 shares of IBM stock. These shares are an example of a general intangible.

Corporate **stocks** are documents that represent the owner's percentage interest in the company that issued the stock. Either these **shares** are traded in the open market (the New York Stock Exchange, the American Stock Exchange, NASDAQ, and so forth) or are **closely held,** meaning that the shares are only owned by a few people. In either event, these shares are known as securities whose value represents the value of the company that issued the shares. Shares that are publicly traded on the open market have values that fluctuate each day; the value, or selling price, is reported in the newspaper. Closely held stock, on the other hand, is not publicly traded, so its value is determined each time the shareholder wishes to transfer his shares. Additionally, most closely held companies restrict the transferability of their shares, meaning that the shareholder may not have the right to sell, give, or leave by will the share to whomever he or she wants.

 EXAMPLE:

> Three friends decide to start a business that they establish as a corporation. To limit the number of owners, they do not sell shares to the public. Furthermore, to maintain control of the business, they sign an agreement whereby none of them can sell his shares to an outsider. These shares thereby become non-transferable.

Bonds can be issued either by companies or by the government, and are evidences of indebtedness. Bonds operate by having the bondholder lend money to the issuer for a set number of years, and during the period of the loan the bondholder receives interest on the loan. At the end of the period, the bondholder gets her money back. Bonds are usually publicly traded like stock. Bonds are **secured investments,** meaning that the debtor must set aside some property that the bondholder can attach in the case of default. If a bond is issued that does not have some secured property attached to it, it is called a **debenture.**

 EXAMPLE:

> To raise money, a corporation issues a bond for $300,000. It agrees to pay the holder 4% interest on the bond for 30 years. The corporation puts $30,000 into a trust account as security for the bondholder in case it defaults on the bond.

Another form of debt intangibles are **promissory notes** that are loans evidenced by a document stating interest payments and a payback date. They are similar to bonds and debentures except that they are issued for a shorter period of time. They are considered items of value because they represent the promissee's right to receive the money indicated in the note.

 EXAMPLE:

> A man lends his friend $250 and has the friend sign a promissory note, due in three months. The note represents the man's right to the return of the money, and he may sue the friend on the note if the friend does not repay the loan.

Another example of intangible property is a mortgage, discussed in previous chapters. The mortgage and underlying note represent a debt, an intangible, secured by realty.

Intellectual Property

Intellectual property is any property that was created by a person to which he or she has exclusive use. Intellectual property falls into three categories: copyrights, patents, and marks.

Copyrights are government grants to the author of a writing or the creator of a work of art. Anyone who creates a book, a poem, or any work of art automatically has a common law right to the exclusive use of the work. However, in order to document and protect this right, the work can be statutorily copyrighted with the federal government in Washington, D.C. Once copyrighted, the author or creator has an exclusive right to use the copyrighted property for his life plus 75 years, meaning that it is an asset that can be inherited.

 EXAMPLE:

A lawyer decides to write a text on property law. Once the work is finished, she has the exclusive right to the material for her life, plus 75 years.

The monetary value of a copyright comes from the owner's licensing of that right. A **license** allows the licensee to use the copyrighted work, paying the copyright owner a fee for the use. As a typical example, a book is copyrighted by the author, and the publisher is licensed to print and sell that book, paying the author a fee known as a **royalty.**

A **patent** is a government grant of exclusive use of an invention, given to the inventor. The patent must be registered with the U.S. Patent Office, and the exclusive right is good only for a period of 20 years, at which point it passes into the public domain. Like a copyright, a patent can be licensed to produce an income to the patent holder.

A **trademark** is the exclusive right to use a name, symbol, or group of words that signify a particular product or service, distinguishing it from similar products and services. If the item is a product, the mark is called a trademark; if the item is a service, the mark is called a **service mark.** Examples would be "Calvin Klein" for a trademark because it identifies a clothing product, or "Schleppers Movers" for a service mark because it represents a moving company.

Marks are registered with the federal government, and the government grants the owner the exclusive right to use the mark for ten years. The mark may be renewed for unlimited ten-year periods, but if not renewed, the owner loses his rights. Additionally, if the owner permits someone to use the mark without his authorization, the owner will lose this exclusive right to the mark.

Methods of Transferring Personal Property

Gifts

A **gift** is a transfer of property from one person to another without a mutual exchange of consideration. If each party receives consideration, the transfer would be a contract of sale (see Chapter 4). With a gift, the titleholder, known as the **donor,** transfers her title to another, the **donee.** Gifts are characterized by the time and method of their transfer:

1. **Inter vivos gift:** This transfer occurs during the life of both the donor and the donee. Typical examples of inter vivos gifts are birthday and wedding presents.
2. **Testamentary gifts:** These are transfers of property that occur upon the death of the donor. The donor's intent to make the gift is evidenced by a legal document called a **will** that operates to transfer title to a person's property upon the person's death according to his or her expressed intention.
3. **Gifts causa mortis:** These transfers are gifts made in contemplation of the donor's imminent death. Unlike the other types of gifts, a gift causa mortis may be revoked by the donor any time prior to death, and, if the donor does not succumb to the imminent death, the gift is revoked by operation of law. Furthermore, should the donee predecease the donor, the gift is likewise deemed revoked.

To effectuate a gift, three elements must exist:

1. The donor must evidence a **donative intent,** the present intent to make a gift.
2. There must be a delivery of the gifted object to the donee or the donee's agent in the same fashion as the transfer of a deed discussed in Chapter 5.
3. There must be an acceptance of the gift by the donee; the law presumes acceptance absent an indication to the contrary.

Gifts and sales form the two primary methods of transferring property. Although personal property may be transferred without documentation, to transfer realty by gift the donor must still execute a deed as previously described.

 EXAMPLE:

To celebrate her graduation from law school, a woman's friends get together and buy her a pearl necklace. They present it to her at the graduation ceremony. All three elements to perfect a gift of personal property have been met — intent, delivery, and acceptance.

Bailments

A **bailment** is the transfer of possession of personal property from one person, the **bailor,** to another person, the **bailee.** A bailment does not transfer title to the object, simply the right of the bailee to possess, and sometimes use, the object until the item is returned. A bailment may be created by an express agreement. The agreement may be either oral or written.

No bailment exists until the object is physically transferred. Several jurisdictions indicate that possession alone may not be sufficient to create a bailment. To create the bailment, an essential feature is the ability of the bailee to exercise control over the object.

Some states will imply a bailment if mere possession exists, but in those jurisdictions the possession, while creating a bailment, does not impose duties on the bailee. Duties do attach once control is demonstrated (see below). Also, a person may become a bailee even if he or she does not know the precise value of the object but has in fact demonstrated the intent to exercise control over the item. This situation is referred to as a constructive bailment.

EXAMPLE:

A woman brings a cloth coat to a dry cleaner. The owner of the store accepts the coat. Unbeknownst to the owner, the coat is a designer original valued at $8000, and the woman has left a diamond brooch in the coat's pocket. The dry cleaner is a bailee for the coat, even though he was not aware of its value, but not for the diamond brooch because he did not know of its presence in the pocket, would not expect such an item in the pocket, and cannot have a bailment thrust upon him.

Several specific situations with respect to bailments have given rise over the years to particular rules of law:

- *Pledges.* A **pledge** is a bailment in which the possession of personal property is transferred to secure a debt, somewhat like the collateral for a loan. The bailee, in this instance the creditor, has possession of the object until the debt is repaid. If the debtor defaults, the bailee acquires title to the property. A pawnbroker typifies this type of relationship. In the normal bailment situation, the transfer of title is not an element.
- *Safe deposit boxes.* Because both the bank and the bank customer have keys to the box, the law has determined that a bailor-bailee relationship exists, holding the bank liable as a bailee.
- *Cloakrooms.* A customer leaving a coat with a cloakroom attendant creates a bailment; however, the liability of the owner of the cloakroom may be limited by specific state statute.

- *Parking lots.* Leaving a car in a parking lot does not in and of itself create a bailment, because no actual transfer of possession has occurred. However, if the car owner leaves the keys to the car with the parking lot attendant, a bailment is been created because the attendant now has control of the car.
- *Health clubs and retail stores.* The owner of a health club is a bailee for the customer's clothing left in a locker while the facility is being used, even if the customer keeps the key to the locker. A retailer is a bailee for items set aside while the customer shops, such as putting down packages while trying on clothes.

A bailment only transfers the right of possession, and sometimes use, of the property. It does not transfer title, as would be the case with a sale or a gift.

Typically, a bailee is entitled to absolute possession of the object during the period of the bailment, and may maintain legal actions against anyone who attempts to interfere with this possessory right. Also, a bailee may have certain rights with respect to the use of the property:

- *Express use.* The parties to the bailment may contract, or agree, that the bailee may use the property during the term of the bailment.
- *Implied use.* Certain types of personal property by their nature indicate that the bailee may use the property.

EXAMPLE:

A man puts his dog in a kennel while he is away on a business trip. As part of her responsibility to care for the dog the kennel owner can take the dog for long walks.

- *Incidental use.* Certain necessary use by the bailee may be expected in order to complete the bailment.

EXAMPLE:

A woman lends her friend a diamond necklace. As an incidental use, the friend can clean and polish the gems.

If a bailee uses a bailed item for purpose that is not expressly agreed upon, implied, or incidental to the bailment, the bailee will be held liable to the bailor for any damage that results from such unauthorized use of the item.

EXAMPLE:

A couple lends their boat to a neighbor so that the neighbor can row across the lake to the town center rather than drive. While it is in his possession, the neighbor decides to rent the boat to some tourists, who damage the boat. The neighbor is held liable because of this unauthorized use of the item.

The modern trend of the law is to hold the bailee liable for ordinary negligence that causes damage to the bailed items. However, the bailee may be held to a standard of absolute liability if the bailee departs from the terms of the bailment or misdelivers the bailed item to someone other than the bailor.

The parties may agree to a limitation of liability clause in their contract, but a blanket waiver of liability is usually disfavored. The bailor may maintain an action against the bailee for breach of contract, or for any injury or destruction of the item.

Common Carriers and Innkeepers

A **common carrier** is a commercial enterprise that transports goods and people for consideration. The definition does not include public agencies that perform the same services. A common carrier is held to the responsibility of an insurer for all goods it transports, meaning that the common carrier is liable for the value of goods if they are damaged or destroyed, even if the injury or destruction is caused by an act of God. However, unless there is an agreement to the contrary, the carrier will not be liable if goods are not delivered according to its printed timetable or its estimated time of delivery. Note that the common carrier is only held to a standard of ordinary care for any injury to the passengers.

An **innkeeper** is a commercial enterprise that rents temporary accommodation to members of the public. As such, the innkeeper is considered an insurer of the guests' property, similar to the common carrier. However, the innkeeper is not liable if the damage to or destruction of the property is caused by the guests' own negligence or fault, an act of God, or a fire not caused by the innkeeper's lack of care. Moreover, the innkeeper is liable for any loss due to burglary, theft, or negligence. The burden is on the innkeeper to evidence that she was not negligent. The innkeeper may limit her liability for loss if she conspicuously posts a notice of such limitation of liability.

Both common carriers and innkeepers have insurer liability with respect to goods left in their possession. Both types of businesses are entitled to a lien on the property in their possession. A **lien** is a right (intangible personal property) of a person who has improved property to retain possession of that property until the cost of the improvement has been paid. To create a lien, there must be a debt created by the lienor having performed a service on the item. Title to the property remains in the debtor, but possession of the property is in the lienor.

A common carrier is given a common law lien on all items it has agreed to transport. No lien attaches if the property is received from people other than the owner. Innkeepers have liens on all property a guest brings into the inn, even if the property does not belong to the guest. The lienor has the right to retain possession of the items until the debt is discharged, and if it is not discharged, title will vest in the lienor.

 EXAMPLE:

A man travels on the Metroliner from Boston to New York. At the train station in New York someone steals his suitcase. The thief checks into a motel with the suitcase. The thief stays one night and then departs without paying his motel bill. Amtrak is liable to the man for the value of his suitcase unless it has limited its liability, and the motel can keep the suitcase left by the thief, even though the suitcase did not belong to the thief.

Other Issues

In addition to the above-discussed methods of transfer, property may be transferred from one person to another without a specific interest or relationship having been created. These methods of acquiring property — accession and confusion — may operate to transfer both personal and real property.

Accession

Accession occurs when one person's labor or materials are added to another person's property so as to increase the value of that property. If this additional value can be severed (removed) from the original item, the court will order such removal. If removal is impossible, the original party may sue for damages. If the change in the nature of the property is deemed so significant that the object is completely altered and its value is greatly increased, the title to the property will pass to the person whose labor or property caused the change.

 EXAMPLE:

A person takes lumber from a hardware store and builds a cabinet with the wood. The hardware store owner is entitled to the value of the lumber taken, but the person who made the cabinet may retain the cabinet because the nature of the lumber has now been completely changed. This result is true if the person took the lumber unintentionally, believing that he had purchased it. If the person intentionally took the lumber knowing that he had no right to it, the cabinet will belong to the hardware store owner.

Confusion

Confusion occurs when the personal property of two individuals is mixed together. If the goods are of the same kind and quality and the mixture occurred by inadvertence, the mixture is deemed owned by both parties as tenants in common. If the confusion was caused by the willful act of one of the parties, the wrongdoer is required to identify his or her portion. If identification is impossible, the entire mixture belongs to the innocent party. If the mixed property can be separated, the court will order such separation.

EXAMPLE:

Two farmers send their grain to the same mill to have it ground into flour. The mill owner fails to realize that two different farmers have brought the grain because they both use the same carrier. He innocently mills all the grain together, and it cannot be determined how much each farmer owns. In this situation, both farmers as tenants in common will own all the flour.

Practice Tips

- Document transfers of personal property in writing to avoid problems with respect to ownership later on.
- Remember that titles to personal property are the same as those for real property, with all the same rights and obligations.
- Transfers of property may be subject to gift taxation — always check the tax implications of the transfer of valuable property.

Chapter Review

No discussion of the law of property is complete without an examination of the law concerning personal property. Personal property is divided into two broad categories: tangible property, moveable property that has intrinsic value, and intangible property, items whose value is representative.

Tangible property is exemplified by clothing, jewelry, art, antiques, electronic equipment, cars, and so forth. It is the type of property that most people own or possess. Intangible property is exemplified by stocks and bonds, bank savings and checking accounts, loans, and the various types of intellectual property such as copyrights, patents and marks. The intangible aspect of intellectual property is the grant of exclusive use of the item given by the government to the item's creator, inventor, or owner.

Personal property is transferred using procedures that differ from the general methods of conveyancing used to transfer realty. The most common methods of transfer are by gift, in which title passes from the titleholder to another without consideration; by bailment, in which possession, not title, is transferred to a person not the titleholder; and by accession and confusion. Furthermore, specific rules apply to common carriers and innkeepers when they acquire possession of another person's personal property.

Ethical Concern

The legal professional often acts as the agent of the client, and is called upon to keep the client's property. The legal professional may not place the client's property with his or her own, which is known as commingling. Such a practice violates the ethical standards of the legal profession. All client property must be kept separate and distinct from that of the legal professional.

Key Terms

Accession	Intangible property
Bailee	Inter vivos gift
Bailment	License
Bailor	Lien
Bonds	Patent
Chose in action	Pledge
Closely held	Promissory note
Common carrier	Royalty
Confusion	Secured investments
Copyright	Service mark
Debenture	Share
Donative intent	Stock
Donee	Tangible property
Donor	Testamentary gift
Gift	Trademark
Gift causa mortis	Will
Innkeeper	

Exercises

1. Determine the type of duty that is owed by innkeepers in your jurisdiction.
2. Differentiate between tangible and intangible property.
3. Indicate how one might demonstrate donative intent.
4. Give three examples of your own experience with bailments.
5. Briefly discuss the concept of intellectual property.

Situational Analysis

A famous artist finishes a painting just before he leaves for a vacation. He gives the painting to a friend to keep it safe while he is away. The artist says that if anything happens to him the friend can keep the painting. On the flight home the plane on which the artist is traveling crashes and the artist is killed. Both the friend and the estate claim the painting. Argue for both sides and decide the matter.

Edited Cases

The two cases that follow highlight some concepts discussed in this chapter. *Pitchford v. Commonwealth of Virginia* underscores the obligations incident to bailments, and *In the Matter of the Estate of McGeath* provides insight into gifts causa mortis.

Pitchford v. Commonwealth of Virginia
50 Va. Cir. 266 (1999)

"In this [case] involving a bailment, [the court] must decide what standard of care is imposed upon the bailee by the relationship." *Morris v. Hamilton,* 225 Va. 372, 302 S.E.2d 51 (1983).

The case was tried to the court on September 8, 1999. The court took the decision under advisement after all the evidence. The term bailment is used advisedly because the defendant argues that no bailment is involved for lack of proof that it ever came into possession of the plaintiff's property. A summary of the salient facts are as follows.

Plaintiff, a nurse employed at the Medical College of Virginia, arrived for work around 8:00 to 8:30 on the evening of May 8, 1999. After parking her vehicle in a parking deck adjacent to the hospital, she was accosted there by two men who attacked and beat her. The two ran away after plaintiff said she thought she heard one of them say others were approaching. Plaintiff testified that the next thing she remembered was looking up at the face of a medical resident who found her lying face up on the parking deck floor.

After being attended to by ambulance personnel and fitted with a neck collar at the scene, the plaintiff was transported to the MCV emergency room. While in the receiving room, nurses in attendance removed her jewelry consisting of earrings and a necklace. This was necessary to take x-rays of her upper extremities. Plaintiff testified that she was told to keep still and close her eyes. She was bloodied and beaten about the face, and blood was present over one eye due to a head wound.

At issue is a diamond pendant which was attached to the necklace plaintiff was wearing. Plaintiff has alleged in four counts that the pendant, though taken, was not returned with her other personal effects. Plaintiff testified that she felt the pendant in the back and around the side of her neck during the process of removal by the nurse. The two nurses who were present, one of whom actually removed the necklace while the other observed, both testified that, when the necklace came off, no pendant was present. During the hearing, the court examined the necklace. There was no visible sign of damage to it.

After remaining in the emergency room for about six to eight hours, plaintiff was released without being admitted to the hospital. As mentioned, after removal of the necklace and after personal items were placed in a bag, the bag was put on the table beside plaintiff's bed. The bag was eventually turned over to plaintiff's supervisor who in turn gave it to plaintiff or plaintiff's daughter after plaintiff's release. Later at home, she discovered that, while the necklace was present, the pendant was not. The parties have stipulated that the diamond pendant has a value of $6,000.

The court will assume that for purposes of a ruling that the diamond pendant was attached to the necklace at the time of removal. Thus, contrary to the position of the hospital, the court assumes a bailment arose. Again, the question is what standard of care is applicable. As I mentioned during the proceedings, it depends on how the bailment is classified. Applicable here, the circumstances suggest either a bailment for mutual benefit or a gratuitous one.

In a bailment "for the mutual benefit of the bailor and bailee, the bailee must use ordinary care for the protection, preservation, and return of the bailed property. If the bailee fails to use ordinary care, he is liable to the bailor for any loss or damage to the property resulting from the bailee's failure." *Volvo White Truck Corp. v. Vineyard,* 239 Va. 87, 91, 387 S.E.2d 763 (1990) (citation omitted). A gratuitous bailment, on the other hand, is one where the possession is given the bailee solely for the benefit of the bailor. "A bailee who acts gratuitously is not held to the same standard of care as one who enters upon the same undertaking for pay. The latter owes a duty of reasonable or ordinary care, while a gratuitous bailee owes only a duty of slight care. Thus, in order for a bailor to recover from a gratuitous bailee, he must prove the bailee was guilty of gross negligence." *Morris v. Hamilton* at 375 (citation omitted).

As noted, plaintiff was asked to remove her personal effects including the necklace, to facilitate the taking of x-rays of her upper extremities, where she had sustained injury. There was testimony that this was needed to exclude skull and bone fracture, among other things. Under these circumstances the hospital came by possession of the necklace for the benefit of plaintiff in the rendition of medical care.

As has also been noted, plaintiff was not admitted to the hospital, but was rather treated in the emergency room and released. Contrary to plaintiff's contention, the evidence does not establish a contract of bailment. Were this the case "[a] different set of principles would apply." *Volvo White Truck Corp. v. Vineyard*, 239 Va. 87, 92, 387 S.E.2d 763 (1990). In such an instance the bailee, here the hospital, would have the burden of persuasion of showing the exercise of "due care to prevent the damage." Id. at 92.

Here, the proof falls short of demonstrating the applicable standard, gross negligence in the instance of a gratuitous bailment; given this finding, plaintiff cannot recover on this basis.

This outcome applies to three of the counts plaintiff has raised: detinue, contract of bailment, and tort of bailment. To the extent that the plaintiff relies on bailment as a basis for detinue, her action fails.

As to the remaining count, conversion, the court will not rely on the assumption that the property was given over. This count alleges essentially a theft of the pendant to the extent that there was an unauthorized exercise of dominion and control with intent to permanently deprive the plaintiff thereof, either by taking or embezzlement. Here the testimony is equally believable as to a taking and a non taking, plaintiff's testimony that she felt the pendant around her neck when the nurses were removing it and the nurses' who both testified they did not observe it when the necklace was pulled away. There is no evidence of who may have deprived the plaintiff of the pendant after it came in rightful possession to constitute an embezzlement. Accordingly, the conversion count also fails.

For the foregoing reasons, the court has entered judgment for the defendant.

Case Questions

1. What factors did the court look to to determine that a bailment existed?
2. How does the court define a "conversion"?

In the Matter of the Estate of McGeath
2001 Ohio App. LEXIS 2470

Suzanne C. Munger appeals from a judgment of the Montgomery County Court of Common Pleas, Probate Division, which sustained exceptions to the final account she had filed as executrix of Joyce A. McGeath's estate.

The record reveals that on August 9, 1996, McGeath died as a result of a brain tumor. Her will was admitted to the probate court and it appointed

Munger to be the executrix of the estate. At the time of McGeath's death, she had had $17,652.34 in a Universal 1 Credit Union Account. The disagreement in this case concerns that money.

Munger testified as follows. On the day before McGeath's death, Munger was in Michigan. During a phone conversation with McGeath, she told Munger that she was having a second brain tumor surgery the next day and that she knew that she would "likely be a vegetable" after the surgery "or that she would pass away[.]" She told Munger that there was approximately $17,000 in her checking account. McGeath said that she would leave a check with her mother, Dorothy Yacchari, and that Yacchari would give that amount of money to Munger. McGeath told Munger that if she became a vegetable, Munger should use the money to take care of her and to make sure that she was placed in a nice nursing home. McGeath told Munger that if she died, she wanted Munger to pay her funeral expenses from the money and then to use the remaining funds to go to Italy, a place the two of them had previously planned to go together. McGeath wrote the check and gave it to Yacchari.

Munger returned to Ohio on the day of McGeath's death. When she arrived, Yacchari told Munger that she had the check. Munger told Yacchari to "just hold on to" the check so that the funeral expenses could be paid from that amount.

Yacchari deposited the check into her own account. Yacchari later wrote a check to the funeral home in the amount of $5,825.84. Yacchari also wrote a check to Munger for the remaining amount of $11,826.50. Debra Shaw, McGeath's daughter, testified as follows. McGeath had two brain surgeries "within a matter of days." While McGeath was in the hospital, Shaw and other family members visited her. During one of those visits, McGeath told Shaw that she wanted the $17,652.34 to be used to take care of her if she survived. McGeath stated that if she died, the money should be used to pay her funeral expenses and any outstanding bills and that the remainder of the money was to go to her estate.

McGeath told her that a check was being written to Yacchari and that Yacchari was to give the check to Munger so that Munger could pay the funeral expenses and outstanding bills from that amount and such expenses and bills would not be charged to the estate. McGeath also stated that she was writing the check "because she did not want money tied up in probate."

Munger filed the final fiduciary's account with the probate court on October 25, 2000. The account did not list the $17,652.34. The court appointed a guardian ad litem for the minor beneficiaries of the estate. On December 4, 2000, the guardian ad litem filed exceptions to the account. On that same day, some of McGeath's family members, acting as "guardians for the benefit of minors," also filed exceptions to the account. One of the exceptions filed by both asked the court to determine whether the $17,652.34 was a gift causa mortis or an asset of the estate.

A hearing was held on December 13, 2000. On January 3, 2001, the court filed its decision, finding that Munger had not proven that McGeath had made the gift causa mortis and thus that the amount of $17,652.34

should have been included as an asset in McGeath's estate. The court decided that the payment of the $5,825.84 funeral bill had been "correct" however and decided not to disturb such amount. The court sustained the exception as to the remaining $11,826.50 and ordered that such money belonged to the estate.

On January 17, 2001, Munger filed a notice of appeal of the probate court's decision. She now raises a single assignment of error.

THE TRIAL COURT ERRED IN SUSTAINING THE EXCEPTIONS OF THE GUARDIAN AD LITEM AND THE PRO SE FAMILY AS TO THE AMOUNT OF $11,826.50.

Munger argues that the trial court erred in concluding that the $11,826.50 belonged to the estate. She claims that she proved that the money was a gift causa mortis and thus such money should not have been part of McGeath's estate.

The essential elements of a gift causa mortis are as follows:

1. It must be of personal property.

2. The gift must be made in the last illness of the donor, while under the apprehension of death as imminent, and subject to the implied condition that if the donor recovers of the illness, or if the donee dies first, the gift shall be void; and

3. Possession of the property given must be delivered at the time of the gift to the donee, or to some one for [her], and the gift must be accepted by the donee.

In re Estate of Newland (1946), 34 Ohio Op. 235, 236, 70 N.E.2d 234, *affirmed* (1946), 47 Ohio L. Abs. 252, 70 N.E.2d 238. Although courts do not favor gifts causa mortis, they will be given effect when the elements are proven by clear and convincing evidence. Id. at 237-238; *Adams v. Fleck* (1961), 171 Ohio St. 451, 455-456, 172 N.E.2d 126, 129-130, paragraph 3(b) of syllabus.

Munger argues that she presented evidence to meet all of the essential elements of a gift causa mortis. While her testimony might have presented evidence to support that conclusion, Munger's testimony was disputed. Shaw's testimony contradicted Munger's testimony. Thus, the question of whether McGeath made a gift causa mortis was a question of credibility. See *Citizens Natl. Bank v. DeLuca*, 2000 Ohio App. LEXIS 4413 (Sept. 27, 2000), Crawford App. No. 3-2000-12, unreported. Credibility issues are within the discretion of the trial court. Id. Thus, in this case we will not interfere with the trial court's determination that Munger failed to prove that McGeath made a gift causa mortis where there was competent, credible evidence that McGreath had not done so.

The assignment of error is overruled.

The judgment of the trial court will be affirmed.

Case Questions

1. How did the decedent attempt to transfer her funds?
2. Why was this not a gift causa mortis?

Glossary

Abatement: Reduction of rent due to lack of habitability.

Absolute ownership doctrine: Allows an owner the unrestricted use of ground water.

Abstract of title: Summary of title transfers of realty maintained by the county recorder's office.

Acceleration payment: Mortgage clause that requires immediate repayment of the outstanding balance if certain occurrences take place.

Accession of the loan: Increase in value of property caused by an act of someone not the property's owner.

Adverse possession: Obtaining title to property by possessing the property in an open and notorious manner that is adverse to the interests of the true owner.

Alienate: Transfer property.

Ameliorative waste: Action of a life tenant or possessor that changes the character of the property in a way that increases its value.

Appropriation rights doctrine: Allows water use based on historical use; used in several western states.

Articles of incorporation: Document filed with the secretary of state to create a cooperative or condominium board.

Assessment: Financial obligation of condominium and cooperative unit owners to maintain common areas.

Assignee: Transferee of contractual rights.

Assignment: Transfer of contract rights.

Assignor: Transferor of contractual rights.

Assume the mortgage: The mortgagor's transferee becomes primarily liable on the mortgage.

Assumption agreement: Contract by which a mortgage is assumed.

Attractive nuisance: A natural or artificial situation on land that would entice children onto the realty.

Bailee: Person who acquires possession of personalty.

Bailment: Transfer of possession of personalty.

Bailor: Transferor of the possession of personalty.

Base line: Artificial line used to create rectangular indexing of land; runs east-west.

Block and lot index: Method of recording title to land by the land's description.

Board of directors: Manager of the condominium and cooperative.

Boilerplate: Standard clauses not specifically related to real estate.

Bond: Underlying loan for a mortgage. When issued by the government or a company it is evidence of indebtedness.

Building code: Government rules regarding construction of buildings.

Bylaws: Document establishing day-to-day operations of an enterprise.

Certificate of non-foreign status: IRS document filed by U.S. citizens involved in a real estate transfer.

Certificate of occupancy: Document prepared by the government indicating that a building is safe to be occupied.

Chattel: Tangible personal property.

Chose in action: Another name for intangibles.

Closely held: Corporation whose shares are not publicly traded.

Closing: The formality of completing the transfer of realty and transferring title; can also refer to the date on which title to property is transferred.

Closing statement: Document determining all costs of a closing.

Cloud on title: Any break in the chain of title that could give rise to a lawsuit with respect to ownership of the property.

Co-tenant: A person who shares title to property.

Commission: Broker's fee.

Common carrier: Transporter of goods and people.

Common enemy: Concept of draining and removing surface water by any method the landowner chooses.

Common law covenants: Covenants of seizin, right to convey, against encumbrances, quiet enjoyment, warranty, and further assurances.

Community property: Form of title in nine jurisdictions in the United States for legally married couples in which each spouse is deemed to own one-half of the property outright.

Concurrent ownership: Title to property shared by two or more persons collectively.

Condemn: To destroy property for public welfare and safety.

Condition: Fact or event that creates or extinguishes a contractual duty.

Condition precedent: Condition that must occur to create a contractual duty.

Condominium: Form of ownership in which a person owns a portion of the property outright and is a tenant in common with others for common areas.

Condominium association: Group that oversees regulation of the condominium and has authority to maintain common areas.

Condominium declaration: Document used to create a condominium.

Confusion: Mixture of personal property that cannot be separated after the mixing.

Consideration: Benefit conferred or a detriment incurred at the request of the other party.

Constructive eviction: Action by the landlord that interferes with tenant's possession.

Contingent remainder: Future interest that takes effect only if a condition is met.

Contractual capacity: Legal ability to contract.

Conveyancing: The process of transferring title to land.

Cooperative: Ownership of shares in an association that permits the holder to possess a unit of the association's property.

Copyright: Exclusive right to a work of art.

Correlative rights doctrine: California doctrine permitting landowner reasonable use of ground water.

Covenant: Permanent restriction on land use.

Covenant against encumbrances: Warranty that there are no liens, mortgages, or clouds on the title on the property.

Covenant of further assurances: Warranty that the grantor will protect the grantee from claims on the title in the future.

Covenant of quiet enjoyment: Warranty that no one else has a lawful claim on the property.

Covenant of right to convey: Warranty that the grantor has the legal ability to transfer the title.

Covenant of seizin: Warranty that the grantor has title to and possession of the property.

Covenant of warranty: Warranty that a good title will be passed.

Damages: Monetary remedy.

Debenture: Unsecured corporate loan.

Deed: Document that transfers title to realty.

Defeasible fee: Interest that can be totally lost upon the occurrence of a specified event.

Defect: Condition that causes a significant reduction in the value of property.

Deposit: Money paid to secure a sales contract; a portion of the purchase price.

Doctrine of equitable conversion: Risk of loss passes to the buyer on the signing of the contract.

Dominant tenement: Property that holds an easement.

Donative intent: Desire to make a gift.

Donee: Recipient of a gift.

Donor: Giver of a gift.

Down payment: Portion of the purchase price given to the seller to secure the sale.

Earnest money: Another name for the deposit given when the sales contract is signed.

Easement: The right of access over or use of another's property.

Easement appurtenant: Easement created by adjoining properties.

Easement by necessity: Easement that arises in landlocked situations to give property owner access to public roads.

Easement by prescription: Easement that is created over time in a manner similar to adverse possession.

Easement in gross: Easement that is created for non-adjoining properties.

Emblements: Profits from land use, such as crops, minerals, and timber.

Eminent domain: Power of the government to take private property for the welfare and safety of the public.

Encumber: Place a cloud on title; give a third person some right to the property.

Encumbrance: Anything that puts a cloud on title.

Equitable mortgage: Mortgage is assumed if deed is transferred to secure a loan.

Equitable redemption: A right of a defaulting mortgagor to reacquire the property by paying the loan prior to the foreclosure sale.

Equitable servitude: Restriction on land use enforceable by an injunction.

Equitable waste: Waste arising from the failure to exercise good husbandry.

Escrow: Trust account where funds are held until contract is completed.

Estate: Title to real or personal property.

Estoppel by deed: Doctrine whereby a purchaser of property not owned by the seller will acquire title if the seller subsequently acquires ownership.

Estoppel certificate: Document provided to the buyer by the seller's mortgagee in a sale of commercial realty.

Estoppel letter: Letter provided by tenants in a commercial building indicating the accuracy of their leases.

Eviction: Process of having a tenant removed from a leased premise.

Exclusive listing: Only broker or owner may sell the property.

Exclusive right to sell: Broker receives commission regardless of who sells the property.

Execution: Signing of an agreement.

Executory interest: Future interest that takes effect after a gap in an earlier interest.

Express grant: Easement created by agreement.

Fee: Type of freehold estate.

Fee simple absolute: Complete, unfettered ownership of property.

Fee simple determinable: Fee interest that is lost if a specified use of the property changes.

Fee simple subject to a condition subsequent: Fee interest that can be lost if a specified condition occurs.

Fee simple subject to an executory interest: Fee interest that takes place after a gap.

Fee tail: Fee interest that can only pass to lineal descendants.

Fixture: Chattel that is permanently affixed to the land.

Foreclosure: Right of the mortgagee to sell the land to satisfy the debt.

Foreclosure by advertisement: Foreclosure permitted without court order.

Form 1099-S: IRS tax form filed for real estate sales.

Four unities: The elements a conveyance must contain to create a joint tenancy: time, title, interest, and possession.

Freehold: Estate in land held for an indefinite period of time.

Fructus industriales: Emblements arising from a possessor's efforts.

Fructus naturales: Emblements naturally growing on the land.

General warranty deed: Deed with the common law covenants.

Gift: Transfer of personalty without consideration.

Gift causa mortis: Gift made in contemplation of donor's imminent death.

Grantee: Transferee.

Grantor: Transferor.

Grantor-grantee index: Method of recording titles to realty by transferor and transferee names.

Gross lease: Lease in which the tenant is liable for rent plus utilities.

Ground water: Underground or percolating water.

Hold-over doctrine: Right of landlord against tenant who remains in unlawful possession after the termination of a lawful lease.

Homeowners' association: Another name for the condominium association.

Horizontal privity: Original parties to a covenant must share a common interest.

HUD-1 Uniform Settlement Statement: Government form generally used for all real estate settlements and mandated for those backed by government loans.

Implied easement: Easement that arises by actual use of adjacent property without consent.

Indefeasibly vested remainder: Future interest that cannot be lost.

Indemnification: Agreement to be financially responsible if another is held legally liable.

Innkeeper: One who offers public accommodation.

Installment sale: Sale in which the purchase price is paid over a number of years.

Insurable title: Less clear than marketable title but one that can be insured against claims.

Intangible property: Personal property that represents something of value.

Inter vivos gift: Gift that is transferred during the life of both donor and donee.

Invitee: Person who lawfully enters land for his or her own benefit.

Joint tenancy: Multiple ownership of property with an undivided interest and a right of survivorship.

Judicial foreclosure: Foreclosure sale authorized by a court.

Landlord: Person who grants the use of property through a lease.

Landlord-tenant law: Law concerned with leaseholds.

Land use: Right of access to land permitted to persons who are not owners/possessors of the land.

Lease: Contract for the right to possess property, creating a leasehold.

Leasehold: Possessory estate in property.

Lessee: Tenant.

Lessor: Landlord.

License: Permission to enter property for a specific act or series of acts. Allows use of a copyrighted work.

Licensee: Person who can enter land subject to a license.

Lien: Claim on property to satisfy a debt.

Life estate: Freehold held for the term of a person's life.

Life estate pur autre vie: Life estate held for the life of a person other than the titleholder.

Life tenant: Person who holds title to a life estate.

Listing agreement: Real estate broker's contract.

Marketable title: Title without any encumbrances.

Measuring life: Person whose life determines duration of the life estate.

Mechanic's lien: Lien automatically given to anyone who performs work on property.

Merger: Where dominant and servient tenement titles are owned by the same person.

Metes and bounds description: Method of describing land by following a course around the boundaries.

Mitigation of damages: Duty of non-breaching party to lessen the money owed by the breaching party.

Mortgage: Security interest to guarantee repayment of a loan.

Mortgage insurance: Insurance to protect against a default on a mortgage loan.

Mortagee: Creditor who receives a mortgage.

Mortgagor: Debtor who gives a mortgage.

Natural flow theory: Owner may use water from watercourses in a manner that does not affect quality or quantity of the water.

Net rent lease: Landlord remains responsible for utilities.

Note: Underlying debt used to create a mortgage.

Notice: Recording statute giving priority to bona fide purchaser with no notice of other claim.

Notice to attorn: Notice to tenants of a change in ownership of the property.

Nuisance: Interference with the use and enjoyment of real property.

Offer: Proposal to enter into a contract.

Offeree: Person to whom an offer is made.

Offeror: Person who makes an offer.

Open listing: Owner engages several brokers to sell the property, and the commission only goes to the one who consummates the sale.

Ouster: Court-ordered termination of a co-tenant's rights because of failure to meet an obligation.

Partial eviction: Act that interferes with a tenants possession of a portion of the leased property.

Partition: Court-ordered division of property among tenants.

Patent: Exclusive use of an invention.

Payoff amount: Outstanding amount owed by seller to be paid off by the buyer.

Percentage breakpoint: Type of commercial lease in which the landlord receives a portion of the tenant's gross sales or profits above a set amount.

Percentage rent: Rent based on a percentage of commercial tenant's gross sales.

Percolating water: Ground water.

Periodic tenancy: Tenancy for successive specific periods of time.

Permissive waste: Decrease in value of land due to failure to maintain the property.

Personal property: All property not classified as real property.

Personalty: Personal property.

Plat book: Record maintained at county recorder's office that describes parcels of land.

Plat description: Method of describing property based on a survey.

Pledge: Bailment of property for money.

Possibility of reverter: Automatic reversion of title to grantor in a fee simple determinable.

Premises: Leased realty.

Principal meridian: Artificial line used to describe rectangular divisions of land; runs north-south.

Prior appropriations doctrine: Water rights determined by historical use.

Private nuisance: Interference with an individual's right of enjoyment of his or her own land.

Promissory note: Evidence of indebtedness.

Proration: Division of rent between the buyer and the seller.

Public nuisance: Interference with the health or safety of the community.

Punch list: Itemized list of remaining problems in newly constructed premises.

Quiet title: Action to have a court decide ownership of property.

Quitclaim deed: Deed in which no covenants are given.

Race: First to record has priority.

Race-notice: To acquire priority, the person must be the first to record without notice of any prior claim.

Radius clause: Provision prohibiting a commercial percentage rent tenant from operating a similar business within a specific geographic area.

Real covenant: Covenant that touches and concerns the land and "runs with the land."

Real Estate Settlement Procedure Act: Federal statute governing real estate closings for all federally guaranteed mortgage loans.

Real property: Land and anything permanently affixed to the land, including vegetation and mineral resources.

Release: Document that relinquishes legal rights.

Realty: Real property.

Reasonable use: Ordinary and foreseeable use.

Reasonable use doctrine: Permits landowner all reasonable use of the property.

Recording act: Statute that establishes the method of acquiring priority with respect to claims against property.

Rectangular survey description: Description of land created by intersection of base and principal meridian lines.

Redemption: Ability of a defaulting mortgagor to reacquire the property.

Redemption in equity: Mortgages may redeem the property at any time prior to the foreclosure sale by satisfying the debt.

Remainderman: Person who ultimately receives a fee interest after intervening estates.

Rent: Fee for use of a property.

Rent escalation clause: Lease provision providing for rent increases over the term of the lease.

Retaliatory eviction: Unlawful eviction of a tenant for asserting legal rights.

Right of entry: Landlord may gain access to premises in the event of a breach of the lease by tenant.

Right of re-entry: Ability of a grantor to regain title to a fee simple subject to a condition subsequent.

Right of survivorship: The right of a joint tenant to succeed to title to property after the death of another joint tenant.

Riparian doctrine: Landowner has unfettered use of watercourse.

Royalty: Fee for use of a copyright, patent, or mark.

Rule Against Perpetuities: All interests must vest, if at all, within 21 years after the death of the lives in being on the date of the initial conveyance.

Salvage doctrines: Statutes enacted to prevent conveyances being found invalid by violating the Rule Against Perpetuities.

Secured investment: Debt with property the bondholder can attach.

Security deposit: Money given by a tenant to the landlord to be held in a trust account in case of the tenant's default.

Service mark: Trademark that designates a service.

Servient tenement: Property subject to an easement holder's rights.

Settlement: Another name for the closing.

Settlement statement: HUD-1 Statement

Share: Intangible that represents ownership in a corporation.

Special warranty deed: Deed that only covenants against specific acts of the grantor.

Specific performance: Equitable remedy in which the breaching party is required to perform the contract.

Statutory redemption: Ability to redeem property after a foreclosure sale.

Stock: Another name for a share.

Strict liability: Being held legally responsible for one's actions regardless of any care taken.

Subjacent support: Anyone who occupies the area beneath the property must support the surface and buildings on the property.

Subject to the mortgage: Transferor remains principally liable on the debt and the property can be attached if the transferor defaults.

Sublease: A transfer of a portion of the tenant's rights under a lease.

Surface rights: Rights to use the land.

Surface water: Water that accumulates on the land.

Survey: Creating a description of a parcel of land.

Tangible property: Personalty that can be touched and moved, and whose value is intrinsic.

Tenancy by the entirety: Joint tenancy for married couples.

Tenancy in common: Multiple ownership of property with transferable interests and no right of survivorship.

Tenancy in partnership: Multiple ownership of property for business partners.

Tenancy in severalty: Title held by only one person.

Tenancy at sufferance: Tenancy resulting when the tenant remains in unlawful possession of the premises.

Tenancy for years: Tenancy for a specific number of years.

Tenancy at will: Tenancy created by agreement of the parties with no specific term.

Tenant: Lessee.

Testamentary gift: Gift made at death by a will.

Time is of the essence: All obligations in a contract must be fulfilled on the dates and times specified or the contract is deemed breached.

Title: Interest in property.

Title insurance: Insurance to protect against a defect in title.

Title search: Making sure the title to property is clear and capable of being transferred.

Touch and concern the land: Requirement to create a real covenant that restricts or requires certain actions.

Tract index: Title recorded by description of the property.

Trademark: Exclusive right to use a name, symbol, or words that designate a product or service.

Trespasser: Person who unlawfully enters onto another's property.

Usual covenants: Common law covenants without the covenant for further assurances.

Variance: Government permission to use property in a manner inconsistent with zoning regulations.

Vendor and Purchaser Risk Act: Statute that passes risk only after the buyer takes possession of the property.

Vertical privity: Necessary relationship from transferor to transferee to create and enforce a real covenant.

Vested remainder subject to complete divestment: Future interest that may be lost due to the happening of a specified event.

Vested remainder subject to a condition subsequent: Future interest that can be lost.

Vested remainder subject to open: Future interest in a class to which members may be added.

Vesting: Having legally enforceable rights.

Voluntary waste: Waste occasioned by deliberate action.

Warranty: Guaranty.

Warranty of habitability: Guaranty that the premises are livable according to local standards.

Waste: Action that lessens the value of the land.

Watercourse: Water on the land coming from rivers, streams, and lakes.

Zoning regulations: Laws designed to limit use of property for governmental geographic design purposes.

Zoning board: Governmental agency that enforces zoning regulations.

Index